# Using Flash® MX to Create e–Learning

### 1st Edition

Sharon Castillo, Steven Hancock, and Garin Hess

Rapid Intake Press™
books and more for e-learning developers

www.rapidintake.com

# Using Flash MX to Create e-Learning

by Sharon Castillo, Steven W. Hancock, and Garin A. Hess

ISBN: 0-9715080-4-6

Published by Rapid Intake Press.

Rapid Intake, Inc.
13215-C8 Mill Plain Blvd #641
Vancouver, WA 98684-6991

Toll Free (866) 231-5254
FAX (360) 838-0828
www.rapidintake.com

## Printing History
October 2004:                     First Edition

## Warning and Disclaimer
The authors and publisher of this book have made their best efforts in the preparation of this book and all the electronic examples to make them complete and as accurate as possible. The authors and publisher make no warranty, express or implied, on the information and programs in this book.

## Trademarks
Numerous trademark names are used throughout this book. Every effort has been made to place indication marks on the first occurrence. The publisher cannot ensure the accuracy of this information. All trademark names have been used for the purpose of communicating the information in the book and for the benefit of the trademark owner with no intention of infringing upon that trademark.

 Rapid Intake Press™
books and more for e-learning developers

http://www.rapidintake.com

# About the Authors

**Garin Hess** is an e-learning developer with a history in instructional design and instructor-led training. With over twelve years of experience in the training and education field, his previous work includes positions as a trainer, e-learning development team leader, and training manager. He is currently CEO of Rapid Intake Inc., a firm specializing in custom e-learning design and development. Garin lives in the United States in the state of Hawaii with his wife and three children.

**Steven Hancock** is an instructional designer with a strong background in e-learning development. His instructional design and e-learning experience began at Utah State University where he worked on Dr. David M. Merrill's research and development team. He then took that experience to Brooks Air Force base in San Antonio, Texas to work with Dr. Robert Gagne to develop a prototype of an instructional design system. During the many years since, he has worked on various projects as an Instructional Designer, Trainer, Team Leader, CBT developer, and WBT developer. He is currently the President of Rapid Intake, Inc. Steve lives in the United States in the state of Utah with his wife and eight children.

**Sharon Castillo** is an instructional designer with a history in e-learning, media based training, and instructor led training. Over the past 15 years she has created and delivered customized training to industry leading high-tech, financial, publishing, and educational companies. She is currently President of Creative Interactions, an instructional design and development firm. Sharon lives in the state of Massachusetts in the United States with her husband and three children.

**Rapid Intake**, owned and operated by Garin and Steve, is a custom e-learning design and development company, which also offers products and services to aid other e-learning developers. In addition to the e-Learning Developer's series (4 books targeted at e learning developers), Rapid Intake offers these services and events:

- On-site training on e-learning development topics
- Recorded webinars on e-learning topics
- E-Learning development tools
- E-Learning developers support
- The CleanCourse project management tool
- The ClearCourse LMS

- The e-Learning Developers conference (www.elearndevcon.com)
- The free WBT Tips online newsletter

You can obtain more information about Rapid Intake's custom e-learning development or services by visiting www.rapidintake.com.

# Acknowledgements

We have felt for a long time that Flash holds a lot of promise as an e-learning authoring tool. The completion of this book further solidifies that belief. I'm grateful for the chance to participate in the writing of this book. I have learned a lot more about Flash as an authoring tool than I originally knew.

This book is a collaborative effort, and I need to thank Garin and Sharon for the many meetings we had discussing ideas and directions for this book. I have worked with Garin for many years and find him the same steady, patient person no matter the project. I'm grateful for his friendship and many talents. Sharon fits into a similar mold and we were able to work well together as a team.

I also need to thank many of our colleagues in the e-learning field for valuable feedback and encouragement.

Finally, I need to thank my wife and children. I work in the house on a constant basis, and they are patient with me and give me the time I need to finish projects like this one.

*Steven Hancock*

Of all of the books that we've written, this book has been the most challenging to get out the door. Flash has so many possibilities; we kept revisiting and revising the Table of Contents. What should we include? What should we exclude? In the end I think we've hit the right balance.

I want to first acknowledge Steven Hancock and Sharon Castillo who wrote the bulk of this book. They have been so good to work with. Sharon was so patient with all of our stops and starts over the last two years. And Steve has been so doggedly determined to get this project wrapped up--he has worked tirelessly on all of the details required to get to publication.

Writing is not unlike cooking (at least for me). I love cooking, and when I cook, I make a mess. It may taste good at the end, but the kitchen looks like a disaster area. On that note, I want to thank Mark Brewer and Jill Garner, our editors, who have had to clean up the messes that have resulted from the "cooking" process.

I also want to acknowledge Scarlett Cabral. Scarlett was a project manager when I was a lone and unknown freelancer and she gave me one of my first commercial Flash projects to work on. This increased my confidence in Flash as an authoring environment, as well as boosted my own confidence.

Lastly, I want to thank my wife Kristin. She has always expressed optimism and hope in all of the projects we have undertaken. The positive effects of that on me cannot be measured, for which I'm deeply grateful.

*Garin Hess*

I would like to thank Garin and Steve for including me on this project. I had read their previous books and attended their CourseBuilder class. I liked their straightforward, practical approach, which included solid instructional design—not just focusing on the technology. Over the past two years in developing the book, they made the process very enjoyable and rewarding.

One of the things I value most about being an instructional designer is that I learn something new on every project. Creating courseware for me is a collaborative process. I have been fortunate to work with so many talented people over the years that I could not possibly list them all here. Each one has taught me new skills, new approaches to solving problems, better ways to provide effective learning, and most of all how to have fun in the process. I would especially like to thank two of my mentors, Colin Grant and Jerry Poulin, who provided invaluable support early in my career. They gave me the confidence to see that anything was possible.

Of course, I am most thankful for the loving support of my family. My parents, who got me started down the path that I have chosen. My husband and partner in life, Robert, with whom I have been able to dream of where I want life to take me and to help me make it happen. And, my children whose energy, joy, and passion for life help me keep it all in perspective.

*Sharon Castillo*

# Contents at a Glance

# Table of Contents

# Introduction

Welcome to the world of e-learning. We hope you find this book useful. We have enjoyed writing it. We feel this book provides you with the information you need to use Macromedia's Flash as an e-learning authoring tool.

Many e-learning Developers have used Flash as a component of their e-learning projects. In such settings, Developers usually relegate Flash to a supporting role—a tool to create an animation that helps teach a concept. This book considers a broad range of uses for Flash, with a special emphasis on using Flash as the main authoring tool.

This introduction lists recommended prerequisite knowledge, details the organization of the book, and provides basic information about using the book.

## Prerequisite Knowledge

To get the most out of this book, you should have a working knowledge of Macromedia's Flash® MX or Flash® MX 2004 (here after referred to as Flash). A few topics in this book require you to have a copy of Flash MX 2004 Professional. The professional edition of Flash MX 2004 contains advanced functionality that is sometimes used in the book.

If you are unfamiliar with Flash, consider reading a book that teaches Flash basics or visiting one of the many Flash sites before continuing with this book.

We suggest that you have a working knowledge of these Flash topics:

- Using the Flash work environment
- Creating objects using the Flash drawing tools
- Using panels and the Properties Inspector
- Working with timelines and frames
- Creating basic animations
- Creating and using symbols

# How this Book is Organized

The first chapter of this book introduces e-learning and explains how Flash fits into that discipline. We present some advantages and disadvantages for using as well as a few tips to help you maximize Flash as an e-learning authoring tool.

The remainder of the book is presented in five sections. Each section is described here.

## Section I—Using Flash for Interactivity and Illustration

This first section focuses on many of the traditional applications of Flash in e-learning. We cover interactions, demonstrations, simulations, and multimedia.

The exercises and applications in this section can be used for any e-learning project whether or not Flash is the main authoring tool. For example, if you are creating an e-learning course using HTML pages, the interactions presented in this section can still be used.

## Section II—Using Flash Interactions for Assessment and Interactivity

The second section covers Flash learning interactions in detail. Learning interactions make it easy to develop interactions, reviews, quizzes, and tests. This section is broken down into six chapters each of which covers a learning interaction in detail. We also spend a good deal of time discussing how you can expand the current functionality of each learning interaction.

## Section III—Creating Course Architecture with Flash

An important part of any e-learning development project is the creation of the architecture that supports the e-learning course. In this section we define course architecture and look at several ways you can build that architecture. These methods range from the simple to complex.

## Section IV—Tracking Student Data

In this section we discuss what is required to track student data in an LMS. We look at how you can use Flash learning interactions and Quiz templates to create AICC- or SCORM-compliant courses.

## Section V—Working with Flash Components

In the final section we introduce you to the promising world of components, and you will learn how to use the standard Flash components. You will learn to customize those components as well as how to make additional customizations to the Flash learning interactions. Finally, we introduce the process of creating your own components.

## Appendices

The CD-ROM consists of several appendices that cover topics associated with Flash and e-learning. To access these appendices, insert the CD-ROM into your computer and access the PDF files stored in the appendices folder.

# Conventions

We have used icons and a few typographical conventions in this book to make information more readily identifiable.

## Icons Used

There are 6 icons used throughout this book.

 **Note:** The note icon is placed beside a note that contains extra or important information about the current topic.

**Caution:** The exclamation point icon is placed beside a caution. Pay close attention to this information.

**Tip:** The light-bulb icon is placed beside a tip. Tips in this manual are practical and helpful.

**More Information:** The books icon is placed beside a cross-reference. A cross-reference directs you to another place in the book or separate information altogether.

**On CD**: The CD icon is placed next to information that is also contained on the companion CD. You can find more information about what the CD contains in the section What is on the CD-ROM? later in this introduction.

The hands-on icon is placed next to a section header. This icon indicates that the section contains step-by-step instructions and sample files on the CD-ROM that lets you follow along. At the completion of a hands-on exercise, you will have created an interaction or made some change to a Flash file.

**Note:** The visual design of any of the interactions you create in this book will still need a bit of work before presenting them in a real course. We created them to teach functionality, not visual design. You can learn good visual design principles from any number of good books on visual design.

# Typographical Conventions

This book uses a few typographical conventions that you should be aware of:

- We reference menus using an arrow between each menu option. For example, Window → Design Panels refers to the menu option "Design Panels" that is inside the menu "Window".

- **Code font** indicates ActionScript code. If a lengthy piece of code is included, we set it off in its own paragraph. This font is also used to identify file names on the CD

- We always number step-by-step procedures. This will make it easy for you to follow.

- The instructions in this book work in both Macintosh and Windows environments. If there is a difference, we will indicate the difference for the Macintosh environment.

- We indicate keyboard keys by using small caps. (For example, press the ENTER key.)

# What is on the CD-ROM?

The CD-ROM contains sample files and appendices. If you want to work through the hands-on exercises, you will need to access the sample files. Some sample files are building blocks for creating interactions; others are completed Flash movies you can view.

**Note:** When possible, sample Flash files have been saved in Flash MX format. However, certain files require Flash MX 2004. You will not be able to open those files unless you are using a copy of Flash MX 2004. Sample FLA files in chapters 6 – 11, 15–16 and 19–22 require Flash MX 2004 to open. You can still work through the exercise using Flash MX, but you won't be able to open the sample files.

You can find the appendices in the appendices folder on the CD-ROM. The appendices cover a number of different topics that apply to Flash and e-learning yet are not part of the focus of the book. This table identifies the appendix and provides a description of what it contains.

| Appendix | Description |
|---|---|
| **Appendix A–Using FlashforMobile e-Learning.pdf** | Providing e-learning on PDAs or cell phones is an area that will grow in the future. This appendix provides basic information about developing e-learning for mobile devices. |
| **Appendix B –Other Flash Authoring Tools.pdf** | There are several other software programs that generate Flash SWF files. In this appendix we provide an overview of those software programs. |
| **Appendix C - Customizing Version 1 Flash Components.pdf** | Customizing Flash MX components is different from customizing Flash MX 2004 components. This chapter is the Flash MX version of Chapter 21 in the book. |
| **Appendix D - Creating Version 1 Flash Components.pdf** | Creating Flash MX components is different from creating Flash MX 2004 components. This chapter is the Flash MX version of Chapter 22 in the book. |

| Appendix | Description |
|----------|-------------|
| **Appendix E-Using_Flash_Movies_in_HTML_Files.pdf** | If you are developing an e-learning course using HTML, you may still want to include Flash movies. This appendix provides basic instruction for including Flash movies in HTML pages. |

Here are the minimum system requirements to use the files on the CD-ROM:

- **Windows**. An Intel® Pentium® processor, or equivalent, running Windows® 98 or later. You also need a minimum of 64 MB of available RAM and a CD-ROM drive.
- **Macintosh**. A Macintosh running Mac OS 9.x or later. You also need 64 MB of available RAM and a CD-ROM drive.

# Using Flash for e-Learning 1

In its early days, developers probably did not envision Flash as a robust e-learning development tool. Initially, web designers used Flash to make web pages more engaging by spicing up plain web pages with animation, audio, and interactivity.

Today you can use Flash for creating e-learning in many different ways. You may use it simply as a support tool to create a movie that explains a difficult topic, or you can create effects that grab the learner's attention. You may use it to insert assessments into an On-line course, or you can choose to use it as the main development tool.

In this chapter you will learn:

- What e-learning is.
- About advantages and disadvantages of using Flash for e-learning.
- About the benefits of using ActionScript, Flash's scripting language.

# What is e-Learning?

There are probably as many definitions of e-learning as there are organizations that use e-learning. We prefer this definition: e-learning is using technology to promote learning.

Companies and organizations use e-learning to describe any education initiative that includes technology. This may include web-based training (WBT), video conferencing, or something as simple as electronic documentation. These are all mediums for delivering electronic content.

In today's high-tech world it is important for companies to take advantage of quality e-learning solutions. We stress the term "quality" because that is what makes the difference. E-learning delivered just because it is the latest buzzword will not solve a company problem; effectively designed e-learning will.

Many organizations assume training to be the quick-fix solution to their problems, problems that may actually exist for other reasons (i.e., organizational, managerial, economical, etc.). Having said this, if you've done your homework and you really believe that training is the issue, your effective use of e-learning will, over time, reach more employees at less cost than traditional training methods. An ineffective e-learning solution will waste your money and erode your company's trust in future e-learning opportunities. Many people may not know how to do the Needs Assessment to make the determination.

### The Importance of Instructional Design

As with any educational program, quality instructional design is the key to effective e-learning. For that reason, you will find instructional design tips and techniques scattered throughout this book.

If you choose to use e-learning to solve your current training issues, then you will want to understand how to use Flash in your e-learning efforts. How you choose to use Flash in your e-learning projects needs to be decided up front. In the next section, we will present different ways you can use Flash in e-learning, including their respective advantages and disadvantages.

# Why Use Flash to Develop e-Learning?

While Flash was not initially created for e-learning development, it is gaining acceptance and becoming recognized as a tool to create effective on-line courses— or to create smaller course components to be embedded in courses created using other e-learning products.

Let's begin by looking at ways in which you can use Flash to create e-learning. Then we will discuss the advantages and disadvantages of using Flash for this purpose.

# e-Learning Uses for Flash

There are numerous ways to use Flash in your e-learning projects. This table shows some different e-learning applications for Flash:

| Application | Description |
| --- | --- |
| Movies or animations that can more effectively explain a difficult topic | If a still picture is worth a thousand words, an animated illustration can be worth ten thousand. Flash animations allow you to explain procedures step-by-step, illustrate difficult processes piece-by-piece, or show the relationship of parts to the whole. See Chapter 4: *Multimedia* for an example. |
| Eye-catching introductions | Grabbing and maintaining the learner's attention is important in any educational endeavor. Animated introductions can help in this area without increasing bandwidth beyond necessary limits. See Chapter 4: *Multimedia* for an example. |
| Audio-enabled web based training (WBT) | Flash is a great medium for delivering audio over the web. Even if you don't show any animation, you can still include audio by embedding a Flash file. See Chapter 4: *Multimedia* for an example. |
| Learning interactions | Learning interactions require the learner to become involved in the e-learning instead of just viewing content. Flash has the power necessary to create these types of interactions. The Flash MX Learning Extensions can do this for you, or you can create your own interactivity using ActionScript. See Chapter 2: *Adding Interactivity to a Course* as well as Section II: *Using and Extending Macromedia's Built-In Learning Objects* for examples. |
| On-line assessments | You can use Flash to provide quizzes and track results. Once again the Flash MX Learning Extensions can do this quickly and easily. See Section II: *Using and Extending Macromedia's Built-In Learning Objects* for examples. |

| Application | Description |
| --- | --- |
| Course architecture and course navigation | You can use Flash to create customized buttons the learner will use to navigate through the course. Or, you can use Flash to provide the entire architecture for your course, complete with navigational elements. See Section III: *Creating a Custom Course Architecture* for examples. |
| Interactions that keep the learner's interest | Because of the interesting effects that you can create with Flash, learning interactions created using Flash can help keep the learner's interest. |

# Advantages of Using Flash for e-Learning

There are many advantages to using Flash as an e-learning development tool. In this section we look at some of those advantages.

## Versatility

Versatility is a strong point for Flash. You can do an amazing variety of things with this tool. We mentioned several e-learning applications earlier in this chapter, but there are also numerous other uses of Flash. Browse the Internet and you'll soon realize that Flash is a popular solution being used by many companies and organizations to create or enhance their content.

You can easily incorporate Flash into a multitude of development tools. This means that you can embed Flash into standard HTML pages or courses created with other e-learning development tools. For example, you could create a demonstration of a software application in Flash and then embed that demonstration into an HTML page, an Authorware or ToolBook course, or a course created by almost any other authoring tool.

**More Information:** For more information about incorporating Flash into other development platforms, see the appendices at the end of this book.

## Designed for Cross-platform Web Delivery

Unlike some e-learning development tools, Flash's primary application is to create web-delivered content. This provides two major benefits:

- Because Flash uses a plugin, it can run on multiple hardware platforms. In addition, there is very little effect when viewed in different browsers. For example, fonts, colors, and layout will display just like what you developed. Not only does this give you more control over your content, it also means that you can cut down on the amount of time it takes to test your finished course.

- Bandwidth is always an issue that e-learning developers need to be concerned about, particularly if you want to include animation, audio, or video. Flash files are small compared to other authoring tools, which makes Flash an ideal tool for authoring web-delivered training.

### Substance Over Style

Since Flash makes it so easy to create a slick presentation, some designers get carried away with the effects and styles.

Remember, the most effective courses focus on content and use effects and style to support the learning.

If you let your instructional design drive the development, you will have a better chance of avoiding this problem.

## Deliver a Professional Looking Product

It is cumbersome to create a professional looking page in HTML because you have fewer ways to control the look of the page. With Flash it is relatively easy to create professional-looking presentations without being a professional graphic artist. The drawing tools are intuitive and they give you many options to modify the look to best suit your needs. You can also use Flash to include animation, audio, imported images, and sound effects in your courses.

## Flash Learning Extensions are More Secure

Using Flash to create questions for on-line quizzes or assessments is much more secure than regular HTML solutions. Learners can often view the HTML source file to discover the answer. This is not the case with Flash Learning Extensions. All quiz information is stored in the Flash object and is not accessible to the learner.

### Flash is Evolving to Better Facilitate e-Learning

Flash 5 introduced major enhancements that increased its power and flexibility. It introduced built-in learning interactions, such as Multiple Choice and Drag and Drop questions. It also introduced Quiz templates and more powerful scripting capabilities.

In Flash MX, Macromedia enhanced the learning extensions and templates to track the results from a series of learning interactions. Tracking information can then be sent to a learning management system (LMS) that conforms to either the AICC or SCORM standards. Macromedia continues to show its support for Flash as an e-learning development tool through their marketing and development efforts.

# Disadvantages of Using Flash for e-Learning

We have discovered some disadvantages to using Flash for e-learning as well. Knowing some of these disadvantages will help you avoid associated problems.

### Increased Development Time

The biggest drawback of Flash is that there are a limited number of built-in objects that specifically aid in the creation of e-learning. If you have worked with other e-learning development environments, you will notice that the there are fewer interactions available in Flash and that the ones available are not as flexible.

**Note:** We address limitations specific to each interaction in the chapter dedicated to that interaction.

Additionally, the Flash MX templates assist only minimally in course structure development. Fortunately, Flash is a very powerful and flexible tool. Through the use of ActionScript—Flash's scripting language—you can build interactions, assessments, and the navigation system for your e-learning course.

**More Information:** We discuss specific methods and techniques in greater detail in individual chapters throughout the book.

**On CD**: The CD-ROM contains many examples that you can use or adapt as needed to help you save time.

## Plugin is Required

Probably the biggest disadvantage of using Flash for e-learning is that it requires a plugin. A plugin allows the learner to view the file you have created. If you want to include a Flash element in an On-line course you have created, your learners must either install the plugin on their own or you will need to install it as a part of an installation program.

 **Note**: Different versions of Flash require different versions of the plugin. Therefore, if a learner has the Flash 4 plugin installed, but your course uses Flash 5, the learner will need to install a new plugin in order to view the file.

You could package a Flash movie as an executable (also known a projector file). It is much more difficult to integrate a projector file into another program. If you are trying to deliver the course over the web, you cannot use a projector file.

On the positive side, the Flash plugin is integrated in the current version of the most popular browsers on the market. Therefore, it is likely that the Flash plugin has penetrated such a large percentage of users that the majority of your learners will not need to install the plugin. Those who do need to install it can easily access it from Macromedia's web site at no cost.

## Timeline Metaphor

As you probably already know, Flash uses a timeline metaphor for development. The reasons for this are obvious. The original intent of Flash was to create movies that could be delivered over the web and the timeline metaphor works great for that purpose.

The timeline metaphor is not always intuitive for creating non-linear training course architecture. Accordingly, we will teach you techniques for creating non-linear course components in Section III: *Creating a Custom Course Architecture*.

## Graphic Limitations

If you have imported bitmap graphics into Flash, you know that the quality of those graphics can be compromised. In many cases this is due to smoothing. This problem is correctable but adds time to development. Be aware of this limitation if your project contains numerous bitmap graphics (for example, a simulation or training that requires numerous outside graphics).

# Maximizing the Power of Flash

You can create some very basic e-learning without knowing a lot about ActionScript. You have probably used some simple ActionScript such as the *stop*, *goto*, and *play* actions. However, to create robust, flexible courses you will need to learn more about ActionScript.

ActionScript is a scripting language similar to JavaScript. You will use it to control the flow of your content and to enable learner interaction. As with most scripting languages, it is easier to use than a full-blown programming language such Java or C++ but still requires intensive study to master.

**Note:** You do not need to know JavaScript to learn ActionScript.

ActionScript enables you to create interactive, flexible applications. As your knowledge of ActionScript increases, you will find that there are more elegant solutions to certain problems; that you can customize learning interactions; that you can create e-learning objects that build the content dynamically; and that you can create e-learning that can communicate with external data sources.

**More Information:** We discuss the specific methods and techniques for creating e-Learning using Flash in greater detail in individual chapters throughout the book. This book does not claim to be a complete resource for ActionScript. For exhaustive coverage of ActionScript, see one of the many excellent ActionScript titles currently available on the market. Our choice is ActionScript, The Definitive Guide, by Colin Moock, published by O'Reilly.

## Using ActionScript and XML Together

XML (EXtensible Markup Language) is a method for describing data using tags, similar to HTML tags. However, while HTML uses standard pre-defined tags to specify the format of a web page, XML lets you actually define your own tags that describe the structure of the data. This gives you a method for passing data into and out of Flash—offering you a lot of flexibility and power. For example, you can:

- Create a course where the content and the structure can be modified dynamically to best meet the needs of the learner, such as offering the text in a different language or assembling only those topics with which the learner is unfamiliar.
- Send learner information such as topics completed and quiz scores out to a database or a learning management system.

**More Information:** For more information on creating the structure of your course, see Section III: Creating a Custom Course Architecture or Section IV: Tracking Student Data.

# Summary

e-learning uses technology to enable a learner to achieve a learning objective. This book focuses on a subset of e-learning—learning delivered via the web (or WBT). Flash is an excellent tool to create e-learning courseware because it is versatile and was developed to take advantage of the benefits that the web has to offer.

In this chapter, you have been introduced to the ways that you can use Flash in your e-learning development efforts. We have also looked at its benefits and limitations. Throughout the rest of this book you will be shown how to maximize your use of Flash and how to get past the limitations so that you can create effective, media-rich e-learning courses. Now, that's good!

# Section I:
# Using Flash for
# Interactivity and
# Illustration

**Ready to get started? This section will get you started creating interactions using Flash.**

---

# Adding Interactivity to a Course **2**

Many early e-learning courses were merely On-line books? using large amounts of text and a few quiz questions at the end. Dense text is hard for learners to read on-line and makes the learner passive. It is difficult, if not impossible, for a passive learner to effectively absorb and retain new information. The best courses are dynamic and engage the learner.

Design your e-learning to be as interactive as possible. There are many ways to get the learner to interact with your course content. These interactions can take the form of learning activities or assessments. This chapter covers how to use mouse interactions for learning activities.

In this chapter you will learn how to:

- Make e-learning interactive.
- Create button interactions.
- Create mouse over interactions.
- Create links for non-linear navigation.

# Ways to Make e-Learning Interactive

Interactions require the learner to learn by doing. By clicking the mouse on (or in some cases moving the mouse over) an object on the page, the learner can choose to explore a topic in more detail. This table shows several applications of mouse interactions in e-learning:

| Application | Description |
|---|---|
| Reveal additional content | Instead of dense paragraphs or tables of information, use a list of items that the learner rolls the mouse over to see more detail. This enables you to focus the learner's attention on specific information or allow the information to build over time. For example, you can display:<br><br>• A process one step at a time.<br>• Details about a concept.<br>• Secondary information such as tips and notes.<br>• Descriptions of parts of a graphic. |
| Enable the learner to explore a concept or a product | The learner can try out different scenarios by interacting with a mock-up of a tool. For example, the user can work through the steps to perform a process in a software application, or the user can move pieces of a diagram. |
| Create a link to a web page | Some courses need to be designed for both instruction and reference. You can create links to supporting web pages that contain additional information for more advanced users. You could even create a link to a supporting document such as a PDF file. |

 **More Information:** Interactivity also takes the form of assessments and course navigation. Assessments are covered in Section II: Using Flash Interactions for Assessment and Interactivity. Course navigation is covered in Section IV: Creating Course Architecture with Flash.

## Parts of an Interaction

All interactions have the same basic parts; you can vary how you use them:

- **An event**. A learner causes an event by clicking on a button or a hot spot, clicking on a link, rolling the mouse over a hot spot, dragging an object from one spot to another, or pressing a key on the keyboard.
- **An action or a series of actions**. Once the event occurs a resulting action takes place. For example, when the user clicks on a hot spot, additional text and graphics display. Or when the user clicks on a link, a web page displays in a secondary window.

In each of the scenarios shown in this lesson, you will define the events and the actions for each interaction.

# Using Buttons for Interactivity

Buttons allow you to create interactions that respond to mouse clicks. A button is basically a clickable image. Typically, the look of the button changes when the learner moves the mouse over it.

Flash ships with pre-made buttons that you can use as is; or you can modify buttons to meet you needs. In many e-learning projects you will create buttons from scratch to best meet the needs of your particular course.

**Tip:** Once you've created buttons, you can store them in a shared library so that you can reuse these buttons in later projects.

**Note:** Flash's pre-made buttons reside in the Common Libraries (Window → Other Panels → Common Libraries → Buttons).

## Button Basics

In Flash, a button is a symbol that resides within a frame of the timeline. Symbols are elements like graphics or buttons that you store in your library and can use repeatedly. Each time you place a symbol on the Stage, you are creating an instance of that symbol.

**Tip:** Use symbols when you plan to use an object multiple times. This not only reduces the file size (since Flash only stores the symbol once), it also enables you to make a change in one place and the change is applied across all instances of that symbol. You can also modify the properties of an instance without affecting the symbol itself. For example, you can resize the instance or modify its color.

The button symbol has its own unique timeline, which contains four frames—Up, Over, Down, and Hit. Each frame is described in this image:

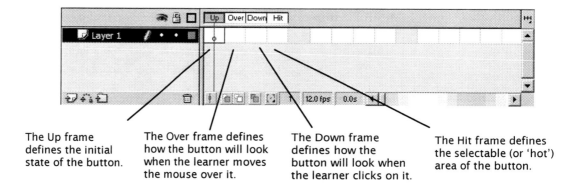

The Up frame defines the initial state of the button.

The Over frame defines how the button will look when the learner moves the mouse over it.

The Down frame defines how the button will look when the learner clicks on it.

The Hit frame defines the selectable (or 'hot') area of the button.

## Methods for Creating a Symbol

As mentioned a Flash button is merely a Flash symbol with a specific purpose. There are two methods for creating symbols:

- Create a new symbol in the library and then drag it to the Stage.
- Create a graphic on the Stage and then convert the selected graphic to a symbol.

With either method you associate events and actions with an instance of the symbol, not the original that resides in the library. This enables you to reuse the button and vary the actions to match the context of the situation in which you use it.

# Creating an Interactive Button

This step-by-step tutorial takes you through the process of creating a button and associating an event and an action with it.

## Viewing the Finished Interaction

Before you create the button, take a look at the finished product.

**On CD**: Take a moment and try out the finished interaction: samples/chapter02/sample_2-1.swf.

As you explore this interaction, notice what happens when you move the mouse over the button. Then click on the button to see what action occurs.

## Creating the Button

Using the steps in this section, you will create a button that causes some text to display when the learner clicks on it. You will need to have the Flash file samples/chapter02/sample_2-1_start.fla open. This file already has the needed background and text.

**Use these steps to create a new button symbol:**

**1** Open samples/chapter02/sample_2-1start.fla to begin the exercise.

**2** Create a new symbol (Insert → New Symbol).

The Create New Symbol dialog box displays:

A symbol may be a movie clip, a button, or a graphic. In this case, you will create a button.

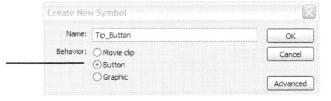

**3** Enter the settings as specified in this table:

| Property | Setting |
|----------|---------|
| Name | *Tip_Button* (This is the name that will appear in the library.) |
| Behavior | *Button* |

**Tip:** Each symbol must have a unique name. It is a good idea to determine a standard naming convention at the beginning of your project. This enables you to locate your objects more easily in your library. For suggestions on how to organize and name library symbols, see Section III: Creating Course Architecture with Flash.

**4** Click **OK.**

You can now edit the button, using the drawing tools (located in the Tools palette).

**5**  Use the Rectangle tool to draw the Up state of the button. Select #66CC66 as the color and make the rectangle about 78 x 26 pixels. Don't include a stroke color. Position the button as shown here. (If you prefer exact dimensions x is 0 and y is 0.)

The button's timeline displays 1 frame for each state: Up, Over, Down, and Hit.

Use the Rectangle tool to draw the Up state of the button.

When editing the button, you see the button's Stage, which resides within the scene's Stage.

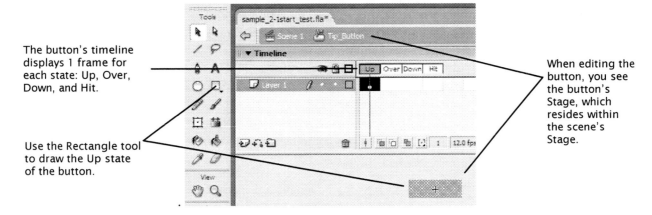

The button can have multiple layers, so that you can modify each button element independently. In this case, you will use one layer for the button graphic and one for the text.

**6**  Rename the current layer as **Background** and add insert a layer (Insert → Timeline → Layer) and rename it **Text**.

Use the insert layer button as a quick way to add a layer to the timeline.

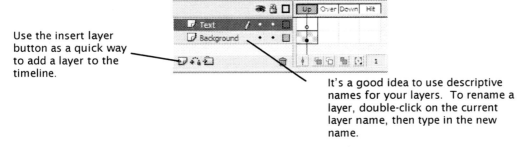

It's a good idea to use descriptive names for your layers. To rename a layer, double-click on the current layer name, then type in the new name.

**Note:** Be sure to add the Text layer above the Background layer. This ensures that the text will display in front of the background graphic. To rearrange the layers, simply select the layer and drag it until you have the correct order.

**7**  In the text layer, enter the text **Tip** (using the Text tool located in the Tools palette). We used Comic Sans MS 18 point as the font.

**8**  Select the Hit frame of the Text layer and insert a frame (Insert → Timeline → Frame). This forces the text to display in each of the button states.

Use the Text tool to add the text to your button.

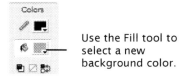

Notice that your changes are reflected in the library as well.

**9**  Select the Over state in the Background layer and insert a new keyframe (Insert → Timeline → Keyframe).

**10**  Change the color of the rectangle in the Over state of the button to be a lighter shade (#00FF00).

Use the Fill tool to select a new background color.

**11**  Select the Hit frame of the Background layer and insert a new frame (Insert → Timeline → Frame) to extend the Over stat across the Down and Hit state.

Note: In this button we chose not to use three states. The only time the button will change is when the cursor is first moved over it.

**12**  Return to the main timeline (Click on **Scene 1** above the timeline).

**13**  Select the **Buttons** layer in the main timeline and drag the button you created from the library onto the Stage and position it as shown here:

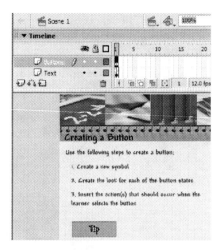

**14** Save the file (File → Save).

You will add actions to the button in later sections of this chapter.

**Tip:** To create a button from an existing graphic (or text), right-click (CONTROL-click on Macintosh) on the object and select Convert to Symbol from the pop-up menu. Then continue to create the button in the same manner as when you created a button from scratch. When you have finished designing the button, you can return to the main timeline by clicking on the scene name at the top of the timeline.

## Editing the Button

If you need to make changes to a button, you have a few options. You can right-click (CONTROL-click on Macintosh) on the button and select **Edit** from the pop-up menu. You can also select the **Edit in Place** option or double-click the button. This option enables you to edit your button and see how it will look in the context of the scene on the Stage.

Notice that the button's timeline displays and you can see the button in the context of Scene 1. The Stage appears semi-transparent.

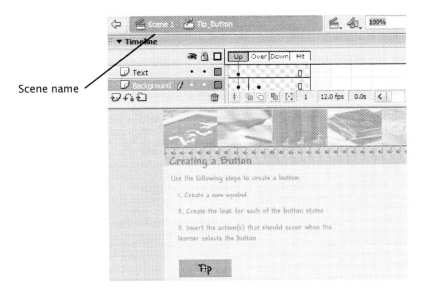

Scene name

Make any changes as necessary. Then click on the scene name at the top of the Stage to return to the Stage.

**Note**: If you have used a particular button multiple times in a movie, any edits to the button symbol will be reflected in all of the instances of that button. If you want to create variations on the button, for example a button with the same look but a different text label, then you will need to create a duplicate symbol. To do this, right-click (CONTROL-click on Macintosh) the button instance on the Stage. Then select Duplicate Symbol from the pop-up menu (or right-click the symbol in the library and select Duplicate). Be sure to provide a unique name for the new button.

# Setting Up the Interaction

You now have a button, but it doesn't perform any actions when the learner clicks on it. As a continuation of the previous exercise, you will add the actions to make some text appear when the learner clicks the button (the event). There are several ways to make the text appear. In this exercise, you will learn two methods:

- **Using multiple frames in the main timeline to display results.** One frame contains the button with no text displayed and another frame contains the button and the resulting text. The result of the learner clicking on the button is to advance the playhead to the frame that contains the display text.

- **Using Dynamic Text fields to display results.** This approach uses a blank text field where text is added to it when the learner clicks on the button.

In this next section of the tutorial, you will learn both methods and look at the pros and cons of each.

## Using the Multiple Frames in the Main Timeline to Display Results

This method uses two frames in the main timeline, one for the initial state and one to show the results of the learner's interaction.

**Use these steps to display the text when the learner clicks on the button:**

You will first need to extend each layer to fill 2 frames (select the first frame in each layer and insert a frame). This has already been done for you in the sample movie.

**1**　In the Result Text layer, insert a keyframe at frame 2 (Insert → Timeline → Keyframe).

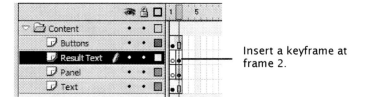

Insert a keyframe at frame 2.

**2**　In the Result Text layer at keyframe 2, create a text box (using the Text tool on the Tools palette) on the right-hand side of the screen and enter the following text: *You can create a button from an existing graphic (or text) by selecting the graphic on the Stage and then converting it to a symbol.*

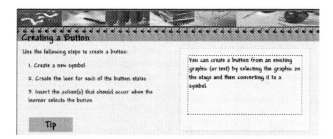

We added a background rectangle to the panel layer to help set the text off from the rest of the Stage.

Now you will add the action to the button that will move the movie playhead to frame 2 when the user clicks on the Tip button.

**3**    Select the **Tip** button and open the Actions panel (Window → Development Panels → Actions).

**4**    Enter this ActionScript code into the Actions panel:

```
on(release){
    gotoAndStop(2);
}
```

The first line of code on(release) is the event. This event occurs when the button is clicked. The second line is the action that causes the movie to go to the second frame. The text you created shows because it exists in the second frame.

**Tip:** In Flash MX 2004 you can select the button and add a Goto and Stop at frame or label behavior from the behaviors panel. When you add the behavior you must enter 2 as the frame number.

**5**    Test your movie (Control → Test Movie).

When you test the movie you will notice that the playhead goes immediately to the 2nd frame and then loops back to the first frame. You need to insert a **stop** action in frame 1 to prevent this from happening.

**Tip:** When you add actions to frames, it's always a good idea to create a separate layer in the timeline for the actions. This makes it easier to find the actions later on.

**6**    Create a layer called Actions (Insert → Timeline → Layer) above the Buttons layer.

**7**    Select the first frame Actions layer and open the Actions panel. Enter **stop();**.

**8**    Retest your movie and make adjustments as necessary. Save the file when you are done.

## Using Dynamic Text fields to Display Results

The multi-frame method requires very little coding, but it is inflexible and becomes cumbersome to use when you have many interactive elements in the movie. For example, if you have five buttons on the page, you would have to keep track of which frame each button's text resides in.

While you could use frame labels to help you keep track of this information, a more elegant solution is to use a Dynamic Text field. A Dynamic Text field is similar to a regular text area, except that you are able to change the text via ActionScript actions rather than moving the playhead of the movie.

**Use these steps to display the text in a Dynamic Text field:**

**1**    Open file samples/chapter02/sample_2-2start.fla.

**2**    In the Result Text layer add a keyframe to frame 1 (Insert → Timeline → Keyframe).

**3**    With frame 1 selected draw a text field on the right-hand side of the Stage.

**4**    In the Text field's Properties Inspector, enter the settings as shown:

Choose Dynamic Text as the text field type

Enter a Field name (also known as the Field ID).

Make sure the text field is a multiline text field.

Now you need to enter the code that will place text into the Dynamic Text field.

**5**    Select the *Tip* button, open the Actions panel (Window → Development Panels → Actions) and enter the following code:

```
on (release) {
 _root.description.text = "You can create a button from an existing
graphic (or text) by selecting the graphic on the Stage and then
converting it to a symbol";
}
```

The event is the same as in the previous exercise. However, this time instead of advancing to a new frame, we change the property of a text field. The property that is changed is the text property. We set it to the same text used in the previous exercise. We identify the text field using an absolute path beginning with root (the main timeline).

**6**    Test your movie (Control → Test Movie).

## Using Buttons in Assessments

You can use buttons as part of an assessment using the same techniques as shown in the previous section. For example, you can create a multiple choice question where each of the options are buttons and then use Dynamic Text fields to display the feedback to the user.

**On CD**: The following example is available on the CD in **samples/chapter02/sample_2-3.swf**. It shows a multiple choice question using buttons to enable the learner to make a selection. When the learner clicks on Choice C, the feedback indicates that the learner made the correct selection. For all other selections, the feedback indicates that the learner made an incorrect selection and should try again.

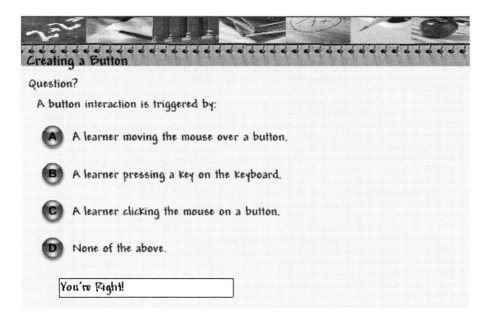

**Note**: While you can use buttons to create multiple choice questions, you could also use Flash's built-in Multiple Choice learning interaction (Window → Other Panels → Common Libraries → Learning Interactions). Using a button gives you a bit more flexibility, but the built-in Multiple Choice learning interaction is a little faster to set up. For more information on the built-in Multiple Choice learning interaction, see Section II: Using Flash Interactions for Assessment and Interactivity for more information.

# Using Mouse Overs to Add Interactivity

Using a mouse over (also known as a rollover) is very similar to using a button. However, the event is triggered *on (rollover)* rather than *on (release)*.

Most mouse overs use transparent hot spots to trigger the event. This enables you to create interactions that have a graphic in the background and several hot spots set at designated locations. When the learner moves the mouse over these locations, text or a graphic appears.

Another application of hot spots is to create a bulleted list that has a hot spot over each list item. When the user moves the mouse over each list item, additional information is displayed.

## What is a Hot Spot?

A hot spot is actually a type of button. To create it, you need two layers on the Stage, one for the background text (or graphic) and one for the hotspot.

**On CD**: The following example is on the CD: samples/chapter02/sample_2-4.swf. It shows how to use hot spots with bulleted lists. The learner moves the mouse over each item to see a more detailed description of that list item. The learner cannot see the hot spots, but you can view them if you open sample_2-4.fla. The hot spots appear as transparent blue areas when you view them on the Stage. (However, they are invisible to the learner in the published course.)

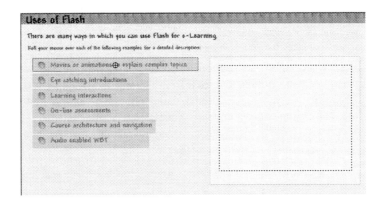

**Note:** Since hot spots are invisible, you should always include directions indicating what you want the learner to do. For example, "Place the cursor over each item in the list for a complete description".

# Creating a Mouse Over

This step-by-step tutorial takes you through the process of creating a series of hot spots over a graphic and then displaying relevant text when the learner moves the mouse over each respective hot spot. In this case, there is a graphic that contains a series of nautical flags. Each individual flag is covered with a hot spot. When the learner moves the mouse over a particular hot spot, some text displays that describes the corresponding flag.

## Viewing the Finished Interaction

Before you try to create the interaction, take a look at the finished product. Think about what causes the actions to be triggered and the result of these events.

**On CD**: Take a moment and try out the finished interaction: samples/chapter02/sample_2-5.swf.

## Creating the Hot Spots

**1**  Open the file samples/chapter02/sample_2-5start.fla.

This file contains the basic page setup and the flag graphics. You will be adding the hot spots, the Dynamic Text field and the code that will place the text in the Dynamic Text field.

The first step is to create the button that will act as the hotspot. In this exercise we will use a slightly different method for creating the button.

**2**  Select the first frame in the Hot Spots layer.

**3**  Using the rectangle tool draw a square that adequately covers the first flag. The color of the square doesn't matter.

**4**  Make sure the entire square is selected and convert it to a button symbol (Modify → Convert to Symbol). Name it *Hot Spot*.

**Caution:** When creating a hot spot make sure that the hot spot is large enough to enable the learner to select it. If you draw a hollow shape (no fill) with thin lines it will be difficult for the learner to select it. Additionally, when there are multiple hot spots on a page, you need to ensure that these areas do not overlap, or you can get some unexpected results.

**5**   Edit the button symbol using one of the techniques discussed earlier in the chapter.

**6**   Click and drag the Up frame to the Hit frame.

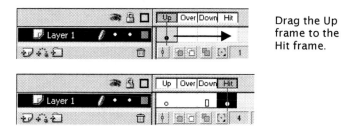

Drag the Up frame to the Hit frame.

This will leave the button without anything in it. The square that is in the Hit frame will identify the "hot" area of the button even though there is no visible image.

**7**   Return to the main timeline.

When you return to the main timeline, notice that the hot spot has a transparent aqua appearance. This occurs because the button has no visual appearance; the Hit frame merely defines the area that is active.

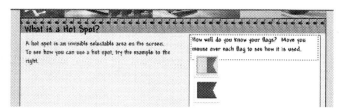

**8**   In the Properties Inspector, enter *hotspot1* in the Instance Name field.

**9**   Create a Dynamic Text field in the Result Text layer to display the results of the user rolling the mouse over the hot spot. Establish the text field's properties as shown in this table:

| Parameter | Setting |
|-----------|---------|
| Field Type | Dynamic Text |
| Name | description |
| Line Type | Multiline |
| Font | Use a serif font of about 12 points. |

**10** Position the text field next to the first flag as shown here:

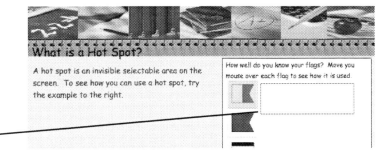

Dynamic Text
field

**11** Select the hot spot, open the Actions panel, and add this code.

```
on (rollOver) {
    description.text = "This is alpha. It means diver down keep clear.";
}
```

Text field's ID

Property to
modify

New value for
the property

This code places text into the text field when the cursor is rolled over the hot
spot.

**12** Set the text field to be blank when the user moves the cursor away from the
hot spot by adding this code immediately below the rollover event handler:

```
on (rollOut) {
    description.text = " ";
}
```

**13** Test the movie and make sure this hotspot is working correctly.

**14** Copy and paste the hot spot object you created so that there is one hot spot
per flag.

**Tip:** If you copy a hot spot, the actions are copied as well. Then you can just adapt the actions as needed. However, if you drag a hot spot from the library on to the Stage, there will be no actions associated with the new instance of the hot spot.

**15** Modify the actions and the instance name of each hot spot according to this table:

| Hot Spot | ID (Instance Name) | Text |
|---|---|---|
|  | hotspot2 | This is Bravo. It means dangerous cargo. |
|  | hotspot3 | This is Charlie. It means 'yes'. |
|  | hotspot4 | This is Delta. It means keep clear. |
|  | hotspot5 | This is Echo. It means alter course to starboard. |
|  | hotspot6 | This is Foxtrot. It means disabled. |

**16** Test your movie and make any changes as needed.

When you tested your movie, did you notice that the description stayed in the same location? It will be easier for the learner to associate the description with the flag, if it appears next to the flag.

**17** Use this sample code to add an action to each of your hot spots–an action that moves the text field to be relative to the hot spot. To do so you need to modify the _y coordinate of the description text box to be similar to that of the hotspot.

```
on (rollOver) {
  description.text = "This is alpha. It means diver down keep clear.";
  description._y = hotspot1._y + 15;
}
```

Modify the text field's y coordinate
to be similar to the hot spot's y
coordinate.

```
on (rollOut) {
description.text = " ";
}
```

**18** Make one final test of your movie to make sure it is functioning correctly.

**Note:** We put the +15 pixels to make the two items align properly. This number may be different for you, depending upon the size of your hot spot and your text field. In this code we used the actual instance name of the button instead of the keyword **this**. In buttons, it refers to the main timeline not the button.

# Choosing the Best Type of Interactivity

Use the following guidelines to determine the best type of interaction to use for a given situation:

- Use mouse overs when there are many interactions on the page and the learner wants to quickly see the result of each.
- Use mouse clicks when there is a large amount of text to reveal. It is hard for the learner to hold the mouse still for the amount of time required to read a large amount of text.

Most people think of Mouse Over interactions as hot spots and Mouse Click interactions as buttons. However, there is nothing that prevents you from using the **on (release)** event for a hot spot so that the learner can click on it to trigger an action. Likewise, you could use the **on(rollOver)** event on a button so that the learner can roll over it to trigger an action. You could also combine these two events to display two types of information.

Keep in mind that most learners assume that buttons are clickable objects. Therefore, if you use a button as a hot spot, you should either code for both the **on(release)** AND the **on (rollOver)** events, or you will want to make your directions extremely clear to the learner.

# Enhancing Your Interactions

So far in this chapter you have created some basic functional interactions. There are many ways to enhance these interactions. The following table describes a few of these enhancements:

| Enhancement | Description |
| --- | --- |
| Modify the properties of the Dynamic Text field | You can control the properties of the Dynamic Text field such as the color, font, alignment, line wrap, and so on. Set these properties in the Properties Inspector for the Dynamic Text field. |
| Use ActionScript to format the Dynamic Text field's text | Another option is to specify text formatting in Dynamic Text fields with basic HTML tags and attributes. This enables you to specify the formatting for a portion of the text rather than the entire text field. To do this, select the Render text as HTML option in the Property Inspector (or use ActionScript to set the HTML property of the Text Field object to **true**). Then, use ActionScript to apply HTML tags to text field. In the following example, the word "correct" is in bold and appears below the word "That's", `Result.html = true;` `result.htmlText = "That's<B>Correct!</B>";` See your Flash documentation for more information about HTML text. |

| Enhancement | Description |
|---|---|
| Play a movie clip | Sometimes you want to display text when the learner clicks on a button (or hot spot); other times you'll want to display graphics or multimedia instead. |
| | Creating a movie clip object is similar to creating a button object. The movie clip has its own timeline in which you place graphics, animation, or audio as needed. You would then place that movie clip in the main timeline. |
| | For more information on creating multimedia movie clips, see Chapter 4: *Adding Multimedia to a Course*. |

# Creating Links to Web Pages

It is very useful to be able to link to additional information from within an e-Learning course. This puts the learner in control of the level of depth that he or she wants to explore. You can provide links to external web sites or to pages that you create to support the e-learning course. For example, you could create a glossary page or a site that contains the complete product reference guide.

In a typical HTML editor, you can easily associate a link to a URL (i.e., a web page) with any piece of text using the <A HREF> tag. However, in Flash MX you will use the link property as shown here:

Highlight the text that you want to have linked.

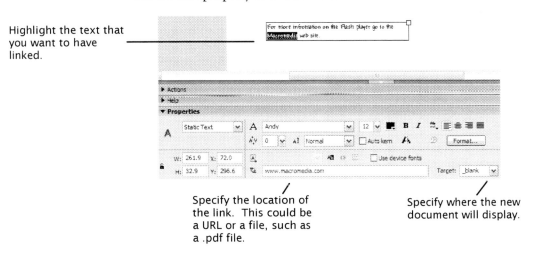

Specify the location of the link. This could be a URL or a file, such as a .pdf file.

Specify where the new document will display.

The options for the target setting include:

- **_self** Specifies that the new URL will replace the contents of the current frame in the current window. This means that the contents of the current page will go away. Select this option when you are using the link to navigate to another page in a course.
- **_blank** Specifies that the new URL will appear in a new window. Select this option when you want to display secondary reference information in your course.
- **_parent** Specifies that the new URL will appear in the parent of the current frame.
- **_top** Specifies that the new URL will appear in the top-level frame of the current window.

In cases where you want to display the page in a new window you would select the **_blank** option.

Once you have set up the link, you may want to format it to look like a link. This inlcudes drawing a line under the text to indicate that it is a link. (Flash has no underline property.)

After you set up and format the link, you will want to test it to ensure that it links to the correct location.

 **Tip:** If you want to provide a link from a button or a hotspot, use the getURL action. Specify the link and the target as shown in the following example:

```
getUrl ("lesson01page02.html", "blank");
```

# Summary

Learner interactivity is a key ingredient to successful e-learning. Interactivity helps the learner explore the information in a more hands-on fashion. This is more motivating for the learner. It creates interest and improves retention of the material.

In this chapter, you have been introduced to button click and roll over interactions. You learned to create buttons and hot spots and use them in a learning activity. You also learned multiple ways to enhance these types of interactions.

The remaining chapters in this section build on these techniques and enable you to do more complex interactions such as simulations.

# Creating Simulations **3**

At times you may want to design an e-learning course where the learner can perform the actual steps of a task. For example, if your course teaches the learner how to use a software application, you may want the learner to be able to expore the use of the toolbar icons, or perform a complete task without actually invoking the live application. This is known as a *simulation*. You can use simulations for on-line activities or quiz questions.

To create a simulation, you combine the use of interactive elements that you worked with in the previous lesson such as hot spots, buttons, and links. In addition, you need to add other types of interactivity such as responding to keyboard input and drag-and-drop elements. For some types of simulations, your movie will branch based upon the learner's responses.

In this chapter you will learn how to:

- Plan a simulation and when you should use it.
- Arrange the components of a simulation.
- Specify hot areas in a simulation.
- Specify keyboard input in a simulation.
- Process learner actions and provide feedback.
- Navigate through the steps of a simulation.

# Using Simulations

The term simulation means different things to different people. Frequently, simulations are activities where the user clicks on active areas to perform a task or receive additional information or instruction. These active areas can contain graphics, text, or be empty. Another way to perform a simulation is to play a video or audio clip that simulates a real-world scenario. The learner then responds to questions or performs tasks to work through the scenario.

The following are examples of simulated applications:

- Software applications
- Mechanical devices
  - Home electronics (VCR/DVD Player, Stereo, Cell Phone, PDA, etc.)
  - Motors/engines
  - Medical equipment
  - Manufacturing equipment
  - Dashboards
- Case studies
  - Customer service
  - Management interactions
  - Doctor/patient interactions

**Note:** In simulation design a wide range of realism and sophistication is possible. For example, when a tool or an application has multiple ways to perform a task, your simulation will be more realistic if you include all possibilities. This can be a time-consuming proposition; accordingly, you should plan up front how realistic your simulation needs to be in order to meet the objectives of your course.

**Note:** Some e-learning Developers consider a demonstration (a screen movie that shows the user how to complete a task in an application) to be a simulation. A demonstration that does not require the learner's input is not a simulation. We only address simulations in this chapter.

## Types of Simulations

Simulations fall into two basic categories, open-ended and structured. The following table highlights the differences between the two types:

| Open-Ended | Structured |
|---|---|
| Enables the learner to freely explore a simulated environment. | The learner is guided through the steps of a process. At each step, the learner is given alternatives where there are correct and incorrect options. The next step in the simulation is based upon the learner's response. |
| Here are some ways that you may want to use a open-ended simulation:<br><br>■ Teach the parts of an object:<br>　● Pieces of a machine<br>　● Parts of a map<br>　● Parts of the human body<br>　● Components of a software application's user interface<br>■ Teach a process:<br>　● Tasks in a flowchart<br>　● Milestones in a timeline<br>■ To allow learners to apply what they have learned by presenting them with a task in a simulated environment and letting them complete the task. | Here are some ways that you may want to use a structured simulation:<br><br>■ Walk the learner through a sequential process<br>■ Teach a series of concepts or tasks that build upon one another<br>■ Assess the learner's ability to perform a task that must be performed in a prescribed way |

# Simulation Components

Simulations should contain the following basic elements:

■ A clear description of the purpose of the simulation. For structured simulations, you need to include specific directions for each step of the activity.

■ An initial graphic or diagram that represents the simulated environment.

■ A method(s) that the learner will use to interact with the simulation. There are several methods that you can use:

　● Click on hot spots
　● Rollover an image
　● Enter text

- Press a key on the keyboard
- Drag objects (joysticks, dials, sliders, or take objects)
- Feedback (for both correct and incorrect actions)
- Branching. The learner may be asked to perform one set of steps if his action is correct and a different set of steps if his action is incorrect.

# Getting Organized

Your simulation will turn out better if you are well organized before you begin.

**When you create a simulation, you will need to follow these steps to get organized:**

**1**  Plan out how you want the simulation to flow.

Many tasks that you normally think of as one step really require more than one step. Be prepared to take as many screen shots or create as many images as necessary to complete all of these tasks. For example, making a selection from a drop down list requires the user to first click on the arrow ▼ to the right of the box, highlight the appropriate selection, and then click on it. Entering text in a field may require tabbing to the field first.

**2**  Create the graphics to make your simulation work.

Depending upon the simulation this may mean:

- Taking digital photographs.
- Drawing the graphics using a graphic development tool such as Adobe® PhotoShop® or Macromedia Freehand®.
- Taking screen captures (for software application simulations) using a screen capture utility such as TechSmith's SnagIt® or Jasc's PaintShop™ Pro®.

**Note:** When you take screen shots, make sure that they are all aligned, so there is no jump from step to step. Likewise, if you forget a shot in a sequence, you may need to retake the entire sequence to ensure continuity.

**3**  Import the graphics needed for the simulation.

**4**  Determine how big the Flash document will need to be in order to accommodate the graphics. You can adjust the height and width of the screen by selecting Modify → Document and providing the appropriate width and height settings.

You may be surprised by how much screen real estate simulations take up. You may be tempted to resize the graphics; however, the graphics often get blurry when they are scaled even if you are careful to maintain the aspect ratio of the graphic. Resizing the graphics may also make the screens too small for the learner to work with effectively. If you do need to resize a graphic, it is generally best to resize the graphic in a graphics program.

**5**  Organize your layers to include: graphics, hot spots, text, and feedback.

# Creating a Software Simulation

Since computer software simulations are prevalent in e-learning, you will create a software simulation in this step-by-step tutorial. The components used for software simulations are the same for other types of simulations. In this example, your simulation takes the learner through the task of creating a symbol in Flash.

## Viewing the Finished Simulation

Before you try to create the simulation, take a look at the finished product. Walk through each step of the interaction. Notice the types of interactions that you need to do in order to perform the task. What happens when you perform a step correctly? What happens when you perform a step incorrectly?

**On CD**: Take a moment and try out the finished interaction:

**samples/chapter03/sample_3-3.swf.**

## Laying Down the Text and Graphics

First you need to create the starting state of the simulation. This includes the text directions and graphics that represent the software.

**Use these steps to set up the simulation:**

**1**  Open samples/chapter03/sample_3-3start.fla.

Notice that several layers have already been created and all the screen shots have been imported into the library (using File → Import → Import to Library). In the Actions layer we have included a **stop** action. We have also created a Hot Spot button, similar to the one that you created in Chapter 2, and a **Hint** button.

The starting image and text have been added to the first frame of the appropriate layers.

*The starting graphic appears on the Stage in the Picture layer:*

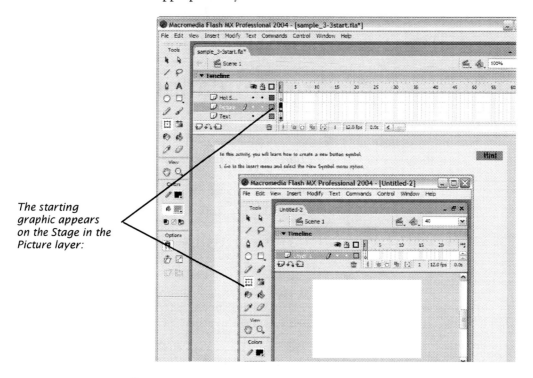

**2**   On the timeline, extend each of the layers to include 70 frames. Select frame 70 and insert a new frame (Insert → Timeline → Frame).

**3**   In the Picture layer, insert a keyframe (Insert → Timeline → Keyframe) and place the associated graphics from the library according to this table:

| Keyframe | Graphic |
| --- | --- |
| 1 | Sim1 |
| 10 | Sim2 |

| Keyframe | Graphic |
|----------|---------|
| 20 | Sim3 |
| 30 | Sim1 and Sim4 |
|    | Sim1 will sit behind Sim4. Use (Modify → Arrange) to force Sim4 in front if it is not already in front. |
| 40 | Sim1 and Sim5 |
|    | Sim1 will sit behind Sim5. |
| 50 | Sim1 and Sim6. |
|    | Sim1 will sit behind Sim6. |
| 60 | Sim7 |

**Tip:** By inserting a keyframe instead of a blank key frame, the original image is copied to the new keyframe. This will help you position the new image. You may need to delete the old image if it is not needed.

**4**   Test the position of the images by moving the playhead through the entire movie. Make changes as needed.

It is likely that your graphics jumped from frame to frame. Use the Info panel or the Properties Inspector to ensure that your graphics are properly aligned. You can modify the X and Y coordinates for each of the graphics to make sure they line up in sequence.

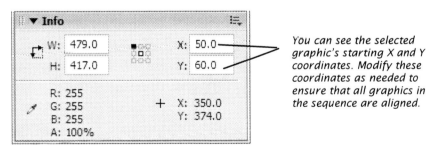

*You can see the selected graphic's starting X and Y coordinates. Modify these coordinates as needed to ensure that all graphics in the sequence are aligned.*

**5**   In the Text layer, insert a new keyframe at the frame indicated and change the text as shown in this table:

| Keyframe | Text |
| --- | --- |
| 1 | *1. Go to the Insert menu and select the New Symbol menu option. (Already done for you.)* |
| 30 | *2. Press Delete to remove the default name.* |
| 40 | *3. Enter "My Button" as the new symbol name and click OK.* |
| 60 | *Good Job! You have created a symbol and could begin adding images.* |

Since the movie will not play continuously, you will need to add **stop** actions for each step.

**6** In the Actions layer add a **stop** action to the first keyframe. To add a **stop** action, select the frame, open the Actions panel (Window → Development Panels → Actions) and enter **stop( )** ;.

Now you are ready to begin adding hot spots.

## Adding Hot Spots

At this point, you will add hot spots to enable the learner to interact with the simulation.

**Use these steps to set up the hot spots:**

The first step in the simulation is to have the learner select the Insert menu item.

**1** In frame 1 of the Hot Spots layer, drag the **Hot Spot** button from the library to the Stage and place it over the part of the graphic where the Insert menu appears.

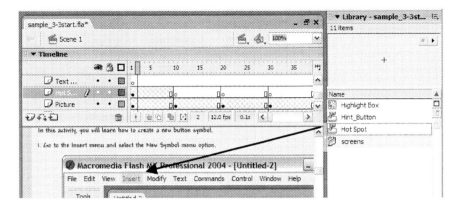

**2**   Resize the instance of the hot spot object to fit the Insert menu.

# Controlling the Flow

For a structured simulation, you need to determine how the simulation will flow. For now, we will only focus on the flow when the learner correctly performs a task. We will deal with incorrect responses later in the tutorial.

**Use these steps to set up the flow of the simulation:**

When the learner clicks on the hot spot, the play head should advance to the next step. In this case, the play head should advance to frame 10.

**1**   To make the playhead advance, enter this code for the hot spot:

```
on(release) {
    gotoAndStop(10);
}
```

**2**   Insert a new keyframe at frame 10 in the Hot Spot layer and move the hot spot over the New Symbol option on the menu. Resize the hot spot to cover the menu option.

To fit over the menu option the width of the hot spot will need to be about 160 pixels. You can make this change in the Properties Inspector.

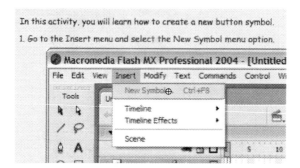

**3**   Modify the actions for the hot spot to reflect two possible learner actions:

- If the learner moves the mouse over the hot spot, then the menu item should highlight (this is the graphic in frame 20).
- If the learner clicks on the hot spot, then the New Symbol dialog box should appear (this is the graphic in frame 30).

```
on(rollOver) {
    gotoAndStop(20);
}
on(release) {
    gotoAndStop(30);
}
```

We need to include both actions because this hotspot is used for both menu images (frame 10 and frame 20).

**Tip:**  To make this simulation even more realistic, you can include a hot spot for each of the menu choices. If the learner selects an incorrect choice, he or she will receive feedback indicating that an incorrect selection was made. You will learn more about feedback in the next section.

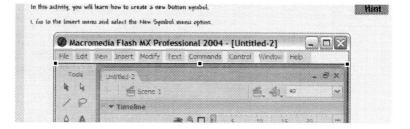

**4**   Insert a new keyframe at frame 30 in the Hot Spot layer.

The first thing the learner should do at this point in the simulation is to press the DELETE key. Once the DELETE key is pressed we need to advance the play head to frame 40.

**5**   Delete the hot spot since it is not necessary for this step.

Since the next step is to press the DELETE key we do not need the hotspot on this frame. To determine whether or not the DELETE or BACKSPACE key is pressed we need to create a listener that will watch for these events.

Listeners are an ActionScript technique that lets you assign an event handler to an object. The object may be a symbol or text field or it can be a newly created object as shown below.

**Note:** Many ActionScript coders recommend the use of listeners for all of your code. This way the code remains in the frames and is not attached to individual objects. This makes it easier to find the code. In this exercise we use a listener so that we can detect when the key is pressed.

**6**   Select frame 30 in the Actions layer, open the Actions panel (Window → Development Panels → Actions) and change the code to look like this:

```
myListener=new Object();
myListener.onKeyDown = function(){
    if(Key.isDown(Key.DELETEKEY)){
            gotoAndStop(40);
    }
    if(Key.isDown(Key.BACKSPACE)){
            gotoAndStop(40);
    }
}
Key.addListener(myListener);
stop();
```

The first line of code creates a new object in Flash called **myListener**. The purpose of this object is to give us a place to attach a listener that will check for a key press.

The next eight lines define a function that will execute whenever a key is pressed (onKeyDown). This function checks to see if the DELETE key or BACKSPACE key was pressed. If one of these two keys were pressed, the playhead is advanced to frame 40.

The last line of code that was added, assigns the **myListener** object as a listener for any events that occur for **Key**. **Key** is the object that controls keyboard input and contains the onKeyDown event. This line activates the entire script.

**Tip:** In order to test the onKeyDown event for the DELETE and BACKSPACE keys, you will need to publish the movie. The standard testing method (Control → Test Movie) does not respond to these two keys.

**7**  Insert a keyframe at frame 50 in the Hotspot layer (Insert → Timeline → Keyframe). Copy the hot spot from frame 30 to frame 50 and place it over the **OK** button.

**8**  Modify the **on(release)** action to advance the play head to frame 60. Delete the **on(rollover)** handler.

The width of the hotspot will need to be about 70 pixels.

We will take care of the text field for frame 40 in the next section.

**9**  Insert a keyframe at frame 40 of the Hot Spot layer. Copy the hot spot from frame 50 to frame 40 and place it over the **OK** button so that it is available while the learner is typing the name of the symbol.

**10**  Test your movie.

Remember to test the DELETE key you will need to publish the movie and open the SWF file. In most cases Control → Test Movie will not respond to the DELETE or BACKSPACE key. Most other keys should work.

The hot spots should work correctly; however, there are still some pieces missing.

## Creating Text Fields

While many simulations contain hot spots, there are additional elements that you will likely include. For example, the learner needs to type in a name for the new button. Any typing activity will require text fields.

**Use these steps to create a text field:**

**1**  Insert a layer just above the Hot Spots layer. Name your new layer Text Fields.

**2**  Insert a keyframe at frame 40.

*keyframe*

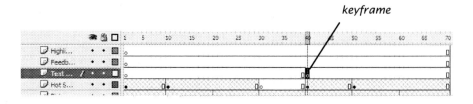

**3**    In frame 40 of the Text Field layer draw a text input field over the top of the
**Name** field.

*Use the Text tool to place
an input text field over
the screen capture in the
location where the
learner will enter the
symbol name.  Make sure
the text field fills the
entire Name field.*

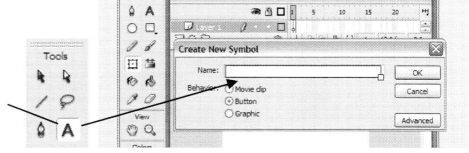

**4**    In the Properties Inspector, make sure that the font is Microsoft Sans Serif. Set
the size to 11 and the color to black. Select *Input Text* as the text field type.

*Select Input Text
as the text field
type.*

These font properties closely match the real application.

**5**    In the Properties Inspector name the text field *symbolname*.

You'll use this Instance Name later on to capture the text that the learner
entered.

**6**    In the Text Field layer insert a blank keyframe at frame 50 (Insert → Timeline
→ Blank Keyframe).

We don't want the text field available after the name is entered; therefore, we
insert a blank keyframe. Frame 50 will be used in a later section to provide a tip
the learner if needed.

When the movie advances to the frame with the field, the cursor needs to be in
the text field. In order to make this happen we need to add a line of
ActionScript.

**7**    Select frame 40 in the Actions layer and open the Actions panel (Window →
Development Panels → Actions).

**8**   Add a line of code to the Actions panel that sets the focus to the text field. Setting the focus to the text field will cause the cursor to appear.

```
Selection.setFocus("symbolname")
stop();
```

The simulation needs to know when the learner is done typing the symbol name. In this case, the learner will click on the **OK** button that already includes a hot spot.

**9**   Publish the movie and test it.

The next step is to evaluate if the learner made the correct entry. You will learn more about evaluating learner input and providing feedback in the next section of this tutorial.

# Responding to Learner Actions

At this point, the learner could step through the simulation. However, the learner does not receive any feedback when the task is not performed correctly. There are several methods that you can use to provide feedback to the user:

- Provide a **Hint** button, which the learner can click on to get some suggestions on how to proceed.
- Provide an error message with corrective feedback if the learner clicks in the wrong area or enters the incorrect text in a text field.

Note: Correct feedback is not necessary for this type of simulation because learners know they are correct if they can continue through the simulation.

Tip: Since you don't want the learner to fail repeatedly, you can provide hints after each successive incorrect attempt. Another option is to provide corrective feedback and then give the learner the option of moving on to the next step or returning to the part of the course where this material is covered.

## Adding Learner Controlled Feedback

In this section, you will add a **Hint** button, which provides hints and visual cues to assist the learner.

**Use these steps to create hints:**

**1**  Create a layer named Buttons above the Feedback layer.

**2**  In the Buttons layer at frame 1, drag the **Hint** button from the library to the Stage and position it as shown.

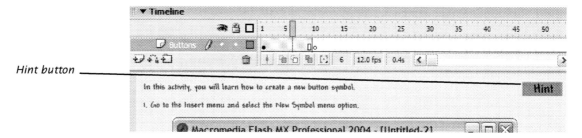

Hint button

**3**  In the Feedback layer, create a Dynamic Text field near the **Hint** button. The text field should have a field name of *hint*. Make sure the text field is **multiline**.

Text Field Type

Name

Multiline text field

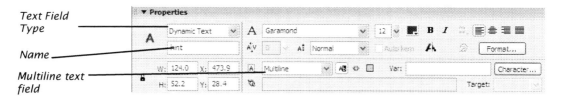

You will want to use a smaller font size and make the text field larger enough to display all the text. Now we will set up the hint text for each area of the simulation.

**4**  Select the **Hint** button, open the Actions panel (Window → Development Panels → Actions) and enter this code:

```
on (release) {
    hint.text = "Click on the Insert menu as shown.";
}
```

When the mouse is clicked, this code sets the text property of the Hint field to the text in quotes. In the next section we will add an image that shows the learner where the Insert menu is located.

**5**  In the Buttons layer insert a keyframe at frame 30 and enter the code in the **Hint** button as shown:

```
on (release) {
    hint.text = "Press the delete key on your keyboard.";
}
```

**6** In the Buttons layer insert a keyframe at frame 40 and enter the code in the **Hint** button as shown

```
on (release) {
    hint.text = "The correct symbol name has been entered. Click the
OK button.";
    gotoAndStop(50);
}
```

**7** Publish and test your movie and make any changes as needed.


## Adding Learner Controlled Feedback with Dynamic Graphics

It is a good idea to include a highlight to reinforce any hint text. Adding a highlight requires that you place a graphic on your simulation.

Since it would be difficult to specify the graphics that you want to display using ActionScript code, you are going to create a movie clip that only gets played when the user clicks on the **Hint** button.

**Use these steps to add a hint graphic:**

**1** In the Highlights layer, create a red box around the hot spot for the Insert menu item as shown.

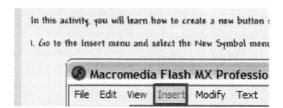

The stroke color should be red. The fill color should be blank. The line width should be 3 pixels.

**2** Turn the highlight into a movie clip symbol (Modify → Convert to Symbol).

The Convert to Symbol dialog box displays. Name this symbol **Highlight Box** and select **Movie clip** as the behavior:

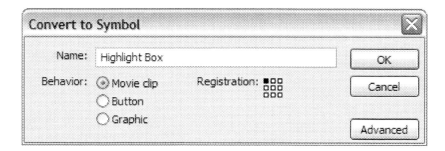

**3**   Click **OK.**

**4**   In the Properties Inspector for the movie clip, give the clip the Instance Name **highlight_clip.**

There are a number of different ways to make the highlight appear. In this exercise you will make the movie clip invisible by changing its alpha setting to 0. Then when you want it to show, change the alpha setting to 100.

**5**   In the Properties Inspector select **Alpha** from the Color drop down box and enter *0%*.

**6**   Select the **Hint** button in the first frame and add a line of code to change the alpha setting:

```
on (release) {
   hint.text = "Click on the Insert menu as shown.";
   highlight_clip._alpha=100;
}
```

So that the highlight doesn't display throughout the remainder of the movie, we need to add some code to make it transparent again.

**7**   Select frame 30 in the Actions layer and add this statement immediately before the **stop();** action:

```
highlight_clip._alpha=0;
```

**8**   Publish and test the movie.

## Capturing User Errors

Previously, you used hot spots to capture correct learner actions. You can also use hot spots to capture incorrect learner responses. For example, you can create hot spots that tell the learner he or she has clicked the incorrect menu.

Create and place as many hot spots as you think you need. For example, you could create hot spots for the individual menu or you could create a larger hot spot covering several menus and give more generic feedback.

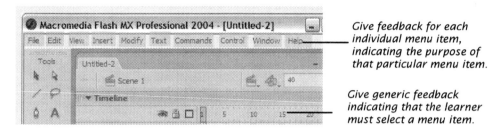

*Give feedback for each individual menu item, indicating the purpose of that particular menu item.*

*Give generic feedback indicating that the learner must select a menu item.*

You will also need to create a Dynamic Text field to display the feedback. In this case, you can just use the same text field that you used when you created the hint.

For the **on(release)** event for each hot spot, set the text property for the Dynamic Text field to provide the appropriate feedback to the learner. For example, for the hot spot over the Help menu, you would use the following code:

```
on (release) {
   hint.text = "Sorry, this menu enables you to get help. Try again.";
}
```

**Caution:** Make sure that the hot spots do not overlap or you will get some unexpected results.

**Tip:** Instead of using hot spots, you could use ActionScript to capture the location that the user clicked (x and y coordinates) and then provide the appropriate feedback based upon the coordinates. This can be a very efficient way to create a simulation; and requires a deeper level of understanding of programming with ActionScript.

## Evaluating Learner Entries to Input Text Fields

In addition to interactions with hot spots, simulations may include learner entries into text fields. When working with text fields you need to determine when the learner's input will be evaluated. The following are some possible scenarios:

- **Evaluate the learner's input in response to a key press on the keyboard**. For example, you want the learner to type in a number between 0 and 9. You will evaluate their input as soon as a number is typed.

- **Wait until the learner has completed typing a text entry and then evaluate the input**. In this scenario, the learner will be typing more than one character, so your simulation needs to determine when the learner has completed the typing.

  For example, the learner might tab to the next field (or click on the next field) upon completion of the entry. Or the learner might click a button as was done in the previous simulation.

In our example, the learner will type the text in the text field and then click on the **OK** button.

*There is a hot spot over the OK button.*

In some scenarios, you may not care if the learner types in a specific piece of text in the text field, while in other situations you might be looking for an exact match. In this example, it doesn't matter what the learner calls the symbol. Therefore, you can just advance the playhead to the next step when the learner clicks on the **OK** button.

If you were looking for something more specific, use an **if** statement to determine if the learner's input matches the required input. If it does, advance the playhead to the appropriate frame, otherwise provide corrective feedback.

```
on (release) {
    if (symbolname.text = "MyButton") {
        gotoAndStop(60);
    } else {
        hint.text="You entered an incorrect name  Try again.";
    }
}
```

# Simulation Enhancements

Using the techniques presented in this chapter, you can create some nice simulations. There are some additional enhancements that you can make to further improve the usability of your simulation. We provide a high-level overview of these enhancements in this section.

# Change the Hand Cursor Over Hot Spots

As you tested your simulations, you may have noticed that the mouse pointer changes to a hand when the mouse moves over a hot spot.

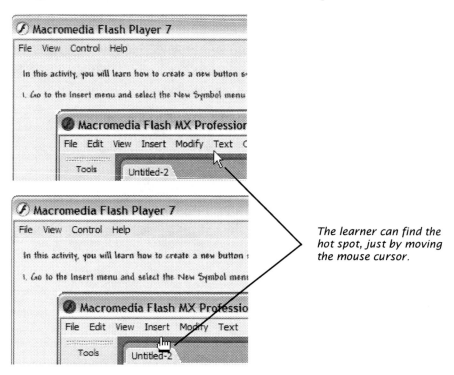

The learner can find the hot spot, just by moving the mouse cursor.

Since you don't want to constantly give hints to the learner, you can turn off this feature by setting the **useHandCursor** property to False. The following is an example of the code that you would use for the hot spot:

*0 means "false" or "off".
1 means "true" or "on".*

```
on (rollOver) {
    hotspot.useHandCursor=0;
}
```

*This is the instance name of the hot spot. You set this in the Properties Inspector.*

## Building Realistic Simulations

Building a realistic simulation isn't complicated, but it does take time and attention to detail. In the current example, when the learner moves the mouse over each menu item, the graphic remains static.

### Attention to Detail

You could make this simulation more realistic by changing the menu item to appear shaded when the learner moves the mouse over it.

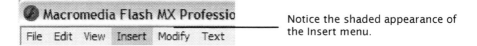 Notice the shaded appearance of the Insert menu.

To do this you would need to take additional screen shots and have some additional keyframes set up to include these graphics. You would then add actions to each hot spot's rollover event to move the playhead to the appropriate location on the timeline

### Providing Multiple Ways to Perform a Task

Most software applications have more than one method for performing a task. For example, in many applications you can perform common tasks by clicking an icon on the toolbar, using a menu, or using a shortcut key. You may need to enhance a simulation to include all input methods.

# Creating Other Types of Simulations

You can use the same principles described in this chapter to produce other types of simulations. For example, you can create a simulation that helps the learner to use a device (such as a cell phone) using hot spots and Dynamic Text fields.

## Device Simulation Example

In the following example, the learner will go through the steps to retrieve voice mail. The simulation has the following features:

- There are hot spots for each button on the phone. Each hot spot has particular actions associated with it.
- When the learner presses the correct button, the movie is advanced to the correct frame that displays the number. For example, if the learner presses the * key, the display window text will update to show a *.
- When the learner presses the incorrect key, the appropriate feedback will be displayed.

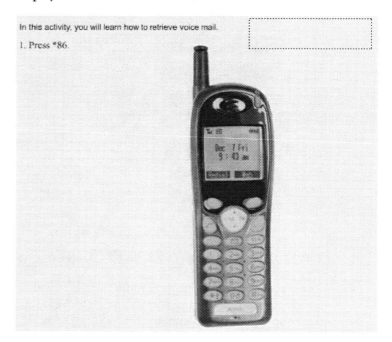

 **On CD**: Take a moment and try out the finished interaction:

**samples/chapter03/sample_3-4.swf.** To see how this simulation was put together open the FLA file.

## Situation Based Simulations

The simulations presented in this lesson required the learner to perform a task with a tool—either a software application or a device. However, sometimes you want to simulate interactions between people. You could play a video or some audio and ask the learner to diagnose a problem or to determine an appropriate course of action.

In the following simulation, the learner will listen to a phone conversation that takes place between a customer support representative and a customer. At different points in the conversation, the learner will be asked to identify the correct way to proceed.

### Troubleshooting a Printer Problem

In this activity, you will listen to a conversation between a customer service rep and a customer. At different points in the conversation, you will have to specify what the the customer service reps next steps should be. *Click on the speaker to start the audio.*

At this point, what should you do?

- Ask the customer for the printer's model number.
- Ask the customer for the printer's serial number.
- Transfer the customer to the sales department.

When building this type of simulation, you use a series of audio clips instead of a series of images. This sample simulation is restrictive. It provides feedback and then moves the learner to the next step in the scenario. The learner is not allowed to stray from the correct path. This is only one of many ways to build a situation based simulation.

**On CD**: Take a moment and try out the finished interaction:

**samples/chapter03/sample_3-5.swf.** To see how this simulation was put together open the FLA file. Because of a component that was used to provide feedback in this simulation, you need Flash player 7 or greater to play it. To open the FLA file you must use Flash MX 2004.

# Using Simulation Tools

The process shown in this chapter can be simplified by using a simulation tool. Simulation tools let you go through a software application task on your own computer. While working through the task, the tool records you actions and builds a simulation from them. You can then edit that simulation and provide feedback as necessary.

Using this type of tool will save you some time in building the simulation. However, the flexibility and the size of the finished movie may not be to your liking.

While all of the products listed here provide different functionality, they also include functionality for simulation. Some of the programs are better than others. While this is not a complete list, this will get you started in your search.

- **Macromedia's RoboDemo®**. For more information go to:
  http://www.macormedia.com.
- **TurboDemo®**. For more information go to:
  http://www.turbodemo.com/eng/index.htm.
- **RapidBuilder**. For more information go to:
  http://www.mjcc.com/rapidBuilder.htm.

These tools can help you build a software simulation, but if you are planning to build some other type of simulation, you will need to use the techniques covered in this chapter.

# Summary

Simulations use mouse actions and text input to step through a task or explore a product. Simulations use a combination of techniques, which were covered in this chapter.

In this chapter, you went through the process of creating a simple software simulation. You learned how to set up the simulation movie, add interactive areas, accept text input, provide hints and feedback, and how to realistically simulate and environment. You also learned how you can enhance that simulation to take it to the next level.

There are software tools available to create software simulations if you choose to go that route, but other types of simulations will require the techniques covered in this chapter.

You can use the same techniques presented in this chapter to create an open-ended exploratory simulation. Rather than the learner being forced through a series of steps, the learner is allowed to proceed in any manner. Short open-ended simulations are easy to create. For example, you could have the user roll over each of the tools in a tool palette to see the tool tips. Longer explorations require significantly more planning and organization.

# Adding Multimedia to a Course 4

Multimedia is a prime reason Developers choose to use Flash in e-learning. This is the area where Flash really shines. There are lots of reasons to use multimedia in e-learning. When used properly, it can engage the learner and enhance the e-learning experience. It can also decrease the amount of reading required by the learner and improve retention of the material.

In this chapter you will learn:

- How to apply multimedia in e-learning.
- How to create a splash screen with moving objects, visual effects, and audio.
- How to add sound to a button.
- Basic information about full motion video.
- How to add sound to HTML-based courses by combining Flash with Dreamweaver CourseBuilder interactions.

# Applications of Multimedia

The term *multimedia* means different things to different people. To some it means full-motion video. To others it is anything that includes audio. And, still others consider animation to be multimedia. In this chapter, we will treat all of these items as multimedia.

The elements you consider to be multimedia are not as important as *how* you use these elements. Since you want to use multimedia for a purpose, rather than gratuitously, we will explore the following applications of multimedia:

| Application | Description |
| --- | --- |
| Splash Screen | Use animation to tell the learner which course (and which version) he or she has accessed in an upbeat and friendly way. In our example, we will animate some text and use some background music. |
| Transition | Use effects to move from one topic to the next. This serves the purpose of orienting the learner as well as keeping the learner's attention. These transitions use effects and animated graphics. |
| Alternative Cue | Use sound or animation to help orient the learner. For example, using supporting highlights, animation, or sound when the learner clicks a button can help the learner to know that the selection has been made. |
| Simplify Complex Concept | Use animation to illustrate a concept such as the flow of a complex diagram or how pieces of equipment fit into a larger logistical process. |
| Case Study | Use still graphics with audio as a low-bandwidth method to show the learner how to apply a concept to a real world scenario. |

| Application | Description |
|---|---|
| Demonstration | Use graphics, animation, and audio to simulate a video presentation. Demonstrations show how to perform a task or use a product. For example, a software demonstration shows the actual movement of the mouse and the data entry on the screen.

Demonstrations can include an audio track (which provides the narration) synchronized with the visuals (screen shots, graphics, text that build, animations, and so forth). See Chapter 5: *Creating Multimedia Demonstrations* for more information on how to create demonstrations. |
| Video | Use full-motion video to show processes that require the learner to master specific techniques such as how to perform a medical procedure, how to paint a picture, or how to play a musical instrument. Additionally, there are times when video has greater impact. For example, a video of a volcano eruption would have more impact than an animated version. |

# Guidelines for Using Multimedia

Let's face it, multimedia is cool, so it is very easy to get carried away with it. Remember, multimedia should support and enhance the e-learning experience, not distract the learner from the content. Before using multimedia in an e-learning course, consider these points:

- Make sure that your learners have the capabilities to use multimedia. For example, the learner should not have out-dated equipment. You also need to consider that the learners may need to have audio capable computers and a reasonably fast connection (depending on the types of media that you are using).

- Make sure to check with your IT department before making fundamental decisions about the use of audio and video over the network. Bandwidth is an important consideration. Even over a local intranet, sound and video can sometimes increase network congestion to an unacceptable level.

- Make sure that your target audience is accepting of multimedia. In some environments multimedia is considered play, rather than learning.

- Make sure that multimedia is being used to support an objective. These types of decisions should be made during the instructional design process.
- Make sure you use a variety of learning methods (text, audio, visuals, etc.) to meet the needs of different learners. You also need to think about the limitations of each of these methods if you are dealing with learners from various cultures, language backgrounds, or those who have disabilities.

**Note:** Remember, some learners work in environments where sound is not acceptable because it is distracting to other workers. Some learners work in environments where it is too loud to be able to hear the sound properly. Make sure that your learners will have access to headphones in these circumstances.

# Using Animation

Animation is simply an object (graphic or text) that changes from frame to frame. For example, you can make the object move across the Stage, change its size, fade in/fade out, change its color, or rotate it. You can have any combination of these things occurring simultaneously for the object. You can also have multiple objects animated at once.

Generally, you create animations by making a change in the object properties from one frame to the next or by creating a tween, where you set a beginning and an end state and Flash figures out the frames in be**tween.**

## Creating a Splash Screen

This step-by-step tutorial takes you through the process of creating a splash screen that contains some simple animation and plays some background music.

### Viewing the Finished Interaction

Before you try to create the button, take a look at the finished product.

**On CD:** Take a moment and try out the finished interaction: **samples/chapter04/sample_4-1.swf.**

## Setting Up the Layers

When creating animations use layers to separate objects so that you can manipulate them independently of one another without introducing unintended changes. If you want Flash to tween the movement of multiple symbols simultaneously, each must be on a separate layer.

Tip: If you have a lot of objects, and thus a lot of layers, you can use layer folders to help keep your layers organized.

**Use these steps to set up the layers:**

**1**   Create a new movie that is 300 x 300 pixels.

**2**   In the timeline, insert and name the layers as shown in this table. If you insert the layers in the order shown in this table, the last layer (Actions) will be at the top.

| Layer | Description |
| --- | --- |
| Audio | Contains the music that will play in the background. |
| Background | Contains static artwork. |
| Title Text | Contains the animated text for the course title. |
| Welcome Text | Contains the animated text for the welcome message. |
| Actions | Contains a simple action to stop the movie. |

**3**   In the Background layer, import the background graphic (File → Import → Import to Stage) from the CD-ROM (**images/pencil.jpg**).

**4**   Resize and reposition the pencil image to fill the Stage. It should be **300 x 300 pixels** and located at position **0, 0** if the image position is in the upper, left-hand corner.

**5**   Make sure the Background layer fills 50 frames. (Right-click, CONTROL-click on Macintosh, on frame 50 and choose Insert Frame.)

**6**   Lock the Background layer.

## Creating the Symbols

The next step is to create symbols for each element that you want to animate.

**Use these steps to create the symbols:**

**1**   In the Welcome Text layer, create the welcome text as shown. To create this
text you will create a dark-gray version of the text and a light-gray version. The
light-gray version will sit in front and will be offset 2 pixels to the left and 2
pixels above the dark-gray version. Use a **Verdana, 30 point** font with a **bold**
style. For the dark gray color you can use **#666666**. For the light gray try
**#CCCCCC**.

**Tip:** Create the text field with the dark gray text first. Copy the text field and use paste in
place (Edit → Paste in Place) to create a second copy. Change the color to light gray and
then use the arrow keys to move the text field 2 pixels up and 2 pixels to the left.

Notice that the text is off the Stage to the right of the background. That is
because we want to bring it in as part of the animation.

**2**   With both pieces of text selected, convert them to a symbol (Modify →
Convert to Symbol).

A dialog box displays:

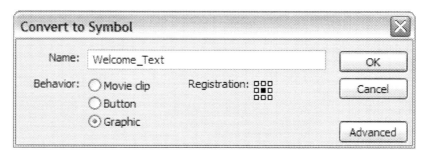

**3** Enter *Welcome_Text* in the name field and select Graphic as the behavior.

**4** Click **OK**.

**5** Insert a frame at Frame 50 (Insert → Timeline → Frame) so that the Welcome_Text fills 50 frames.

**6** In the Title Text layer, create the title text as shown. To create this text you will create a yellow version of the text and a black version. The yellow version will sit in front and will be offset 2 pixels to the left and above the black version. Use a **Verdana, 24 point** font with a **bold** style. For the yellow color you can use **#FFCC00**.

**7** With both pieces of text selected, convert them to a symbol (Modify → Convert to Symbol).

**8** In the Convert to Symbol dialog box, enter *Title_Text* in the name field and select Graphic as the behavior.

**9**   Click **OK**.

**10**  Make sure that the Title_Text fills 50 frames.

## Creating the Animation

Now you are ready to create the animation. First you will animate the Welcome Text so that it appears to slide in and onto the screen. Then you will use effects to make the Title Text fade in.

**Use these steps to animate the text:**

**1**   In both the Welcome Text and the Title Text layers insert a keyframe at frame 25 (Insert → Timeline → Keyframe).

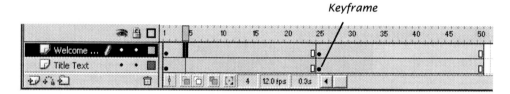

**2**   In the Welcome Text layer, select frame 25. In the Properties Inspector, change the Welcome_Text object's X position to **30**:

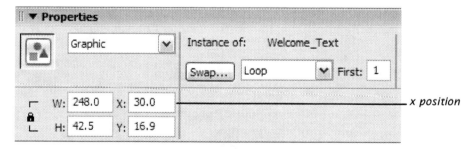

**3**   Select frame 1 in the Welcome Text layer. Then insert a motion tween (Insert → Timeline → Create Motion Tween or choose Motion Tween from the Properties Inspector).

**4**   Test your movie and make any necessary adjustments.

**5**   In the Title Text layer, select frame 1 and delete the text.

**6**   Add a keyframe to frame 50 of the Title Text layer (Insert → Timeline → Keyframe).

**7**   Select the Title_Text instance in frame 25 of the Title Text layer. In the Properties Inspector, change the Alpha channel to be 0% opaque (thus making the object invisible).

*Alpha* channel

**8**   Select frame 25 of the Title Text layer and insert a motion tween (Insert → Timeline → Create Motion Tween or select it in the Properties Inspector).

**9**   Test your movie and make any necessary adjustments.

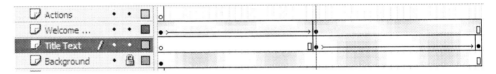

**10**   Insert a keyframe (Insert → Timeline → Keyframe) at frame 50 in the Actions layer.

**11**   Select frame 50 in the Actions layer and open the Actions panel (Window → Development Panels → Actions). Enter a **stop();** command at frame 50.

**12**   Save this file as **sample_4-1a.fla**. You will enhance it with sound later in this chapter.

## Applying Animation to Other Scenarios

In the previous example, you used animation to modify the position and visibility (alpha channel) of symbol instances. You can use tweening to change appearance of graphical objects. For example, you could change the size, color, shape, position, or rotation of the object.

**On CD**: Try *samples/chapter04/sample_4-2.swf* on the CD and look at the animation. Then open up the corresponding FLA file. First, step through the Overview Title layer and notice that the position, size, and alpha channel are all adjusted at different points in the timeline. Then look at the circle layer. Notice how the size, shape, position, and alpha channel are adjusted to make the circle appear to be spinning and then grow until it disappears off the page.

You can also use the same techniques to make effective transitions from page to page or item to item within a page. For example, you can make content appear to fly in or out, just as you might in a PowerPoint™ presentation.

**Caution**: Remember that people read at different rates, so these effects can be very distracting if used improperly. Transition effects work best when the learner initiates an action, such as clicking the next page button, or when they are synchronized with audio.

**On CD**: Try *samples/chapter04/sample_4-3.swf* on the CD and look at the animation. The list of lesson goals moves in and fades up to the lesson description appears.

## Taking Animation To The Next Level

There are some advanced techniques that you can use to create more sophisticated animation. Here are some suggested techniques that you may want to explore in your favorite Flash book.

- Use a mask layer to create a hole through which the contents of an underlying layer(s) is visible.
- Use ActionScript to programmatically move objects through mathematical calculations.
- Use audio effects to make the sound track fade in and fade out or to make the audio loop over a specified series of frames. You will learn more about audio in the next section of this chapter.
- Use third party tools, such as SWISH™ or FlaX™, to create advanced animation effects. These tools cut down on the amount of time you need to spend to get special effects.

**More Information**: Information on these techniques can be found in your Flash documentation as well as in tutorials found in Flash sites on the web. Information on other Flash authoring tools can be found in the Appendices on the CD.

# Using Audio

One of the key benefits of Flash is the ability to work with audio. Audio can make the e-learning more engaging. You can also use it in place of (or as an enhancement to) text, which helps auditory learners retain the information more efficiently. There are many ways to employ audio in e-learning. Here are some examples:

- **Add narrative, voice overs to describe the action occurring on the screen**. In this situation, you will want to synchronize the audio to the action that is occurring on the screen.

- **Create background audio for course introductions, summaries, or transitions**. In this situation, you'll want to play the audio continuously, without regard to the action that is occurring on the screen.

- **Provide an additional method of feedback in response to the learner's actions**. For example, you may want to add a sound to a hot spot button so that the learner has an indication that he or she has made an appropriate selection.

- **Encourage the learner and maintain their attention**. For example, you can add fun sounds when the learner responds correctly to a question.

## Should You Use Audio?

When you design e-learning, you need to evaluate whether audio is appropriate for the project. While a large percentage of learners benefit from the use of audio and the reduction in reading, there are some corporate cultures that find the use of audio to be inappropriate. Additionally, some learners find audio distracting.

If you choose to create a course that uses audio, be sensitive in your selection of sounds. If a sound will be used multiple times within a course, make sure that it will not become tiresome or annoying. For example, if you add background music to your splash screen, keep in mind that the learner has to hear it each time the course launches. Therefore, you may want to pick something that is low key.

You may choose to create a course in which the sound can be turned on or off if the learner finds it intrusive. For background sounds or secondary feedback this is pretty easy to do. If you give the learner the option of turning off the narrative, you should design your content to accommodate both modes. For example, you will provide text in place of the audio narrative. Remember that designing for both text and audio, may affect how you layout your page.

**More Information:** To learn how to create the capability of turning on and off sounds, see Allowing the Learner to Disable Sound later in this chapter.

# Preparing the Audio Files

For background audio there are many sites on the web that sell sound loops and sound effects or you could record your own. For narration, you will need to create and edit your sounds in a third party application, such as CoolEdit® or SoundForge®.

When you save audio using these applications, try to use the smallest size possible, while still maintaining the quality of the sound. Sounds can use up large amounts of RAM as well as disk space. You will need to consider the file format and the file settings:

- **File format:** MP3 is compressed, while WAV and AIF are not. Therefore MP3 will create a smaller file size.
- **Mono vs. Stereo**: In most cases you can use mono rather than stereo without impacting quality. This will cut the file size in half.
- **Bits**: Sounds can be 8 or 16-bit. 8 bit sounds create smaller files, but it can impact quality if you want to create effects after importing the sound into Flash.
- **Sample Rate**: Sounds can be sampled at rates of 11kHz, 22 kHz, or 44 kHz. The higher the sample rate, the higher the quality. Higher sample rates also produce a larger file size. You may need to experiment with the sample rate to determine an acceptable level of quality.

**Tip:** For most narration, we have found mono 16bit 22 kHz to work well, but your results may vary.

# Streaming vs. Event Sounds

Flash has two methods for working with audio: stream sounds and event sounds.

- **Stream sounds** begin playing as soon as enough data for the first few frames has been downloaded. Stream sounds have the capability of being synchronized to specific points on the timeline. Therefore you will want to use stream sounds when you want your narration to be synchronized with the visuals. Stream sounds also work well with long pieces of background music because you do not have to wait for the entire sound to be downloaded before it begins to play.

- **Event sounds** must download completely before playing. The sound continues to play, independently of the timeline, until it is stopped by an action. If the movie stops, the sound keeps playing. Event sounds work best with short pieces of audio such as short sound effects associated with button clicks.

**Caution:** By default, if an event sound is playing and the learner clicks on the button a second time, it will cause a second instance of the sound to begin playing. You can modify this behavior as you will see later in the chapter.

# Using Streaming Sounds for Background Audio

This step-by-step tutorial takes you through the process of importing audio and using it in the background to enhance the animated splash screen that you created earlier in.

## Viewing the Finished Interaction

Before you add the audio, take a look at the finished product. Notice that the audio plays in the background while the animation appears.

**On CD**: Take a moment and try out the finished interaction: *samples/chapter04/sample_4-1.swf*.

**Use these steps to add audio to your movie:**

**1**   Open either the splash screen file that you created earlier in this chapter or *samples/chapter04/sample_4-1a.fla* from the CD.

**2**   Import the sound (File → Import to Library) and select the sound file *audio/jazzy_loop.wav* (or *jazzy_loop.aif* for Macintosh) from the CD.

**3**   Select the first frame of the Audio layer and drag the sound from the library to the Stage.

**4**   Insert a frame (Insert → Timeline → Frame) at frame 50 in the Audio layer.

Notice that the sound shows up in the layer.

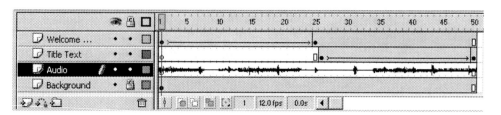

**5**   Select frame 1 and set Sync to **Stream** in the Properties Inspector.

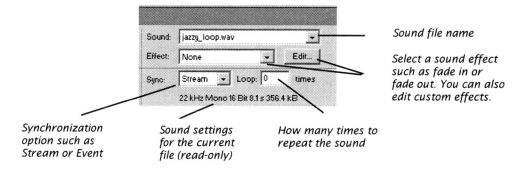

*Sound file name*

*Select a sound effect such as fade in or fade out. You can also edit custom effects.*

*Synchronization option such as Stream or Event*

*Sound settings for the current file (read-only)*

*How many times to repeat the sound*

**6**   Test your movie (Control → Test Movie).

You may choose to change the sound properties. For example, make the sound loop 3 times.

**More Information:** To learn more about sound effects, see Customizing Sounds later in this chapter. If you want to learn how to synchronize your stream sounds to specific events in the timeline, see Chapter 5: Creating Multimedia Demonstrations.

## Using Event Sounds

You can use event sounds to add effects to simulations or in response to buttons. For example, you can use auditory feedback to let the learner know that the mouse is over a hot spot or provide feedback that lets the learner know that the answer to a question was correct.

**Caution:** Using too many sounds with buttons can be distracting to the learner.

# Adding Sounds to a Button

This step-by-step tutorial takes you through the process of adding a sound to a button. When the button is clicked the sound will play to provide feedback to the learner.

## Viewing the Finished Interaction

Before you try to create the button, take a look at the finished product. It is an example of a True/False question. Notice the sound that plays when the learner is correct. Notice the sound that plays when the learner is incorrect.

**On CD**: Take a moment and try out the finished interaction: **samples/chapter04/sample_4-5.swf**.

## Importing the Sounds

The first step is to import the sounds needed into the interaction.

**Use these steps to import the sounds:**

**1**  Open the file **samples/chapter04/sample-4-5_start.fla**.

The file already contains the two question buttons—one for True and one for False. For this exercise you will only need to import the sounds and set them up to play when the learner clicks the button.

**2**  Import the sound file (**audio/correct.wav or correct.aif** for Macintosh) for the correct feedback and (**audio/incorrect.wav or incorrect.aif** for Macintosh) for the incorrect feedback from the CD-ROM (File → Import → Import to Library).

## Associate the Sounds with the Buttons

The next step is to associate the sounds with the Down state of each button. In this example, False is the correct answer choice. Therefore, you will associate the correct sound file with the **False** button and the incorrect sound file with the **True** button.

**Use these steps to associate a sound with a button:**

**1**     Edit the **True** button (double-click the button or select the button and select Edit → Edit in Place from the menu).

**2**     Create a keyframe (Insert → Timeline → Keyframe) in the hit state frame of the Audio layer.

**3**     With the Hit keyframe selected, go to the Properties Inspector and select **incorrect.wav** (or **incorrect.aif** for Macintosh) from the Sound drop-down menu.

**4**     Also select **Event** as the Sync option and set it to repeat **0** times.

**5**     Test your movie and make any adjustments as needed.

**6**     Repeat steps 1-3 for the **False** button, but associate correct.wav (or correct.aif for Macintosh) with the button.

**7**     Test your movie.

       If you try clicking the button multiple times quickly you will notice that the new instance of the sound plays again before the original instance completes. To fix this, go to the Properties inspector and change the Sync. Property to be Start. This option is similar to Event, however, it will only trigger one instance of the sound at a time.

## Taking Sound to the Next Level

There are some techniques that you can use in Flash to customize your audio in order to add special effects. However, for more sophisticated effects you will need to use a third-party audio editing tool. In this section, we will look at the effects that you can create within Flash.

## Creating Audio Effects

There are a limited number of audio effects that you can use to enhance your movie. For example, you can modify the sound properties to gradually fade in or fade out the sound.

*In this case, the sound will gradually fade in.*

If you click on the **Edit** button, you can customize the effect.

*Drag the handles to indicate how quickly each channel will fade in.*

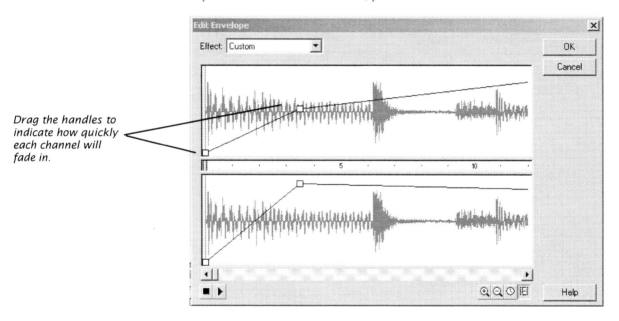

## Provide the Option for Turning Off the Sound

There are many ways to provide an option for turning the sound on and off. One method is to place the audio on a movie clip and play the audio only when the learner selects a button that causes the audio to play. In the following example, if the learner clicks on the **Audio** button, the movie clip that contains the speech's audio begins to play.

Click on the audio button to hear Lincoln's speech.

The Speech_Audio movie clip contains a blank keyframe with a Stop action. The audio begins at frame 2.

*The audio starts in Frame 2.*

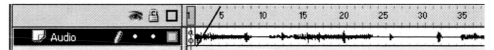

When you place the movie on the Stage you will need to give it an instance name. In this case, the instance name is Speech. Then you will add the following code in the on(release) event for the **Audio** button.

```
on (release){
  Speech.gotoAndPlay(2);
}
```

**On CD**: Take a moment and try out the finished interaction: **samples/chapter04/sample_4-6.swf**. Once you have finished viewing the sample you may want to explore the source file: **samples/chapter04/sample_4-6.fla**.

You could take this idea a step further by allowing the learner to select one of two buttons at the beginning of the course (one to play audio and one to suppress audio). You will then set a variable based upon the user's selection. The variable will change when the learner clicks an **Audio On** or **Audio Off** button. For example, a variable called audioOn could be set to True or False:

```
_global.audioOn = true;
```

In the on(release) event for the **Audio Off** button, set the value of the variable to be False:

```
_global.audioOn = false;
```

Next, place your content into movie clips. Create a version with audio and without audio. In each case where you have some new content to play, you would have an if statement that determines the version that should play:

```
if(_global.audioOn){
  //use the with statement to call the instance of the movie clip
  // that contains audio
else {
  //use the with statement to call the instance of the movie clip
  // that does not contain audio
  }
}
```

**More Information:** To learn more about ways to structure your movies, see Section III: Creating a Custom Course Architecture.

### Working with Sounds at Runtime

Another way to turn sound on and off is to use Flash's sound object to load and control sounds dynamically. For example, when you want to play a sound you can load the sound and then set the volume using ActionScript code. While this is a very elegant solution, this type of manipulation requires a deeper understanding of ActionScript. You should refer to your ActionScript dictionary for a complete description of each of the options associated with the sound object.

# Using Full Motion Video

There are times when true video is required because the subtleties of the content are best conveyed through video. Video can be especially effective when showing procedures with equipment that could be too costly to animate, yet too dangerous or risky to demonstrate to new learners for the first time. For example, video can be especially useful when demonstrating such procedures as manufacturing processes, a scientific phenomenon (such as a volcano erupting), use of military weaponry, proper assembly or disassembly of pieces, and so on. Video is also very effective for behavioral topics like interviewing techniques.

Flash's video support offers some excellent possibilities for demonstrating software procedures. There are already several vendors that offer screen recording software that export to the new Flash video format.

Video can be difficult to implement as it is passive and it requires a lot of bandwidth for effective delivery. Additionally, it can be expensive to obtain or produce high quality video. Therefore, you need to be judicious in your use of video.

On the other hand, digital video cameras are relatively inexpensive, and if your target audience does not require video with expensive transitions and editing cuts, it can be relatively inexpensive to produce.

## Supported Video Formats

If QuickTime 4 is installed, Flash supports .avi, .dv, .mpg, .mpeg, and .mov formats on both Windows and Macintosh. If DirectX 7 or higher is installed, Flash supports .avi, .mpg, .mpeg, .wmv, .asf (Windows only).

Macromedia has developed a new Flash video file format (.flv). If you choose to use this format for video, Flash MX 2004 Professional provides several components that make working with FLV files much easier.

**More Information:** For more details on the supported video formats, see your Flash Documentation under the topic Video import file formats or look on Macromedia's site (**www.macromedia.com**).

# Using Video

In Flash, there are two types of imported video:

- **Embedded Video.** Embedding the video makes it part of the Flash movie just like an imported graphic becomes part of the Flash movie.

  You can synchronize the frame rate of an embedded video to match the frame rate of the main movie timeline. You can also adjust the ratio of the video frame rate to the main timeline frame rate to drop frames from the imported video during playback.

- **Linking Video.** Linking the video maintains it as an independent file. Flash merely maintains a pointer to the source video. Linking is only available for QuickTime (.mov) movies. You cannot edit these files in Flash or publish them as .swf files—they must be published as QuickTime files.

- **Streaming Video**. If you have Flash MX 2004 Professional, you can play back FLV files using the streaming media components.

# Importing and Working with Video Clips

Like audio, you will want to create and edit your video clips in an external video editing application such as Adobe Premier® or Final Cut Pro®. You will then import your video into Flash.

**Use these steps to import a video:**

**1**   Select File → Import to Stage (or File → Import to Library).

   The Import dialog box displays.

**2**   Select the filename and click the **Open** button.

**3**    The Import Video wizard displays. Select either the Embed (as recommended) or the Link option and click **Next.**

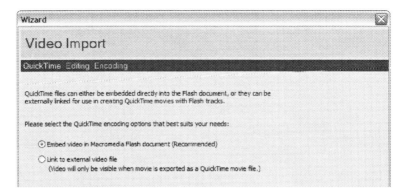

**4**    For embedded files, the Import Video Settings dialog box displays. Select import the entire video and click **Next**.

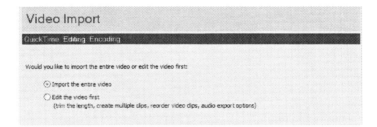

**Note:** If you select the Edit the video first option, Flash displays some simple tools to enable you to edit the length of the video clip and split the video into multiple clips (which you can then reorder). For anything more sophisticated than this type of editing, you will want to use a third party, video–editing tool.

**5**   Specify the compression for the video clip and click **Next**.

*Select a compression profile based on the bandwidth.*

*Edit the advanced settings to resize, crop, colorize, and adjust the brightness/contrast of the imported video.*

*Improve the video quality by increasing the value. However, this will also increase the file size.*

*This option adjusts the frame rate of the video to match the frame rate of the main timeline.*

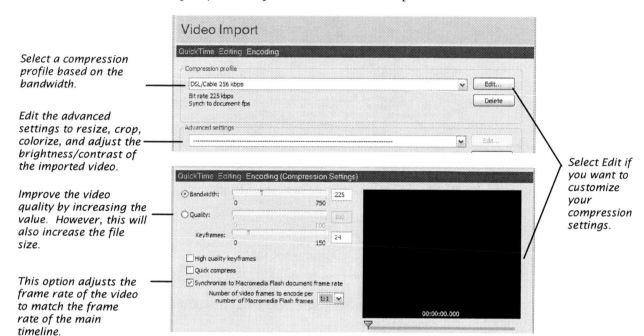

*Select Edit if you want to customize your compression settings.*

Once you click Next Flash prompts you to extend the frames of the movie:

**6**   Click **Yes** to extend the timeline to match the length of the imported movie.

At this point, you can test the movie by using the Controller options.

*Test the playback of the movie using the Controller toolbar options.*

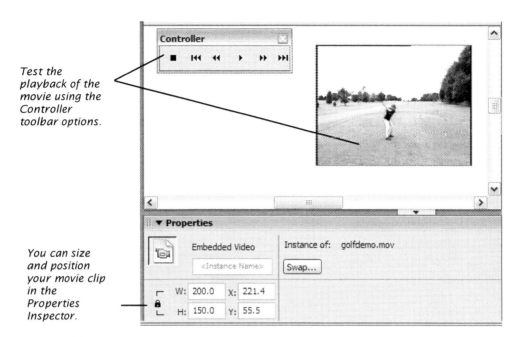

*You can size and position your movie clip in the Properties Inspector.*

**Tip:** You can scale, rotate, or skew your video just as you would any other object in Flash.

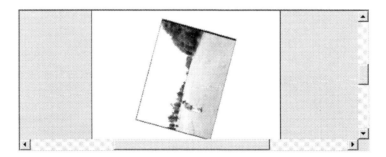

**Note:** In the Properties Inspector, you can specify settings for the instance of a movie. However, if you want to modify the properties for the movie itself, you need to access them from the library.

Double-click the movie to access the Properties *dialog box.*

# Using Flash to Add Sound to CourseBuilder Interactions

The CourseBuilder extension to Macromedia Dreamweaver allows you to create sophisticated, HTML-based interactions. Most e-learning developers use CourseBuilder to create online assessment interactions. You can use Flash to add audio to CourseBuilder interactions.

To use Macromedia Flash movies in CourseBuilder, use the **Control Shockwave or Flash** action in the Action Manager.

**Use these steps to insert and play a Macromedia Flash movie from within CourseBuilder:**

**1** Define a Flash movie by clicking the **Insert Flash** button on Insert panel:

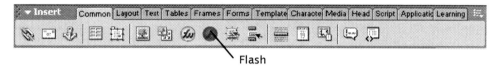

Flash

**2** Specify the Flash file you want to insert.

Dreamweaver displays this visual placeholder to represent the Flash movie:

**3** Open the Properties Inspector (Windows→Properties) and enter a name:

Enter the name in the Name field.

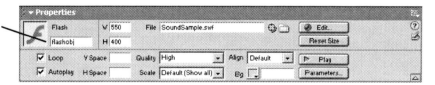

**4** Edit the CourseBuilder interaction and click the Action Manager tab.

**5** Choose **Control Shockwave or Flash** from the drop down list at the top of the tab, to add a **Control Shockwave or Flash** action:

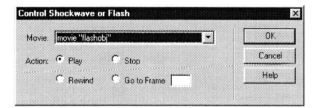

**6** Select the movie from the drop down list in the Control Shockwave or Flash window.

**7** Select **Play** (or one of the other actions: **Rewind**, **Stop**, or **Go to Frame**).

**8** Click **OK**.

The Flash movie is now set up to play based on your Action Manager settings.

 **More Information:** For more information about CourseBuilder, refer to one of our other books in the e-learning developers series: Using Dreamweaver MX to Create e-Learning.

# Summary

Multimedia can be an effective way to communicate information to your learner and keep your learner engaged. It is an area in which Flash is particularly effective. In fact, even designers who use other e-learning development tools use Flash to add multimedia to their courses.

In this chapter, you have been introduced to the ways that you can use Flash to create multimedia elements. You learned how to create a splash screen by including tweened animations and audio. You learned how to trigger and audio clip from a button and several techniques for controlling audio in an e-learning course. You also learned how to add video. At the end of this chapter we briefly discussed using Flash in conjunction with a CourseBuilder interaction.

# Creating Multimedia Demonstrations **5**

In the previous chapter you learned the basic techniques for creating multimedia elements such as animation, audio, and video. In this chapter, you will apply these techniques to create a demonstration. Demonstrations generally include an audio track (providing narration) synchronized with visuals (screen shots, graphics or text, and animations).

Using multimedia to demonstrate a process can be very effective. In on-line courses that teach software, for example, it is often useful for the learner to see the actual movement of the mouse and the data entry on the screen. Multimedia can also be used to demonstrate complex procedures with machinery or other equipment.

The ability to create multimedia demonstrations is one of the key benefits of using Flash to create e-learning.

In this chapter you will learn:

- How to use multimedia in demonstrations.
- About guidelines for creating demonstrations.
- How to create software application demonstrations.
- How to let the learner control the playback of demonstrations.

# Using Demonstrations

Demonstrations show how to perform a task or use a product. The key to a demonstration lies in synchronizing the audio and the text with other visuals on the screen. Examples include:

- How the parts of a piece of machinery work.
- How to use a software application.
- How the organs in the human body work.
- How a financial institution moves money.
- How to create a web page.
- How to follow the procedures required to answer a Customer Support call.

As you can see from these examples, you can use animations to teach everything from concepts, procedures, to actually demonstrating how to use a piece of software.

# Guiding Learners Through Demonstrations

Typically a demonstration plays like a movie, where the visual elements are displayed on the screen while audio narration describes the visuals. The demonstration continues to play until it completes all of the frames in the movie or the learner decides to stop the playback.

The following are some other ways to set up a demonstration:

- **Text-based guidance.** The learner clicks on a **Continue** button to move to the next part of the demo.
- **Audio-based slide shows.** The audio track of the movie controls the advancement of the demo. For example, you could create a demonstration showing how to answer a customer service call. In this example you could show a still photo of the customer and one of the customer service representatives. Then you could have the learner listen to the audio of a conversation that occurs between them.

# Guidelines for Creating Demonstrations

Demonstrations can be time consuming to build. It is easy to underestimate the amount of time needed to prepare the visual and audio elements as well as the time required to ensure that these elements are synchronized. Therefore, you should carefully consider which content is best suited for demonstrations. The following are general guidelines:

- **Demonstrations should not exceed 30 seconds**. Anything longer than 30 seconds is too long for a learner to remain passive. Moreover, long demonstration sequences become very unwieldy to synchronize, test, and maintain. Consider many several short demonstrations rather than one long one.

- **Demonstrations should not launch as soon as the page loads**. Instead, include a button the learned can click to launch the demonstration when he or she is ready.

- **Demonstrations which include audio should be well thought out and scripted**. Avoid using audio to simply repeat what is written on the screen. Here are some suggestions for creating quality scripts:

  - Write for speech, not for the written page. It should sound like a real person talking. For example, people tend to use contractions and dangling modifiers (e.g., "Let's take a look at what this is used for" rather than "We will now look at the purpose for which this is used"). However, make sure you do NOT use idiomatic phrases that may not be understandable in different locations and cultures, such as "Once in a blue moon."

  - Read your script aloud to ensure that it sounds right. The tone of the audio should be friendly and should seem like the narrator is having a one-on-one conversation with the learner.

  - Avoid regional accents or other noticeable speech habits—unnatural pauses, clearing the throat, and weird hesitations are all amplified in this setting. Use a good editing tool so you can modify any problems you encounter with the recording. If you need to re-record a section, start at the beginning of a sentence. This makes editing easier.

- **To reinforce the audio, try to use visual cues such as text labels, bulleted lists, or graphic highlights**. When you use these elements, have them appear with the audio rather than all at once. For example, make each item in a bulleted list appear when the audio discusses that item rather than making all of the bullets appear at the beginning.

- **If your graphics have labels or if you have text that builds, such as a bulleted list, make sure that the terminology and word order on the screen is consistent with the audio**. If the word order on the screen differs from that used in the audio, the learner may become confused.

# Creating a Software Demonstration: Process Overview

After you have planned and scripted your demonstration, you are ready to create it. In this chapter we will use the example of a software demonstration. At the end of this chapter we will discuss tools that make the creation of a software demonstration much easier. However, these tools may not be helpful for other types of demonstrations.

Creating any type of demonstration requires similar high-level steps to those listed here.

**1**   Create the screen shots.

Software demonstrations require a lot of screen captures. Use a screen capture tool such as SnagIt or PaintShopPro to create them. Save these files in GIF format to keep the file size small.

Create one screen capture each time the screen changes in the demonstration. For example, to show how to select File → Save from a menu, you need three screen captures: a shot prior to the menu selection, one of the File menu opened, and one with the Save option highlighted.

Create your screen shots *without* the mouse pointer in the picture. The mouse pointer will be added using Flash.

**2**   Create the audio.

Record and edit the narrative using a sound-editing tool, such as CoolEdit® or SoundForge®.

**3**   Set up the layers in Flash.

**4**   Import the audio files and the screen capture images. Place each of these screen captures in the **Screen Capture** layer according to the order they will appear in the demonstration. Place the audio on the timeline. Roughly synchronize the audio to the visuals.

**5**   Add the mouse image to the timeline in the **Cursor** layer. Animate the mouse movement to mimic the mouse movement in the real software application.

**6**  Add any text entry into the timeline in the **Text Entry** layer. If you want to show the learner how to type in the name of a new Flash symbol, then your demonstration will need to show each letter being typed into the Name field in the dialog box.

**Tip:** You can use special effects utilities, such as Swish, to easily create the typing text effect in Flash. See the appendices on the CD for more information about Swish.

**7**  Choose a synchronization method using the **Sync** property in the Properties Inspector.

**8**  Add highlights and annotations as needed. You can do this by drawing boxes (or arrows) to point out features of the software. Adding text annotations or labels help support the audio and enhances the e-learning experience.

**9**  Publish the movie and test it on the target platform. Make any needed adjustments.

**Note:**  To create a conceptual demonstration rather than a software demonstration, you would follow the same basic process. However, you would use graphics in place of screen captures and you would not need to perform steps 1, 5, and 6.

**On CD**: Try out the following demonstration that steps the learner through a flow diagram: **samples/chapter05/sample_5-3.swf**.

# Creating a Software Demonstration

In this step-by-step tutorial, you will create a software demonstration that shows the learner how to create a symbol in Flash. You may recall that we used this same example to create the simulation in Chapter 3.

## Viewing the Finished Interaction

Before you try to put together this demonstration, look at the finished product.

**On CD**: Take a moment to try out the finished example **samples/chapter05/sample_5-4.swf** on the CD. Pay particular attention to how the audio and the visuals are synchronized as well as how the elements support each other.

# Setting Up the Content of the Layers

We have already created the audio and screen capture files necessary for this exercise. You will start by creating the layers, importing the graphics and audio, and then placing them into the appropriate layers.

**Perform the following steps to set up the content of the layers:**

**1**    Open a new Flash document and set the movie size to **650 x 650.**

**2**    Create these layers in the following order:

| Layer | Description |
| --- | --- |
| Actions | Lets you add actions to your timeline. |
| Cursor | Shows the mouse cursor movement. |
| Text Entry | Shows text entry added to fields. |
| Text | Displays text directions or annotations. |
| Screen Captures | Displays the screen captures. |
| Audio | Plays the audio. |

Make sure that the Actions layer is at the top and the Audio layer is at the bottom.

**3**    Import (File → Import → Import to Library) the screen capture files located on the CD. Import files **images/demo_5-4a.gif** through **demo_5-4f.gif** .

**4**    In the Screen Captures layer place keyframes (Insert → Timeline→ Keyframe) at frames 10, 20, 30, 40, and 50.

At this point, you are allocating 10 keyframes for each screen shot; later, you will adjust the number of frames based upon the length of the audio that you want to associate with each screen shot.

**5**    Place the imported images in the keyframes according to the order shown here:

| Frame | Image |
|-------|-------|
| 1 | demo_5-4a.gif |
| 10 | demo_5-4b.gif |
| 20 | demo_5-4c.gif |
| 30 | demo_5-4d.gif |
| 40 | demo_5-4e.gif |
| 50 | demo_5-4f.gif |

**Note:** Make sure that the graphics in each section of the timeline align with the other graphics in that layer. Using the info panel or the Properties Inspector to do this.

**6**   Import the audio file (File → Import → Import to Library) audio/demo_5-4.wav (or demo_5-4.aif for Macintosh).

**7**   Place the file in the first frame of the Audio layer. Extend the frames so that the entire audio file appears. (Insert a frame at about frame 125.)

*Extend the frames so that the entire audio file displays.*

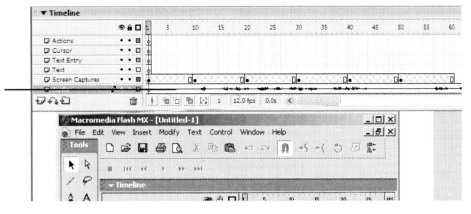

**8**   Set the synchronization option in the Properties Inspector to Stream.

**Note:** The Stream option synchronizes the sound for playing on a web site. If the animation cannot be drawn quickly enough to keep up with the audio, it skips (drops) frames. When the movie stops, the sound stops.

**9**  Roughly synchronize the audio and graphics by playing the movie (Control → Play). Then add (or delete) frames (Insert → Timeline → Frame or Edit→ Timeline → Remove Frames) from the Screen Captures layer as needed.

You will need to test the movie and make adjustments several times to get the synchronization right.

**10**  When you have the screen captures spread out like they need to be, insert a keyframe (Insert → Timeline → Keyframe) in the Actions layer at the last frame of the movie. With that frame selected enter a **stop( );** action in the Actions panel.

## Animating the Mouse

The next step is to add the mouse pointer into the demonstration at the appropriate points.

**Use these steps to add mouse movement to the demonstration:**

**1**  First, import (or draw) a graphic of a mouse pointer in the Cursor layer (File → Import→ Import to Library). We have provided you with a cursor graphic on the CD in **images/cursor.gif.**

**2**   Drag the cursor image to frame 1 of the Cursor layer. Position the cursor on the Stage at the location where you want the mouse pointer to start:

*Place the cursor for the beginning of the sequence.*

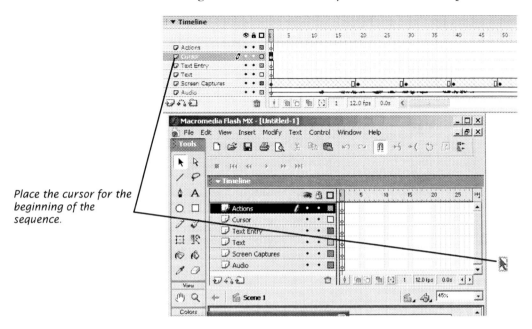

**3**   Insert a keyframe (Insert → Timeline → Keyframe) at the end of the first sequence, where the next image appears (about frame 18).

**4**   Move mouse pointer graphic and position over the Insert menu. This is the first place it must move to.

*Insert a keyframe and place the cursor over the Insert menu.*

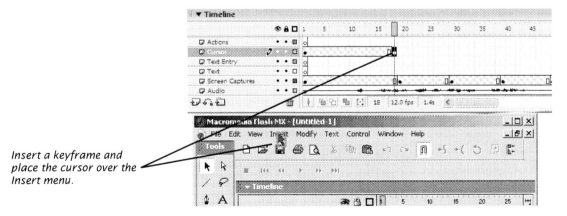

**5**   In the Cursor layer, select the first frame and create a motion tween (Insert → Timeline → Create Motion Tween or select it from the Properties Inspector).

**6**   Insert a keyframe (Insert → Timeline → Keyframe) at the end of the second sequence, where the next image appears, the Insert menu appears (about frame 28).

**7**   Insert another keyframe at the frame where the next image appears (about frame 40). The New Symbol menu is highlighted.

**8**   Position the mouse pointer graphic over the New Symbol menu option.

**9**   Select the first keyframe of that sequence (about frame 28) and create a motion tween (Insert → Timeline → Create Motion Tween or select it from the Properties Inspector).

   This will cause the cursor to move down the Insert menu to the New Symbol menu option.

**10**  Extend the Cursor layer to the last frame of the movie.

   For the remainder of the demonstration the cursor is not moved, but we will keep it visible.

**11**  Test your sequence and make any necessary adjustments.


## Animate Typing

In addition to animated mouse movements, many demonstrations include animated typing to show how learner entries should be made in text fields. For example, in our demonstration, we need to show the name of the new symbol being entered into the Name field. The general idea is to add each character at about 3 frame intervals along the timeline.

**More Information:** You can also use text effects utilities such as Swish to easily create the typing text effect in Flash. There is additional information about Swish in the appendices on the CD.

**Use these steps to show animated typing in the demonstration:**

**1**   At the appropriate point in the timeline, insert a keyframe (Insert → Timeline → Keyframe) in the Text Entry layer. The text field needs to be placed over the Create New Symbol dialog box with a blank Name field. Insert a keyframe in the Text Entry layer where that image appears.

**2** Create a Static Text field in the Text Entry layer and place it over the Name field. Enter just the first character that you want to appear. In this case we'll enter the letter $M$. Set the font to **Microsoft Sans Serif** and the point size to **12**.

This font most closely simulates the normal font used on a computer screen.

*You will enter the characters to spell out* **MyClip** *into this field in the Text Entry* layer.

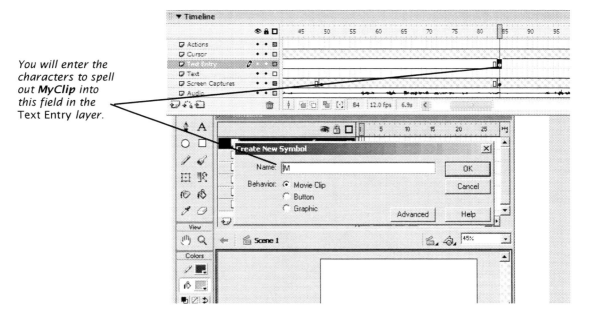

You need to let the new character entry remain the same for 3 frames.

**3** Add a keyframe (Insert → Timeline→ Keyframe) to the Text Entry layer 3 frames after the letter $M$ was entered.

**4** Add the next character into the Text field, the letter $y$.

**5** Repeat this process for each character that you want to show. For this demonstration enter enough characters to spell out *MyClip*.

**6** Extend the final frame to the end of the movie.

**7** Test your movie (Control → Test Movie) and make adjustments as necessary.

# Enabling the Learner to Control Playback

Generally, it is a good idea to allow the learner to control when the demonstration starts and stops. You may also want to give the learner the option of pausing, continuing, or restarting the demonstration from the beginning. You do this with buttons.

You can either create your own buttons or you can use the buttons found in Flash's common libraries (Window → Other Panels → Common Libraries → Buttons). Then select the desired button from the Playback folder.

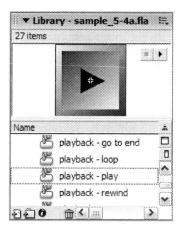

After placing buttons on the Stage (in a Buttons layer), you will add actions to the buttons to control the timeline. For the **Restart** button, use a **gotoAndPlay(2)** action. Use a **stop( )** action in the **Stop** button and a **play( )** action in the **Play** button.

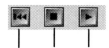

*gotoAndPlay*(2);   *stop( ); play( );*

**Note:** Make sure that the first frame of the movie has a **stop( )** action in it so that the learner can control the start of the movie by clicking on the Play button:

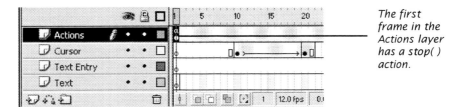

*The first frame in the Actions layer has a stop( ) action.*

We have used a fairly basic example; however, you can add other buttons that enable the learner even more control. For example, you could add a fast-forward (or rewind) button that steps through the movie multiple frames at a time.

**On CD**: To see an example of this demonstration with the control buttons, open **samples/chapter05/sample_5-4a.swf** from the CD.

# Alternative Methods for Creating Demonstrations

While you can use the process described in this chapter to make demonstrations, there are many third-party tools available on the market, which can streamline the process of creating software demonstrations. RoboDemo, Turbo-Demo®, DemoForge®, ScreenFlash®, ViewletBuilder® and Camtasia® are all examples of such tools. While these tools are more efficient, they can also be expensive. You may also be able to achieve a smaller file size developing demonstrations on your own. However, we generally use a tool like this to create a software demonstrations because of the time savings. Other types of demonstrations still require the techniques discussed in this chapter.

**On CD**: For a brief overview of these tools, refer to appendices folder on the CD-ROM.

If you choose to use one of these tools, you will need to create the demonstration in a compatible format, such as .avi. You will then import the video into Flash as an embedded video, as described in Chapter 4.

**Note**: RoboDemo, DemoForge, Turbo-Demo, ScreenFlash, ViewletBuilder, and Camtasia have the option of exporting to a SWF format.

In this chapter we have focused on creating a software demonstration. As we mentioned earlier, you can use Flash to create demonstrations of equipment, such as how to operate a cell phone, or complex concepts, such as a flowchart diagram.

If you need to create these types of demonstrations, you still need to follow the same general steps provided in this chapter.

# Summary

Multimedia demonstrations can be a very powerful part of e-learning when used judiciously. They can address some of the needs that arise due to multiple e-learning styles and can make the e-learning more engaging. In this chapter, you learned how to combine multimedia elements and synchronize them into a complete software demonstration.

# Section II:
# Using Flash Interactions for Assessment and Interactivity

Flash Learning Interactions are a great way to add interactivity to your e-Learning course. In this section you will learn how to take advantage of these interactions.

# An Introduction to Flash Learning Interactions **6**

A learning interaction provides an effective way for the learner to assess his or her progress. While it is possible to create learning interactions from scratch, Flash also provides several built-in learning interactions to simplify your work.

This chapter covers basic concepts for using Flash learning interactions. Subsequent chapters show you how to use and customize the specific types of learning interactions (i.e., True/False, Multiple Choice, etc.).

In this chapter you will learn:

- About uses for Flash learning interactions.
- About types of learning interactions that Flash provides.
- How to insert and delete a Flash learning interaction.

# Uses of Flash Learning Interactions

There are many ways that you can use Flash learning interactions in an e-learning course. Here are some of the most common uses:

- Provide a pre-test to determine the learner's skill level prior to starting a topic.
- Reinforce e-learning as part of a course content page.
- Remediate e-learning in a topic review.
- Assess the student's knowledge/skill as part of a quiz/skill check or a certification test.
- Provide a thought provoking transition to a new topic.
- Provide an attention getting exercise prior to starting a new topic.
- Solicit input from the learner as part of a course survey.

You can include a Flash learning interaction in any Flash document that you create, or you can use an interaction in Flash's pre-built Quiz template.

 **More Information:** To learn more about the Quiz template or about options for tracking quiz information in a Learning Management System (LMS), see Chapter 15: Using Flash Templates for Architecture and Section IV: Tracking Student Data.

## Types of Flash Learning Interactions

Flash includes the following built-in learning interactions: True or False, Multiple Choice, Fill-in-the-blank, Drag and Drop, Hot Spot, and Hot Object. Each particular learning interaction has strengths as described here:

| Type | Use |
| --- | --- |
| Multiple Choice | A good choice when you want to present a closed-ended question. Flash learning interactions enable you to set up a Multiple Choice question that either has a single correct response or multiple correct responses (e.g., "Choose all that apply"). |

| Type | Use |
|---|---|
| True or False | A variation on the Multiple Choice interaction. This type of interaction is useful when you need a question to transition to a new topic or dispel common misconceptions about a concept.<br><br>Since True or False questions are easier to guess, you may not want to use them in scored quizzes. In many cases, it is possible to turn this type of question into a Multiple Choice question, by creating additional distracters. Make sure that these distracters are plausible. |
| Fill-in-the-blank | A good choice when you want the learner to recall information, such as terminology. Since it is based upon recall, rather than recognition, it is more difficult to guess the answers in this type of question. |
| Drag and Drop | A good choice for matching terms with definitions, identifying how parts fit in with the whole, or ordering steps in a process. This interaction works well as a quiz question or an interactive exercise. |
| Hot Spot | A good choice when you want the learner to click on a screen shot or a diagram to indicate the answer or discover information. Examples include: software applications, techincal diagrams, maps, process flow diagrams, and charts. This interaction works well for an explore excercise where the learner discovers information about an object by clicking areas on the object. |
| Hot Object | Similar to Hot Spot questions, however a learner clicks on a hot object (such as a movie clip) rather than a hot spot (which is transparent). This interaction works well for an explore excercise where the learner discovers information about an object by clicking areas on the object. |

 **On CD:** You can view an example of each type of interaction in **samples/chapter06/sample_6-1.html**. This example has a quiz that includes one example of each question type. Be sure to try both correct and incorrect answers.

# Creating Effective Questions

Since the majority of the learning interactions are used in quizzes, reviews, or assessments, think about the educational quality of the questions when you create them. Here are some guidelines for writing effective questions:

**1**  Look at the objectives of your lesson. Make sure that your questions are assessing those objectives.

**2**  Use "how" and "why" questions, rather than questions that require the learner to merely "repeat back" the information presented in the topic.

**3**  Whenever possible, try to base questions upon scenarios that the learner is likely to encounter in the real world. Think of situations where the learner typically makes errors.

**4**  Avoid writing questions in the negative. For example, "Which of the following is NOT a true statement?" This type of question tends to confuse learners— even if they have a thorough understanding of the content.

**5**  For multiple choice questions, create plausible distracters (common misconceptions, mistakes, and nuances that the learner needs to be able to differentiate). The goal is not to trick the learner, but you do want them to think.

**6**  If you have several multiple choice questions in a row, make sure you vary the position of the correct answer. For example, you do not want choice "C" to be the correct answer 75% of the time.

**7**  Be sure to include descriptive text such as "Choose all that apply", so the learner knows what to do.

**8**  When you build a quiz, use a mixture of question types. When selecting a question type for a given topic, consider whether that type of question is most effective for the question that you want to ask.

# Flash MX 2004 Learning Interactions

Learning interactions are available in Flash MX as well as Flash MX 2004. However, all the learning interactions in Flash MX 2004 uses version 2 components. This means that interactions created in Flash MX 2004 cannot be saved in a Flash MX format. Although many of the same techniques shown in this section apply to Flash MX learning interactions, all the samples used in this section were created with the latest version of Flash, Flash MX 2004.

Flash MX 2004 learning interactions use version 2 components, so all movies you create using these interactions must be published with ActionScript 2.0 as the ActionScript version and Flash Player version 6 or 7:

*When publishing Flash MX 2004 learning interactions, choose Flash Player 6 or 7 and ActionScript 2.0 as the version.*

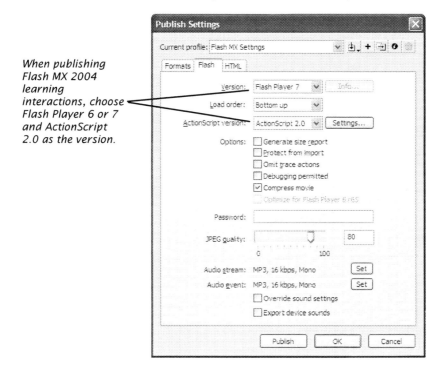

**Use this step to access the publish settings:**

**1**   Select File → Publish Settings to make changes to the publish settings.

# Basic Steps for Creating a Learning Interaction

You can add a learning interaction to any frame in your timeline or to one of Flash's pre-designed Quiz templates. No matter what type of learning interaction you choose, the process is the same.

**Use these steps to create a learning interaction:**

**1**  Select the appropriate frame (and layer) where you want the interaction to appear.

**More information:** Chapter 15 describes what frame and layer you should use if you are adding the interaction to a Quiz template.

**2**  Open the Learning Interactions library (Window → Other Panels → Common Libraries→ Learning Interactions).

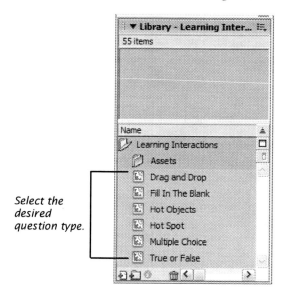

*Select the desired question type.*

**3**  Select the desired question type from the panel and drag it to the Stage.

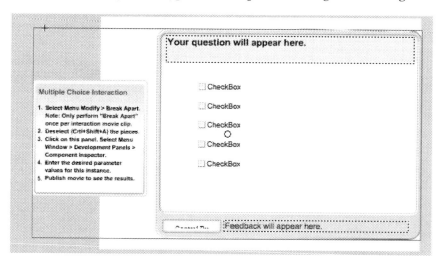

**4** The movie clip contains a number of elements. You need to break them apart (Modify → Break Apart) before you can edit them.

*This object is the **Learning Interaction component**. It gives you directions and it contains the scripts that make the interaction work. Don't delete this object! You will not see it when the movie plays.*

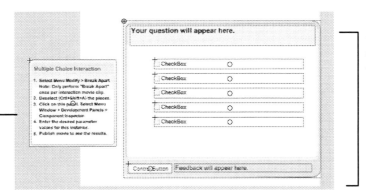

*These elements make up the learning interaction.*

 **Caution:** You should only break the clip apart once. If you break apart the learning interaction component, you will lose its scripts. If this happens, try to undo the action (Edit → Undo Break Apart) or simply delete the learning interaction and drag a fresh copy from the Common Libraries onto the Stage.

**5** Configure the learning interaction by selecting the learning interaction component and opening the Component Inspector (Window → Development Panels → Component Inspector).

*These buttons take you to additional options that you can specify.*

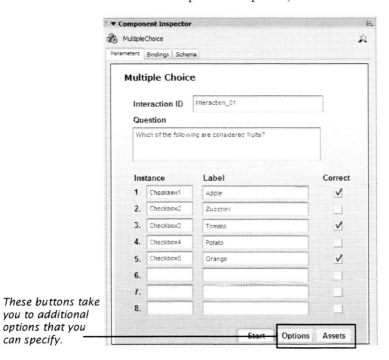

The parameters on the Start tab vary based on the interaction type. This example shows the Component Inspector for a Multiple Choice interaction. For this type of interaction, you specify the question and its associated choices. The Options and Assets tabs are similar for each interaction type. We describe these tabs in the sections that follow.

# The Options Tab

To begin changing feedback, knowledge tracking information (if applicable), and navigation information (if applicable) click the Options tab.

**Drag and Drop**

| | | |
|---|---|---|
| ✓ Feedback | **Tries** | 1 |
| Initial Feedback | Press on an object to drag it. | |
| Evaluate Feedback | Click on the Check Answer button. | |
| Correct Feedback | Yes that is correct. | |
| Incorrect Feedback | No that is incorrect. | |
| Tries Feedback | No that is incorrect. Try again. | |

✓ **Knowledge Track**

Objective ID

Weighting    1

**Navigation**

● Off        ○ Next Button        ○ Auto GoTo Next Frame

GoTo and:  ● Stop   ○ Play    Label

Start    Options    Assets

# Changing Feedback

If you would like to provide feedback to the learner, make sure that the Feedback checkbox is checked. You can then change the feedback text for each of the five types of feedback. The five types of feedback are described in this table:

| Type | Description |
|---|---|
| Initial Feedback | Initial feedback is somewhat of a misnomer. These are actually instructions to the learner. Enter the instructions you would like the learner to see when the interaction first displays. |
| Evaluate Feedback | When the learner chooses a response, the initial feedback changes to provide additional instructions. Enter the instructions you would like the learner to see after choosing a response. |
| Correct Feedback | Enter the feedback the learner receives if the question is answered correctly. |
| Incorrect Feedback | Enter the feedback the learner receives if the question is answered incorrectly. |
| Tries Feedback | Enter the feedback the learner receives if the number of attempts to answer the question has been met (the learner is not allowed to try anymore). You can set the number of attempts by changing the number in the Tries field. |

## Tracking Student Data

If you would like to track information in an LMS, you need to check the Knowledge Track check box. You then need to assign a weight to the question. The weight indicates the importance of a question. For example, if a question is assigned a weight of 2 and another question is assigned a weight of 1, the first question is worth twice as much as the second question.

Optionally you can also enter an objective ID. This lets you correlate a question with an objective.

If you do not plan to track this information, don't check the Knowledge Track check box unless you plan to use the **Auto GoTo Next Frame** navigation option as discussed in the next section.

**More Information:** For more information about tracking data see Section IV: Tracking Student Data.

## Establishing Navigation

Finally, you can determine if and how navigation will take place. When you are adding interactions to a Flash movie, you normally place each interaction in a separate frame. Therefore, to navigate to the next interaction you simply go to the next frame of the movie.

**More Information:** For more information on course architecture see Section III: Creating Course Architecture with Flash.

You have three navigation options to choose from.

- **Off.** If you do not want the interaction to provide navigation, select this option. You should use this option if you have set up a course using the course architectures discussed in Section III: *Creating Course Architecture with Flash.*

- **Next button.** If you choose this option, the **Check Answer** button changes to **Next Question** button once the learner has checked the answer. The movie will proceed to the next frame when the button is clicked. When you select this option the GoTo options become active:

*You must choose one of these options when using the* **Next** *button.*

> GoTo and:   ● Stop   ○ Play   Label [          ]

The **GoTo and Stop** option will proceed to the next frame and then stop. The **GoTo and Play** option will proceed to the next frame and start playing the movie. You can also enter a frame label. In Flash you can assign labels to frames. If you would like the course to proceed to a frame with a specific label then enter the label name. Make sure to enter the correct label name or the navigation will not work.

- **Auto GoTo Next Frame.** Choose this option to automatically have the interaction proceed the next frame once the question is answered. In order for this option to work correctly you must turn off (deselect) the feedback and turn on (select) the Knowledge Track option. Macromedia assumes that you will only use this option if you are tracking student data.

# The Assets Tab

If you have changed the instance name of assets used in the interaction, then you will need to click Assets to register the new names. You can also change the labels of the buttons on this tab.

**Drag and Drop**

| | Text Field Instance Names |
|---|---|
| Question Field | Template_Question |
| Feedback Field | Template_Feedback |

| | UI Component Instance Names |
|---|---|
| Control Button | Template_ControlButton |
| Reset Button | Template_ResetButton |

| | Control Button Labels |
|---|---|
| Check Answer | Check Answer |
| Submit | Submit |
| Next Question | Next Question |
| Reset | Reset |

|  |  |  |
|---|---|---|
| Start | Options | Assets |

## Changing Interaction Assets

Each interaction consists of a collection of assets (fields, buttons, checkboxes, images, and so forth). Some of these assets are referred to in the code that controls how the interaction functions. If you change the instance name of one of these assets, you need to come to this tab and enter the new instance name.

The four assets that you may need to register a new name for are: the Question field, the Feedback field, the **Control** button, and the **Reset** button. The **Reset** button is only found in some interactions.

If you include more than one of the same type of interaction in a single document, you should give the assets different names. In many cases you may not run into problems, but it is better to rename them and avoid problems that could arise in the future.

**Use these steps to change the name of an asset:**

**1**     Select the asset you want to change on the Stage. For example, select the
**Control** button.

**2**     In the Properties Inspector enter a new name.

*Enter a new
instance name for
the asset.* ————

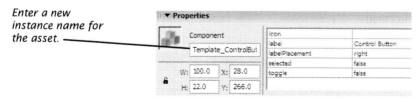

**3**     Access the Component Inspector and click the Assets tab. Enter the new
instance in the appropriate field. For example, enter the new name in Control
Button field.

That is all that is required to change an asset name.

Only common assets are registered on the Assets tab. Assets that are unique to the
interaction type are found on the Start tab. These are covered in more detail in the
chapters that follow.

**More information:** The specific options for each interaction type are described later in this
section. To learn about the options for Multiple Choice and True/False interactions, see
Chapter 7. To learn about the options for Fill-in the-blank interactions, see Chapter 8. To
learn about the options for Drag and Drop interactions, see Chapter 9. To learn about the
options for Hot Spot and Hot Object interactions, see Chapter 10.

## Changing Button Labels

The bottom portion of the Assets tab lets you change the button label that shows
on either the **Control** button or the **Reset** button. When a learner answers a
question the labels may change. Therefore, there are four possible values. Each one
is described in this table:

| Field | Description |
|-------|-------------|
| Check Answer | This is the label that appears on the button when the interaction first displays. This provides some instructions to the learner as to what should be done after answering the question. |

| Field | Description |
|---|---|
| Submit | This is the label used for the **Submit** button. |
| Next Question | If after answering the question you chose to have the **Next Question** button to appear in the navigation options, this is the label that will appear in the button. |
| Reset | If the interaction uses a **Reset** button, this is the label that is used. |

**More information:** To learn more about customizing your interactions, see Chapter 11.

**Tip:** You can include multiple interactions on Flash document by having adding each interaction to its own frame. For example, you can have one interaction in frame 1, another in frame 2, and so on. Be sure to put a stop( ) action on each frame so that the playhead stops and allows the learner to answer the question prior to moving on to the next question.

# Deleting a Learning Interaction

If you need to delete a Flash learning interaction, there are two methods that you can use:

- Select all of the objects from the learning interaction on the Stage and press DELETE.
- Delete the frame where the learning interaction resides (Edit → Timeline → Remove Frames).

# Summary

In this chapter you've learned the benefits of the different types of learning interactions that Flash provides. You have also learned how the basic steps for creating Flash learning interactions and the settings that are available upon each tab.

The following chapters in this section will show you how to work with each specific type of learning interaction and how to customize those interactions to best suit your needs.

# Multiple Choice and True/False Interactions $\mathbf{7}$

Multiple Choice and True/False interactions are the most common types of questions used in assessments. In the previous chapter, we introduced you the basic steps for creating Flash learning interactions. This chapter expands upon those steps and shows you the options used when creating Multiple Choice or True/False interactions.

In this chapter you will learn:

- About uses for Multiple Choice and True/False interactions.
- How to create a Multiple Choice and True/False interactions.
- About ways to enhance Multiple Choice and True/False interactions.

# Uses of Multiple Choice and True/False Interactions

Multiple Choice interactions are a good choice when you want to present a closed-ended question. You can specify whether the interaction can have only one correct response or multiple correct responses (in other words, a choose "all that apply" question). Including multiple correct responses is particularly useful when there is more than one way to perform a task or when you want the learner to select several true points about a particular concept.

The following is an example of a Multiple Choice interaction that has multiple correct responses:

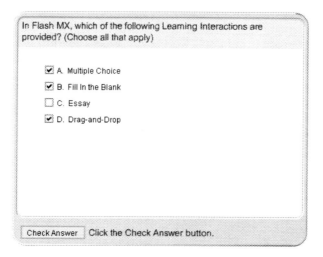

True/False interactions are just a variation on the Multiple Choice interaction. There are only two choices (one correct choice and one distracter). True/False interactions are a good way to transition to a new topic, dispel common misconceptions about a topic, or provide variety from regular Multiple Choice interactions.

**Tip:** Since True/False questions are easier to guess, you may not want to use them in scored quizzes. In many cases, it is possible to turn this type of question into a Multiple Choice question, by creating additional distracters. Make sure that these distracters are plausible.

**On CD:** To help you become more familiar with Multiple Choice and True/False interactions, try **samples/chapters06/sample_6-1.html**. The second to last interaction in the quiz is a Multiple Choice question. The last interaction is a True/False question. The Multiple Choice question has more than one correct response (multiple–correct).

# Creating a Multiple Choice Interaction

This step-by-step tutorial takes you through the process of adding one of Flash's pre-built Multiple Choice learning interaction to your movie. You will then configure and test it.

## Interaction Settings Overview

In Chapter 6 you learned about the different settings on the Options and Assets tab. The Start tab contains settings that are unique to the Multiple Choice or True/False interaction. Those settings are explained here:

| Setting | Description |
|---|---|
| Interaction ID | Enter a name to identify the interaction. This information is mainly used if you are tracking student data. |
| Question | Enter the question that is presented to the learner. |
| Instance | Each instance represents a choice for the learner. The instance names you enter into these fields must correspond to a checkbox with the same instance name. The names are case sensitive. If you do not account for all checkbox instances, the interaction will not function correctly. |
| Label | Enter the text for each choice. When the movie is played, the text entered in these fields will appear in the checkboxes. |
| Correct | Place a checkmark next to those choices that are correct. |

 **More Information:** This tutorial builds on the basic process of creating an interaction that was covered in the Chapter 6: An Introduction to Flash Learning Interactions.

# Viewing the Finished Interaction

Before you create the interaction, take a look at the finished product.

On CD: Take a moment and try out the finished interaction: **samples/chapter07/sample_7-1.swf**. Be sure to test out both correct and incorrect answers.

# Creating the Interaction

To create a learning interaction, you add it to the timeline of your Flash document.

**Use these steps to add a Multiple Choice learning interaction to your document:**

**1**    Create a new file (File → New) or use an existing file.

**2**    Access the Learning Interactions library (Window → Other Panels → Common Libraries → Learning Interactions).

**3**    Select the Multiple Choice learning interaction from the panel and drag it to the Stage. The results should look like this:

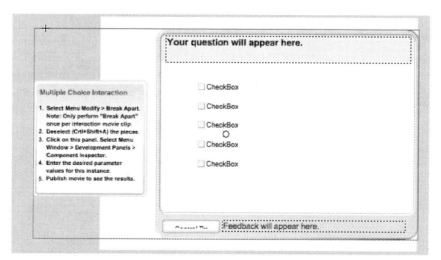

**4**    Break apart the learning interaction (Modify → Break Apart) so that you can edit them.

**Caution:** You should only break the interaction apart once. If you break apart the learning interaction component itself, you will lose the scripts that are associated with this component.

**5**   Deselect all the items on the Stage (Edit → Deselect All) and select only the Learning Interaction component (This is the object with the instructions).

**6**   Open the Component Inspector (Window → Development Panels → Component Inspector).

**7**   In the Start tab of the Component Inspector, make the following changes:

| Field | Value |
|---|---|
| Interaction ID | Interaction 01 |
| Question | In Flash MX, which of the following learning interactions are provided? (Choose all that apply) |
| Checkbox1 | A. Multiple Choice |
| Checkbox2 | B. Fill-in-the-blank |
| Checkbox3 | C. Essay |
| Checkbox4 | D. Drag and Drop |
| Correct | Checkbox1, checkbox2, and checkbox 4 are correct. |

Make sure that you check the correct column for Checkbox1, Checkbox2, and Checkbox4.

 **Note:** In our example, we have only four choices. Be sure to delete all of the information that appears for any of the other choices.

**8**   Close the Component Inspector.

**9**   Test your movie (Control → Test Movie).

Notice that although you removed the information for the fifth option in the Component parameter panel, there are still five choices:

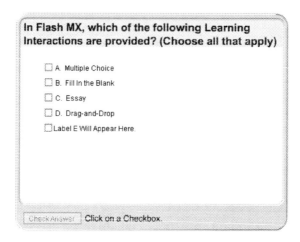

In the next section you will learn to delete these.

# Deleting Choices from the Interaction

The interaction you are currently working on has one extra choice showing up. When you were defining the interaction on the Component Inspector, you should have deleted all information associated with Checkbox5. However, that checkbox still shows up. You have to delete the checkbox component from the Stage to remove it.

**Use these steps to delete extra checkbox components:**

**1**    Select the extra checkbox component on the Stage and press DELETE.

**2**    Test your movie again to make sure the checkbox is removed.

**3**    Save your file.

# Adding Choices to the Interaction

You can have up to 8 choices for a Multiple Choice question. When you want to add a choice, you cannot simply make an additional entry in the Component Inspector. You also need to add a new Checkbox component to the Stage.

**Use these steps to add a choice:**

**1** In the timeline, select the frame (and layer) where the Multiple Choice learning interaction resides and open the Components panel (Window → Development Panels → Components).

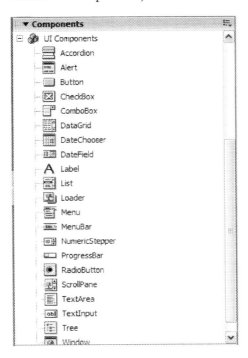

**2** Drag a checkbox component to the Stage.

**Tip:** You may find it easier to duplicate a checkbox component instead of dragging a new checkbox component to the Stage.

**3** Position the checkbox component in relation to the other checkboxes on the Stage.

**4** In the Properties Inspector, name the instance *Checkbox5*.

*Click here if you want to view the component's parameters. You do not need to change them.*

*In this case the instance name is Checkbox5.*

When naming a new instance of a checkbox component, make sure that you do not use a name that is already being used by one of the other checkbox components.

**5**   Select the learning interaction component and open the Component Inspector (Window → Development Panels → Component Inspector).

**6**   Add the instance name and Label Text for Checkbox5 in the Start tab as shown:

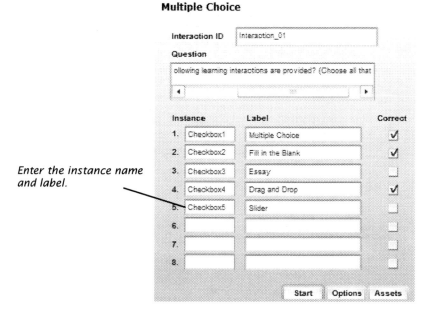

*Enter the instance name and label.*

**7**   Test your movie (Control → Test Movie) and make any necessary adjustments.

# Changing Interaction Options

When you tested your question, you may have noticed that feedback was provided. You can modify this feedback to best meet your needs.

**Use these steps to configure the Options for the learning interaction:**

**1**   Select the learning interaction component.

**2**   Open the Component Inspector (Window → Development Panels → Component Inspector).

**3** Click the **Options** button at the bottom of the panel.

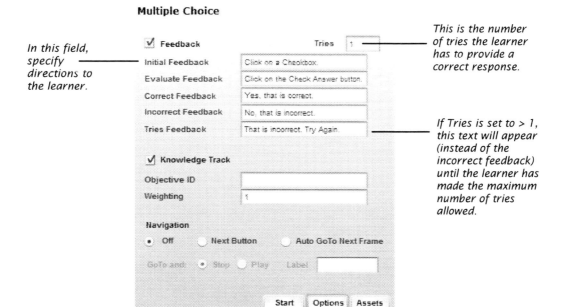

*In this field, specify directions to the learner.*

**Multiple Choice**

This is the number of tries the learner has to provide a correct response.

If Tries is set to > 1, this text will appear (instead of the incorrect feedback) until the learner has made the maximum number of tries allowed.

In addition to the feedback options, you call also specify:

- **Knowledge Track** options enable you to send information about the learner's performance to an AICC or SCORM compliant Learning Management System (LMS).
- **Navigation** options enable you to specify how the movie will proceed after the learner responds to the question. By default the navigation option is set to Off, meaning that no navigation will occur after the learner responds.

**More Information:** For more information about the options available, refer to Chapter 6: An Introduction to Flash Learning Interactions.

# Creating a True/False Interaction

This step-by-step tutorial takes you through the process of adding Flash's pre-built True/False learning interaction to your movie. You will then configure and test it.

# Viewing the Finished Interaction

Before you create the interaction, take a look at the finished product.

On CD: Take a moment and try out the finished interaction:
**samples/chapter07/sample_7-2.swf**. This example includes the Multiple Choice
interaction created in the previous section of this chapter followed by a True/False
interaction. Be sure to test out both correct and incorrect options for these questions.

# Creating the learning interaction

To create a learning interaction, you will add it to the timeline of your movie, just as
you did to create the Multiple Choice interaction.

**Use these steps to add the True/False learning interaction to your movie:**

**1**　Use the file you saved when creating a Multiple Choice interaction earlier in
this chapter or open the file **samples/chapter07/sample6_2start.fla**.

**2**　Add a blank keyframe to the timeline (Insert → Timeline → Blank Keyframe).

**3**　Select the blank keyframe and open the learning interactions library (Window
→ Common Libraries → Learning Interactions).

**4**　Select the True/False component from the library and drag it to the Stage.

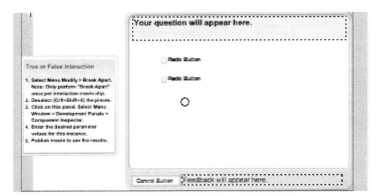

**5**　Break apart the interaction elements (Modify → Break Apart) so that you can
edit them.

**Caution:** You should only break the interaction apart once. If you break apart the learning interaction component itself, you will lose the scripts that are associated with this component.

**6**   Deselect all the items on the Stage (Edit → Deselect All) and select only the instructions. This selects the learning interaction component.

**7**   Open the Component Inspector (Window → Development Panels → Component Inspector).

**8**   Enter the parameters on the Start tab as shown:

| Field | Value |
|-------|-------|
| Interaction ID | Interaction 01 |
| Question | You can have more than one learning interaction in a Flash Document. |

It is not necessary to make any changes to the distracters. However, if you would like to enter a different term you can.

*In this case, the options are labeled True & False, but you could use Yes & No, Correct & Incorrect, or other labels as appropriate.*

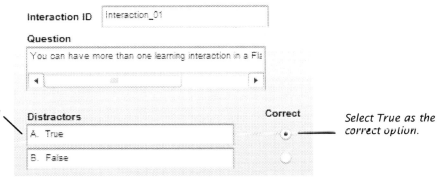

*Select True as the correct option.*

**9**   Click the Options tab.

**10** Modify the Correct and Incorrect feedback as shown:

| Field | Value |
|---|---|
| Correct Feedback | You're Right!! |
| Incorrect Feedback | Sorry, you can have more than one learning interaction in a Flash Document. |

**Note:** Unlike Multiple Choice questions, the learner only gets one try to answer a True/False question.

**11** Test your movie (Control → Test Movie).

Notice that the movie jumps back and forth between the two learning interactions. To correct this problem, you will need to add the navigation between the learning interactions.

**Use these steps to add the navigation between the learning interactions:**

**1** Create a layer called Actions (Insert → Timeline → Layer).

**2** In the Actions layer, add a **stop( )**; action.

Now you need to modify the multiple choice learning interaction component.

**3** Access frame 1 and select the learning interaction component for the Multiple Choice question.

**4** Open the Component Inspector (Window → Development Panels → Component Inspector).

**5** Select the **Auto GoTo Next Frame** navigation option on the Options tab.

This option advances the movie to the next frame automatically once the learner responds to the question.

**Note:** Remember, feedback must be unchecked and Knowledge Track must be checked to use Auto GoTo Next Frame feature. This means that the learner will not get feedback for individual questions because the movie will immediately proceed to the next question. In this scenario, it is likely that you would either send the information to an LMS or you would provide the learner with a score at the end of the sequence of questions. See Chapter 6 for more information about the navigation options.

**6**   Deselect the Feedback option and make sure the Knowledge Track option is checked.

**7**   Test your movie (Control → Test Movie).

# Customizing the Interaction

There are a few interesting ways to customize Multiple Choice and True/False interactions. In this section we take a look at what is possible and provide you with the instructions or we direct you to another chapter in the book.

## Resizing or Changing the Appearance of Text Fields

Multiple Choice and True/False interactions consist of at least two text fields: the question text and the feedback text. These fields come with a preset size, font styles, color, and so forth. You may want to make changes to these fields.

**More Information:** For more information about changing the text fields associated with a Multiple Choice or True/False question see Chapter 11: Customizing Learning Interactions.

# Changing the Components that Make Up a Learning Interaction

There are certain changes that you can make to the components that make up a learning interaction (for example, buttons, checkboxes, and radio buttons). You can change colors and other styles. For more information on making these types of changes see Chapter 22: *Customizing Flash e-Learning Components.*

# Adding Graphical Elements Next to Choices

Since some questions lend themselves to visual information you may want to add an image next to the checkbox. To make this work you will probably need to do the following:

- **Reposition the checkboxes**. This will help you get enough space to place an image. This may require you to position 2 checkboxes on the left side and 2 on the right side.
- **Resize the checkboxes**. When you reposition the checkboxes they may overlap. If that occurs you will want to reduce the width of each checkbox. You can do that by selecting each checkbox component and change the width property in the Properties Inspector.
- **Remove the checkbox labels**. If you are using images a checkbox label may not be necessary. You can remove the label by opening the learning interaction component and removing all text from the label field of each checkbox instance.
- **Import the image to the Stage and position it next to the label.** You may need to work with the positioning so that it is clear to the student which image belongs to which checkbox.

Here is a sample multiple choice question with images:

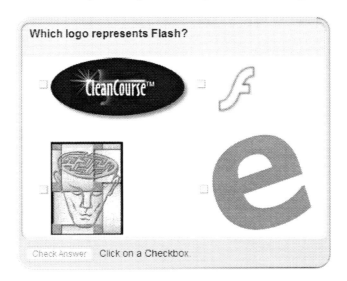

## Forcing Lengthy Answer Text to Wrap

For some multiple choice questions, the text for the answer and its distracters may not fit in the space provided. If the text is longer than the checkbox component the text is simply cut off as shown here:

*Notice that part of the response is cut off.*

☐ Four score and seven years ago our father set forth on this

☐ 87 years ago this nation was formed.

The top response has more text to display but is only able to display a single line. By default the check boxes do not wrap lengthy text. To correct this problem you must use ActionScript.

**Use these steps to force a lengthy answer or distracter to wrap:**

**1**  Select the checkbox that does not show all the text.

**2** In the Properties Inspector increase the height. If you need to show 2 lines of text, double the height (for example from 22 to 44). If you need to show 3 lines of text triple the height.

*Change the height of the checkbox.*

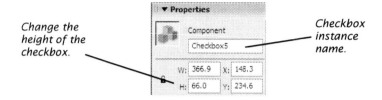

*Checkbox instance name.*

**3** Select the frame that contains the interaction and open the Actions panel (Window → Development Panels → Actions).

You may want to include all the ActionScript in a separate layer. If so, select the frame in the Actions layer.

**4** Enter these 3 lines of code. In place of *Checkbox1* enter the instance name for the checkbox you are trying to fix. You can find the instance name in the Properties Inspector.

```
_level0.Checkbox1.labelPath.multiline=true;
_level0.Checkbox1.labelPath.wordWrap=true;
_level0.Checkbox1.labelPath._height=44;
```

These 3 lines of code change the settings for the *labelPath* field that is a part of the checkbox named *Checkbox1*. The field becomes a multiline field, *wordWrap* is set to *True* and we changed the height. The number that you enter for the height parameter should equal the number you entered in the Properties Inspector for the height of the checkbox component.

There are numerous other settings associated with a checkbox text field that you can change this way. For more information on those settings refer to the Textfield class in the ActionScript Dictionary help.

**5** Save your changes (File → Save) and test the movie (Control → Test Movie).

**Note:** You will notice in Flash MX 2004 that the actual checkbox positions itself in the middle of the text instead of with the first line as shown below. This is not true with learning interactions created using Flash MX.

Four score and seven years ago our fathers brought forth on this continent a new nation...

**Note:** In Flash MX the 3 lines of code will be different because the components in Flash MX use a different name from Flash MX 2004. Here is a sample:
_level0.Checkbox5.fLabel_mc.labelField.multiline=true;
_level0.Checkbox5.fLabel_mc.labelField.wordWrap=true;
_level0.Checkbox5.fLabel_mc.labelField._height=26;

# Summary

In this chapter you've learned how to create Multiple Choice and True/False interactions, which are common question types used in assessments. You learned how to add (and delete) distracters from Multiple Choice interactions, how to specify feedback, and how to establish navigation options.

You also learned some of the customization that can be done with these two interaction types. We will discuss some additional customization in Chapter 11.

# Drag and Drop Interactions 8

In a Drag and Drop interaction the learner clicks and drags an object (called a *drag object*) to a target area (called a *target object*) and releases the mouse button. Drag and Drop interactions are a great way to add interactivity or unique assessment questions to your e-learning course.

In this chapter you will learn:

- About uses for Drag and Drop interactions.
- How to create Drag and Drop interactions as matching exercises.
- How to create Drag and Drop interactions that teach the order of steps in an activity.
- About ways to enhance Drag and Drop interactions.

# Introduction to Drag and Drop Interactions

Drag and Drop interactions are versatile—they can be used for a variety of learning activities as well as in quizzes. The following are some examples:

- **Matching terms with their definitions.** You can have a column of terms on the left and a column of definitions randomly ordered on the right. The learner then drags the term to the correct definition.

- **Assessing placement of parts of a larger whole, such as parts on a machine.** Place the graphic of the machine on the right. The parts are "cut outs" of the machine and placed on the left. The user must drag the part to the correct position.

- **Assessing knowledge of procedural steps.** You can have an object that represents each step in a procedure. The learner then drags the steps into the correct order.

 On CD: To help you become more familiar with the Drag and Drop interaction, open **samples/chapters06/sample_6-1.swf**. The first interaction uses Drag and Drop.

# Creating a Drag and Drop Interaction

This step-by-step tutorial takes you through the process of adding Flash's pre-built Drag and Drop learning interaction to your movie. In this case, you will create an interaction where the learner has to match a series of international marine signal flags with their appropriate names.

 More Information: This tutorial builds on the basic process of creating an interaction that was covered in Chapter 6: An Introduction to Flash Learning Interactions.

## Viewing the Finished Interaction

Before creating this interaction, take a moment to explore the finished exercise.

 On CD: Open **samples/chapter08/sample_8-1.swf** on the CD-ROM to see an example of the Drag and Drop interaction where the learner must match the marine signal flags with their names.

When viewing this interaction, here are some things to look for:

- Drop the drag objects onto an invalid area and see what happens.
- Drop the drag objects near, but not right on, the target elements. How close do you have to be before the drag object snaps to the target?
- Click the **Reset** button to start the interaction over.
- Click the **Check Answer** button to view the feedback.

# Creating the Interaction

Now that you've seen how this interaction works, try creating it yourself. Creating a Drag and Drop interaction involves four major tasks:

- Adding the learning interaction to the timeline
- Creating the drag objects
- Creating the target objects
- Configuring the interaction

## Adding the Learning Interaction

To create any learning interaction, you add it to the timeline of your Flash document.

**Use these steps to add the Drag and Drop learning interaction to your document:**

**1** Open **samples/chapter08/sample_8-1start.fla**. This movie already includes target symbols to simplify this example.

**2** Access the Learning Interactions library (Window → Other Panels → Common Libraries → Learning Interactions).

**3** Select the Drag and Drop interaction from the library and drag it to the Stage.

The result should look like this:

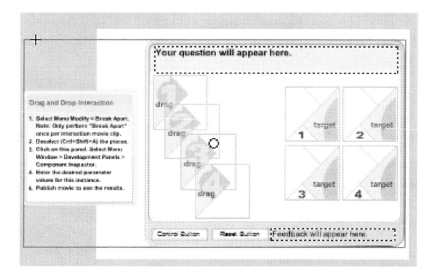

**4**    Break apart the movie clip elements (Modify → Break Apart) so that you can
edit them.

**Caution:**  You should only break the clip apart once.  If you break apart the learning
interaction component itself, you will lose its scripts.  For more information, see Chapter 6:
An Introduction to Learning Interactions.

**5**    Deselect all the items on the Stage (Edit → Deselect All) and select only the
learning interaction component (the object with the instructions).

Now you are ready to customize the objects to look like those in the finished
interaction.

**Tip:** Before you make additional changes to the interaction, test the movie to see the
default behavior of the interaction (Control → Test Movie).  Notice that there are four drag
objects (1–4) that correspond to four target objects (1–4).

In the next section, you will configure the interaction by entering the question,
changing the drag objects to display the flags, changing the target objects to display
the flag's name, and giving the learner 3 chances to get the interaction correct.

## Creating the Drag Objects

This section builds upon the Drag and Drop interaction that you just created.  The
first step in creating the Drag Objects is to create a symbol for each drag object.
Then you can swap the new symbols with the default drag objects.

**Use these steps to create the drag object symbols:**

**1**  Import the following graphic images (File → Import to Library) into the library: images/flagalpha.gif, images/flagbravo.gif, images/flagcharlie.gif, and images/flagdelta.gif.

**2**  Create a new Movie Clip symbol (Insert → New Symbol) using the settings shown:

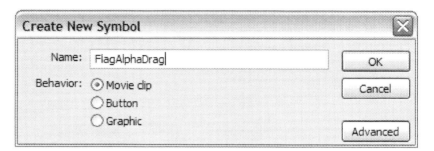

 **Caution:** Make sure you select Movie Clip as the behavior or the drag object will not function properly.

**3**  Open the library and place a copy of **flagalpha.gif** in the center of the movie clip.

*Drag this graphic to the Stage.*

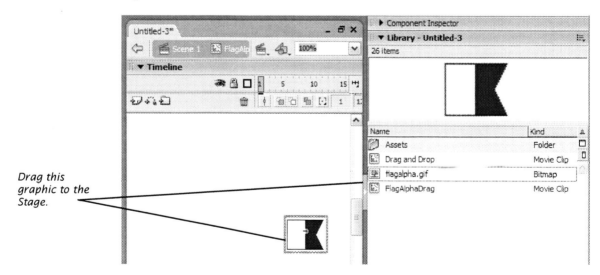

**4**  In the Properties Inspector set the X and Y property to 0. This will position the graphic correctly.

**5**   Repeat steps 2 and 3 so that there is a movie clip for each of the other drag objects: *FlagBravoDrag*, *FlagCharlieDrag*, and *FlagDeltaDrag*.

 Tip: For easy reference, you may want to store these movie clips in a library subfolder. For example you can name it: **Assets/Graphics/Drag and Drop** .

Now that you have created the movie clip objects, you are ready to swap the default drag objects for those that you have created.

**Use these steps to swap the drag objects:**

**1**   On the Stage, select the *DD_drag1* Movie Clip object.

**2**   In the Properties Inspector, click **Swap.**

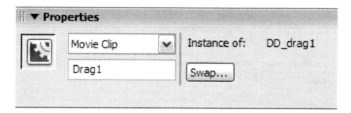

The Swap Symbol window displays:

*Select the new symbol from the list.*

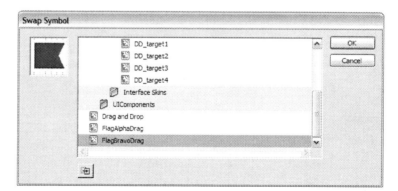

**3**   Select *FlagBravoDrag* as the new symbol and click **OK.**

Notice that the instance of *FlagBravoDrag* maintains the instance name *Drag1*.

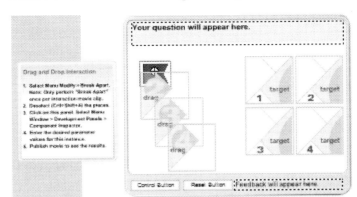

**4**   Repeat steps 1-2 until you have swapped all of the drag objects, as listed here:

| Original | Swap With... | Instance Name |
|----------|--------------|---------------|
| DD_drag2 | FlagCharlieDrag | Drag2 |
| DD_drag3 | FlagDeltaDrag | Drag3 |
| DD_drag4 | FlagAlphaDrag | Drag4 |

Your Stage should look similar to this:

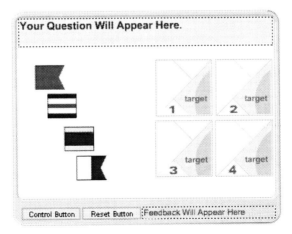

## Customizing the Target Objects

Creating target objects is similar to creating Drag objects. To simplify your work, we have already created movie clips for each of the Target objects. You only need to swap the old targets with the new ones.

**Use these steps to swap the target objects:**

**1**    On the Stage, select the *DD_target1* Movie Clip object.

**2**    In the Properties Inspector, click **Swap** and select *alphatarget* (in the targets folder) as the new symbol.

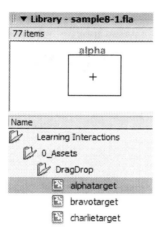

These targets were already created. If you needed to create these on your own, you would create a new symbol (Insert → New Symbol) and use the Flash drawing tools to create the target.

**3**    Click **OK**.

Notice that the instance of *alphatarget* maintains the instance name *Target1*.

**4**    Repeat steps 1-2 until you have swapped all of the target objects, as listed here:

| Original | Swap With… | Instance Name |
|----------|-----------|---------------|
| DD_target2 | bravotarget | Target2 |
| DD_target3 | charlietarget | Target3 |

| Original | Swap With... | Instance Name |
|----------|--------------|---------------|
| DD_target4 | deltatarget | Target4 |

Your Stage should look similar to this:

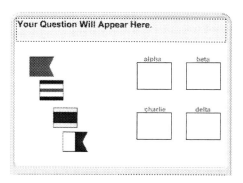

**5** Before moving on to the last part of the exercise, test the movie (Control → Test Movie).

Notice that all of the functionality is there. However, you still need to provide the question text and the feedback. Additionally, the Drag objects and the Target objects are not correctly associated with one another. You configure all of these elements in the Component Inspector.

## Configuring the Interaction

The final task when setting up a Drag and Drop interaction is to configure the learning interaction component. The Start tab is unique to the Drag and Drop interaction. This table describes settings available on this tab:

| Setting | Description |
|---------|-------------|
| Interaction ID | Enter a name to identify the interaction. This information is mainly used if you are tracking student data. |
| Question | Enter the question that is presented to the learner. |

| Setting | Description |
|---|---|
| Drag Object Name | Enter the instance name for each drag object that will be used during the drag and drop exercise. The names are case sensitive. You must account for each drag object you plan to use. |
| Matches Target Name | Enter the instance name for each target object that will be used in the interaction. The names are case sensitive. You must account for each target object you plan to use in the interaction. |
| Snap to Start | Check this box if you would like a drag object to snap back to its original position if the learner does not place on a registered target object. |

**Use these steps to configure the interaction:**

**1**   Select the learning interaction component and open the Component Inspector (Window → Development Panels → Component Inspector).

**Drag and Drop**

Interaction ID    Interaction_01

Question

Match the signal flag with its name.

| Drag Object Name | Matches Target Name |
|---|---|
| Drag1 | Target2 |
| Drag2 | Target3 |
| Drag3 | Target4 |
| Drag4 | Target1 |
| | |
| | |
| | |
| | |

✓ Snap to Start          Start | Options | Assets

**2**   In the Question field, type *Match the signal flag with its name.*

**3** Specify which instance for the drag objects matches which target object as shown here:

**Drag and Drop**

Interaction ID  [Interaction_01]

Question

[Match the signal flag with its name.]

| Drag Object Name | Matches Target Name |
|---|---|
| Drag1 | Target2 |
| Drag2 | Target3 |
| Drag3 | Target4 |
| Drag4 | Target1 |
| | |
| | |
| | |
| | |

✓ Snap to Start          Start    Options    Assets

*Each drag-target pair associates two matching items. If the learner drags and drops the drag objects onto the corresponding target objects, the question is considered correct.*

The settings on this tab determine whether or not the question is correct.

**4** Click the **Snap to Start** box to place a check mark in it.

This will cause the drag objects to snap back to their original position if the learner does not drop them on a defined target.

**5** Click the Options tab.

**6** Set the number of tries to **2**.

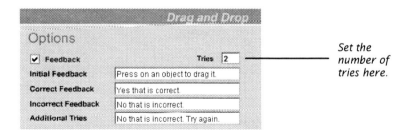

Options

☑ Feedback                                    Tries [2]

Initial Feedback    [Press on an object to drag it.]

Correct Feedback   [Yes that is correct.]

Incorrect Feedback [No that is incorrect.]

Additional Tries   [No that is incorrect. Try again.]

*Set the number of tries here.*

**7** Test your movie (Control → Test Movie). Make corrections as needed.

You have just created a Drag and Drop interaction.

# Adding and Removing Drag and Target Objects

Since the learning interaction comes with only 4 default drag and target objects, you may need to add (or delete) objects to complete the interaction. The Drag and Drop interaction has a built-in limitation on the number of objects. The maximum number you can have is 8 drag objects and 8 target objects.

## Adding a Drag or Target Object

If the default Drag and Drop interaction comes with fewer drag or target elements than you need, you have to add drag and/or target objects using the techniques shown in this section.

**Note:** When you want to add a choice, you cannot simply make an additional entry in the Component Parameters panel. You also need to add a new drag and/or target object instance on the Stage.

**Use these steps to add a drag object or a target object:**

**1**   Create a symbol for each of the new objects (Insert → New Symbol) and select **Movie Clip** as the symbol type).

**2**   Place the image into the symbol. You may need to import the image or draw the image using the Flash drawing tools.

**Note:** When you create an image for a drag object, you need to include a fill color for it to work properly. For example, if the graphic does not contain a fill the learner will try to click on the inside of the object, but the object will not respond because it is not considered a part of the image.

**3**   In the timeline, select the frame (and layer) where the learning interaction resides and drag the symbol from the library to the Stage.

**4**   In the Properties Inspector, give the symbol a unique instance name.

**5**   Repeat steps 1-3 until you have created all the movie clips for all of the drag and target objects that you need.

**6** Select the learning interaction component and open the Component Inspector (Window → Development Panels → Component Inspector).

**7** Add the instance names for the new drag objects in the drag Object Name column.

**8** Add the instance name for the corresponding target object in the Matching Target Name column.

**9** Test your movie (Control → Test Movie). Make corrections as needed.

## Removing a Drag or Target Object

If the default interaction comes with more drag and target objects than you need, you will need to remove a drag and/or target object.

**Use these steps to remove either a drag object or a target object:**

**1** On the Stage, select the object(s) that you want to remove and press the DELETE key.

**2** Select the learning interaction component and open the Component Inspector (Window → Development Panels → Component Inspector).

**3** Remove the deleted object's instance name from the appropriate column (either Drag Object Name and/or Target Object Name).

**4** Test your movie (Control → Test Movie) and make corrections as needed.

# Drag and Drop Variations

All Drag and Drop exercises are by nature a matching activity—where you want the learner to drag an object onto an intended target. However, within the "matching" umbrella there are several different variations:

| Type | Description |
|---|---|
| 1-to-1 Matching | There is a 1 for 1 correspondence between drag objects and target objects. The marine flags example in this chapter is an example of a 1-to-1 Matching interaction. It is the most common type of Drag and Drop interaction. |
| Matching with Distracter Targets | Similar to 1-to-1 matching, but there are target objects that do not have a corresponding drag object. This makes the question more challenging because there are incorrect targets used as distracters. For example, if we created the target *Echo* even through there was no Echo flag displayed.<br><br>You can also use this type of interaction as a visual multiple choice question. In this scenario, you would have only one drag object and several target objects. |
| Matching with Distracter Drag Objects | Similar to 1-to-1 matching, but there are drag objects that do not have a corresponding target object. This makes the question more challenging as there are incorrect drag objects used as distracters. For example, you could have more flags than there are targets. |
| Multiple Drag Objects Share a Target | Similar to 1-to-1 matching, but there is more than one possible correct answer for a given target. For example, in the Component Parameters you could specify *Target3* as the match for both *Drag1* and *Drag2*. |
| Steps in Order | Use this type of interaction when you want the learner to place steps in a particular sequential order. To do this, you could either:<br><br>■ Display a number for each drag object and use each target object to display a description of one of the steps.<br>■ Display a number for each target object. Place the target objects in the correct order (step 1, step 2, and so on). Use each drag object to describe a given step. Set up the drag objects to start in random order.<br><br>You can include distracter steps to make the interaction more challenging. For example, you can place an erroneous step description as a distracter to see if the learner can choose the correct step. |

**More Information:** Some products, such as CourseBuilder, provide the capability of performing 2-way matching. In other words, an object can serve as both the drag object and a target object. This is particularly useful for instructional games. Flash MX learning interactions do not have this capability. However, it would be possible to create your own custom interaction to do this.

# Customizing the Interaction

There are a couple interesting ways to customize Drag and Drop interactions. In this section we take a look at what is possible and provide you with the instructions.

## Resizing or Changing the Appearance of Text Fields

Drag and Drop interactions consist of at least two text fields: the question text and the feedback text. These fields come with a preset size, font styles, color, and so forth. You may want to make changes to these fields.

 **More Information:** For more information about changing the text fields associated with a Drag and Drop interaction see Chapter 11: Customizing Learning Interactions.

## Using Text Instead of Graphics

Using text as a drag object sometimes makes more sense than an image. You can create the text in an external graphics program and import it has an image, but it is much easier to use Flash text.

**Use these steps to create a text Drag object:**

**1**   Create and name a new Movie Clip symbol (Insert → New Symbol).

**2**   Add a text box and enter the text.

 **Tip:** You will want to make your text box a similar shape to your target elements so that it can accurately snap to the target.

**3**    Return to the main timeline and swap the default drag symbol with the new symbol.

## Enhancing What Happens When the Learner Drops the Drag Element

When the learner drops a drag object on a target element, you may want something to happen, like playing a sound. You cause simple actions to occur when an object is dropped without modifying the code that controls the Drag and Drop interaction. If you want something to happen based upon whether the object was dropped on the correct target then you will need to modify the component code.

**More Information:** Refer to Chapter 11: Customizing Learning Interactions for more information on the component code for the Flash learning interaction.

Causing a sound to play when an object is dropped is a simple result that does not require modifying the component code. We will use that example here.

**Use these steps to cause a sound to play when an object is dropped:**

**1**    Add and configure a Drag and Drop learning interaction.

**2**    Import into the library the sound you want to play.

**On CD**: You can import **audio/drop.wav** from the CD if you do not have a sound readily available.

**3**    Right-click (CONTROL-click on the Macintosh) the sound in the library and choose Linkage from the menu.

The Linkage Properties window displays:

In the linkage properties you will assign an identifier to the sound so that you can play the sound using a behavior.

**4**   Check the **Export for ActionScript** checkbox.

The Identifier field becomes active.

**5**   Enter a name for the sound in the Identifier field and click **OK**.

**6**   Create a new layer and name it *Actions* if you have not already created one.

**7**   Insert a blank keyframe to the Actions layer at the same frame position where the drag and drop interaction resides.

**8**   Select the blank keyframe, open the Behaviors panel and select the **Load Sound from Library** behavior.

*Enter the identifier here.*

*Enter a name you can use to reference in the learning interaction.*

*Uncheck this option.*

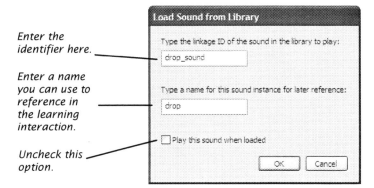

 **Note:** Behaviors are available with Flash MX 2004. They let you quickly add functionality that would normally require ActionScript.

**9**   Enter the linkage identifier in the first field. The linkage identifier is the identifier name you entered in step 3. You can assign a name to the sound in the second field. Make sure the **Play this sound when loaded** option is not checked.

**10**   Click **OK**.

**11**   Make sure the event for the behavior is none.

**12** Select each drag object in turn and add a **Play Sound** behavior.

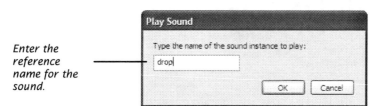

*Enter the reference name for the sound.*

**13** Enter the reference name you assigned to the sound in the **Load Sound from Library** window. This is not the linkage name.

**14** Click **OK** and add the same behavior to the remaining drag objects.

# Creating Drag and Drop from Scratch

There may be times when you would like to include a drag and drop interaction as a learning activity that is not part of a quiz. The drag and drop Flash interaction does not work well for this type of application and you will need to create your own from scratch.

This type of Drag and Drop interaction will not record quiz information. If you need that type of functionality, use the Drag and Drop learning interaction.

In this section we will look at creating a drag and drop interaction from scratch. This hands-on activity will require the use of ActionScript.

## Viewing the Finished Interaction

In this exercise you will create a drag and drop interaction that functions as a learning activity instead of a quiz question. Before creating the interaction, take a moment to explore the finished exercise.

**On CD:** Open samples/chapter08/sample_8-4.swf on the CD-ROM to see an example of a Drag and Drop interaction used as a learning activity.

When viewing this interaction, here are some things to try:

- Drag and drop the arrow next to each number.
- Drop the arrow on top of the number or somewhere else on the Stage. What happens if the arrow is not dropped on a target?

# Creating the Interaction

This interaction is created using ActionScript. To get you started we have created a Flash movie with several objects already included. File

samples/chapter08/sample_8-4_start.fla includes these elements to get you started:

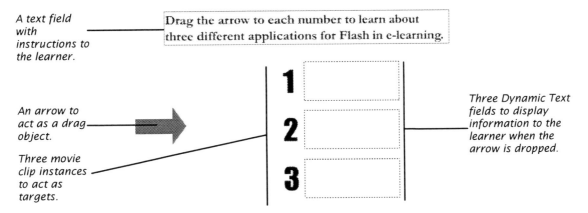

*A text field with instructions to the learner.*

Drag the arrow to each number to learn about three different applications for Flash in e-learning.

*An arrow to act as a drag object.*

*Three movie clip instances to act as targets.*

*Three Dynamic Text fields to display information to the learner when the arrow is dropped.*

Each object has been given an instance name as indicated in this table:

| Object | Instance Names |
|---|---|
| Arrow | dragArrow |
| Target object 1, 2, and 3 | purpose1, purpose2, and purpose3 |
| Dynamic Text fields | text1, text2, and text3 |

These instance names will be used in the ActionScript code.

To complete the interaction you will need to add ActionScript to the arrow movie clip. This code will need activate the dragging when the mouse is clicked. When the mouse is released it will need to do the following:

- Stop the drag action.
- Test to see which target, if any, the arrow has been dropped on.
- Snap the arrow to a location next to the target.
- Place the correct text in the Dynamic Text field.

**Use these steps to complete the drag and drop learning activity:**

**1**   Open **samples/chapter08/sample_8-4_start.fla** from the CD-ROM.

**2**   Select the arrow movie clip instance and open the Actions panel (Window →
Development Panels → Actions).

**3**   Enter the following code in the Actions panel:

```
on(press){
    this.startDrag();
}
```

This code causes the arrow to drag with the cursor once the mouse is pressed.
However, if you test the e-learning activity at this point you will see that there is
no way to stop the arrow from dragging. It follows the cursor around the
screen even when the mouse button is released.

In the next step you will stop the dragging once the mouse button is released.

**4**   To stop the dragging, enter this code beneath the last curly brace.

```
on(release){
    this.stopDrag();
}
```

Once the mouse button is released, this code causes the dragging to stop. Once
the dragging has stopped we need to test to see if the arrow was dropped over
a Target object.

**5**   Enter this code, immediately beneath the *stopDrag* action inside the *on(release)*
handler.

```
if (this.hitTest(_root.purpose1)){

} else if (this.hitTest(_root.purpose2)){

} else if (this.hitTest(_root.purpose3)){

}
```

This if statement uses the *hitTest* action to find out if the arrow (this) intersects
with one of the targets (purpose1, purpose2, or purpose3). We use _root in
order to provide a full path to the target instances. This if statement is adequate
to find out where the arrow was dropped, but it doesn't do anything. You will
begin to add actions in the next step.

**6**    Place this code immediately below the hit test condition for purpose1.

```
this._x=_root.purpose1._x
this._y=_root.purpose1._y
```

This causes the upper left corner of the arrow to snap to the upper left corner of the target. The upper left corner of the target is not immediately next to the number. The symbol was created using a white rectangle to the left of the number. Therefore the X and Y attributes for the upper left corner of the target is to the left of the actual number. You can select this instance in the sample movie to see how large it is.

**7**    Repeat Step 6 for each else statement. Make sure you change the instance name (purpose1) to the instance that is being tested with the hit test.

The only step left to complete is the displaying of text into the field.

**8**    Place this code immediately following the line **this._y=_root.purpose1._y**.

```
_root.text1.text="Create animations to illustrate concepts."
```

**9**    Place this code immediately following the line **this._y=_root.purpose2._y**.

```
_root.text2.text="Create a secure quiz using the Flash learning
interactions."
```

**10**    Place this code immediately following the line **this._y=_root.purpose3._y**.

```
_root.text3.text="Use Flash as the main authoring tool for your e-
learning."
```

The entire code attached to dragArrow should look like this:

*Stops the dragging* ———

*Checks to see which target element the drag object was dropped on. It then positions the arrow and places text in the text field.*

```
▼ Actions - Movie Clip

on(press){
    this.startDrag();
}
on(release){
    this.stopDrag();
    if (this.hitTest(_root.purpose1)){
        this._x=_root.purpose1._x
        this._y=_root.purpose1._y
        _root.text1.text="Create animations for e-learning devloped using other tools."
    } else if (this.hitTest(_root.purpose2)){
        this._x=_root.purpose2._x
        this._y=_root.purpose2._y
        _root.text2.text="Create a secure quiz using the Flash learning interactions."
    } else if (this.hitTest(_root.purpose3)){
        this._x=_root.purpose3._x
        this._y=_root.purpose3._y
        _root.text3.text="Use Flash as the main authoring tool for your e-learning."
    }
}

dragArrow
Line 17 of 20, Col 14
```

**11**  Save and test the movie (Control → Text Movie). If something is not functioning correctly, double-check the code.

You have just created a Drag and Drop interaction from scratch! You can use these same techniques to create other drag and drop activities.

# Summary

In this chapter, you learned how to create Drag and Drop interactions. You can use drag and drop for matching or procedural step interactions. Drag and Drop interactions provide interactivity on instructional pages as well as add variety to quizzes.

You learned how to add new drag and target objects and to configure other drag and drop settings. Finally, you learned to create a drag and drop learning activity from scratch.

# Fill-in-the-blank Interactions 9

Fill-in-the-blank interactions enable you to gather a brief text response from the learner. These responses can be single words or complete phrases.

In this chapter you will learn:

- About uses for Fill-in-the-blank interaction.
- How to create a Fill-in-the-blank interaction.
- About ways to enhance a Fill-in-the-blank interaction.

# Introduction to Fill-in-the-blank Interactions

Fill-in-the-blank interactions are a good choice when you want the learner to recall information, such as terminology. Since it is based upon recall, rather than recognition, it is more difficult to guess the answers. The question can require the learner to enter a single word or a complete phrase. Here is an example of a Fill-in-the-blank interaction:

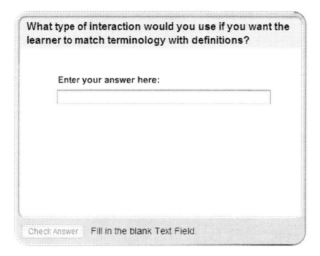

Fill-in-the-blank interactions are particularly useful when you want to assess the learner's ability to recall an exact phrase, spell a particular term, or use appropriate capitalization. They are also quite useful in survey or evaluation forms.

 **Tip:** Since this type of interaction also tests the learner's ability to type and spell accurately, this can be a very difficult type of question for learners with disabilities. Single words are easier than complete phrases, so you may want to take that into consideration when designing your questions.

# Creating a Fill-in-the-blank Interaction

This step-by-step tutorial takes you through the process of adding Flash's pre-built Fill-in-the-blank learning interaction to your movie. You will then configure and test it.

**More Information:** This tutorial builds on the basic process of creating an interaction that was covered in Chapter 6: An Introduction to Flash learning interactions.

## Viewing the Finished Interaction

Before you create the interaction, take a look at a finished interaction. When viewing the interaction make sure to enter both correct and incorrect answers to see how it affects the results.

**On CD:** Take a moment and try out the finished interaction: samples/chapter09/sample_9-1.swf. Be sure to test out both correct and incorrect answers.

## Creating the Interaction

To create any learning interaction, you must add it to the timeline of your movie and configure the parameters.

**Use these steps to create a fill-in-the-blank learning interaction:**

**1** Create a new file (File → New) or open an existing file.

**2** Access the Learning Interactions library (Window → Other Panels → Common Libraries → Learning Interactions).

**3** Select the Fill-in-the-blank interaction from the panel and drag it to the Stage. The results should look like this:

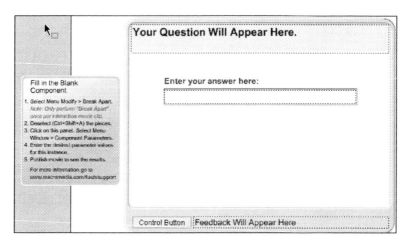

**4** Break apart the movie clip elements (Modify → Break Apart) so that you can edit them.

**Caution:** You should only break the clip apart once. If you break apart the learning interaction component itself, you will lose its scripts. For more information, see Chapter 6: An Introduction to Learning Interactions.

**5** Deselect all the items on the Stage (Edit → Deselect All) and select the learning interaction component only (the object that contains the instructions).

**6** Open the Component Inspector (Window → Development Panels → Component Inspector).

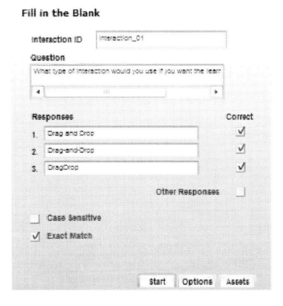

The Start tab contains settings that are unique to the Fill-in-the-blank learning interaction. This table describes each setting:

| Field | Description |
| --- | --- |
| Interaction ID | Enter a name to identify the interaction. This information is used if you are tracking student data. |
| Question | Enter the question that is presented to the learner. |
| Responses | Enter the responses that may be provided by the learner. You may enter either correct responses or incorrect responses, but you are limited to three. |
| Correct | Place a checkmark in the checkbox to indicate that the entered response is correct. If no check mark is present the entered response is incorrect. |
| Other Response | Use this checkbox to indicate whether responses other than those entered in the responses fields are correct or incorrect. |

| Field | Description |
|---|---|
| Case Sensitive | Place a checkmark into this checkbox to specify that responses are valid only if they match the case of the responses you entered. |
| Exact Match | Use this checkbox to specify whether the matching response must be an exact match. If you select Exact Match, a correct response matches only if the user enters the text exactly as the response text. With Exact Match deselected, an answer will be evaluated as correct if it contains the correct word. Other words may be included and the response will still be correct. |

**7** In the Start tab of the Component Inspector, establish these settings:

| Field | Value |
|---|---|
| Question | What type of interaction would you use if you want the learner to match terminology with definitions? |
| Response 1 | Drag and Drop |
| Response 2 | Drag-and-Drop |
| Response 3 | DragDrop |

**8** Make sure you check the **Correct** column for all three responses.

**Tip:** In this example, all of the correct responses were listed. You could also set up the interaction to accept all responses except those listed. In that case, enter all of the incorrect responses, and uncheck the Correct column for each responses. Then check Other Responses to specify that all other responses are correct.

Use the default settings provided on the Options tab. For more information about configuring these settings refer to Chapter 6: *An Introduction to Flash Learning Interactions.*

**9**　Save the file and test the interaction (Control → Test Movie).

# Customizing the Interaction

There are many ways to customize a Fill-in-the-blank interaction. This section covers a few of the ways that you can customize the interaction. Customizations that are valid for all interaction types are covered in Chapter 11: *Customizing Learning Interactions*.

## Resizing or Changing the Appearance of Text Fields

Multiple Choice and True/False interactions consist of at least 2 text fields: the question text and the feedback. These fields come with a preset size, font styles, color, and so forth. You may want to make changes to these fields.

 **More Information:** For more information about changing the text fields associated with a Fill-in-the-blank interaction see Chapter 11: Customizing Learning Interactions.

## Setting the Focus to the Text Field

To make a Fill-in-the-blank interaction a little easier for the learner, you can automatically set the focus to the text field when the interaction appears. This way the learner doesn't need to click in the text box before typing an answer. You can accomplish this using a little ActionScript code.

**Use these steps to set the focus to the text field:**

**1**　Create an Actions layer if one has not been created yet.

**2**　Insert a keyframe in the Actions layer (Insert → Timeline → Keyframe) at the same frame position as the Fill-in-the-blank interaction.

**3**　Select the text component and use the Properties Inspector to find out the instance name of the text field.

The name of the field by default should be *Template_UserEntry*. You can change this instance name, but you need to make sure to record the new instance name in the Assets tab of the Component Inspector.

**4**    Select the keyframe in the Actions layer and open the Actions panel (Window → Development Panels → Actions).

**5**    Insert this code into the Actions panel:

```
focusManager.setFocus(Template_UserEntry);
```

If you changed the instance name, make sure to replace *Template_UserEntry* with the new instance name.

**Note:** We use the focusManager class instead of the Selection class to set the focus because the text field is actually a textInput component not just a standard text field.

**6**    Test your movie and make sure a cursor appears in the text field when the learning interaction displays. The focus will not function correctly if you use Control → Test Movie. You will need to publish your movie and open the SWF file.

## Submitting the Answer with the Enter Key

A natural inclination of most learners when answering a Fill-in-the-blank question is to press the ENTER key after typing a response. For this reason you may want to add some additional ActionScript code to make the ENTER key functional.

**Use these steps to set the focus to the text field:**

**1**    Create an Actions layer if one has not been created yet.

**2**    Insert a keyframe in the Actions layer (Insert → Timeline → Keyframe) at the same frame position as the Fill-in-the-blank interaction.

**3**    Select the **Control** button component and use the Properties Inspector to find out the instance name of the button.

The name of the button by default should be *Template_ControlButton*. You can change this instance name, but you need to make sure to record the new instance name in the Assets tab of the Component Inspector.

**4**   Select the keyframe in the Actions layer and open the Actions panel (Window → Development Panels → Actions).

**5**   Insert this code into the Actions panel:

```
focusManager.defaultPushButton = Template_ControlButton;
```

If you changed the instance name, make sure to replace Template_ControlButton with the new instance name.

**6**   Test your movie (Control → Test Movie) and make sure pressing ENTER submits the answer.

## Resolving the Limited Response Problem

You will undoubtedly run into situations when using the Fill-in-the-blank interaction where you will want to enter more than 3 responses. Since the component only allows 3, you have to make some changes. These changes require the use of ActionScript and a little more knowledge about the component.

**More Information:** For more information about adding additional responses to a Fill-in-the-blank question see Chapter 11: Customizing Learning Interactions.

# Summary

In this chapter you've learned how to create Fill-in-the-blank interactions, which are useful when you want the learner to recall information. You also learned to customize the interaction so that the text field receives the focus and the learner can press ENTER to submit the answer.

In the next chapter, you will learn how to create Hot Spot and Hot Object interactions.

# Hot Spot and Hot Object Interactions 10

Earlier in the book you learned how to add interactivity to your course by creating buttons. You also learned how to create a transparent button, known as a hot spot, and enable the learner to make a selection. In this chapter, you will learn how you can achieve a similar type of interactivity using the Hot Object and Hot Spot learning interactions provided in Flash MX.

In this chapter you will learn:

- About uses for Hot Spot and Hot Object interactions.
- How to create Hot Spot and Hot Object interactions.
- About ways to enhance Hot Spot and Hot Object interactions.

# Introduction to Hot Spot and Hot Object Interactions

In a Hot Spot interaction, the learner clicks a transparent hot spot on the screen to make a selection. You designate one or more hot spots to be correct answer choices. Additional hot spots serve as distracters. A Hot Object interaction is similar; however, the learner will click on a *button or a movie clip—rather than a hot spot* to provide an answer.

Hot Spot and Hot Object interactions are more frequently used to review the parts of some object. For example, the learner could make selections on a map, a diagram of a piece of equipment, a flow chart, or a screen capture of a software application.

 **On CD:** To help you become more familiar with the Hot Spot and Hot Object interactions, try samples/chapter06/sample_6-1.swf. The third interaction uses a Hot Object interaction and the forth interaction uses a Hot Spot interaction.

 # Creating a Hot Spot Interaction

This step-by-step tutorial takes you through the process of adding Flash's pre-built Hot Spot learning component to your movie. You will then configure and test it.

 **More Information:** This tutorial builds on the basic process of creating an interaction that was covered in Chapter 6: An Introduction to Flash Learning Interactions.

## View the Finished Interaction

Before creating this interaction, take a moment to explore the finished product. In this example, the interaction will contain a screen shot with several hot spots over the toolbar buttons. The learner will answer the question by clicking on the appropriate hot spot.

 **On CD:** Open samples/chapter10/sample_10-1.swf on the CD-ROM to see an example of the hot spot interaction.

# Creating the Interaction

Now that you've seen how this interaction works, try creating it yourself. To create a learning interaction, add it to the timeline of your movie.

**Use these steps to create the Hot Spot learning interaction:**

**1** Create a new file (File → New).

**2** Access the learning interactions library (Window → Other Panels → Common Libraries → Learning Interactions).

**3** Drag the Hot Spot component from the library to the Stage.

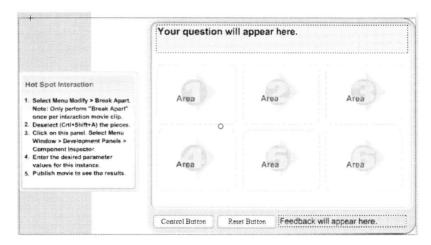

**4** Break apart the movie clip elements (Modify → Break Apart) so that you can edit them.

**Caution:** You should only break the interaction apart once. If you break apart the learning interaction component itself, you will lose the scripts that are associated with this component.

**5** Deselect all the items on the Stage (Edit → Deselect All) and select the only the learning interaction component (the instructions).

**6** Open the Component Inspector (Window → Development Panels → Component Inspector or click the button on the Properties Inspector).

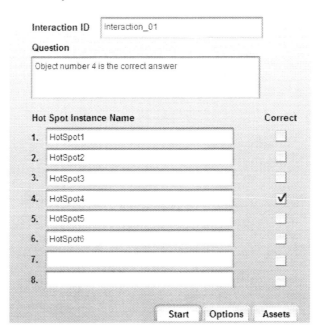

**7** Enter *Click on the button that allows you to fill a drawing object with the current fill color.* as the question.

**8** You only need four hot spots in this interaction, so delete instance names HotSpot5 and HotSpot6.

**9** Specify that *HotSpot2* is the correct answer choice.

**Note:** In this example, we will leave the default feedback as is. However, if you want to customize the feedback, click the Options tab.

**10** Import the **flashfill.gif** graphic from the **images** directory on the CD-ROM (File → Import to Stage).

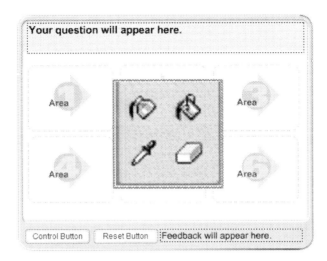

**11** Since you will not need hot spots 5 and 6 delete them from the Stage.

In step 8 you deleted the settings for hot spots 5 and 6. Now you are deleting the actual hot spots.

**12** Select the remaining four hot spots and bring them to the front (Modify → Arrange → Bring to Front).

This places the hot spots above the image of the buttons.

**13** Resize and arrange the hot spots so they are over the four buttons. Make sure hotspot2 is over the paint can.

To resize the hot spots you can use the width and height fields on the Properties Inspector or the Scale tool (Modify → Transform → Scale). The end result should look something like this:

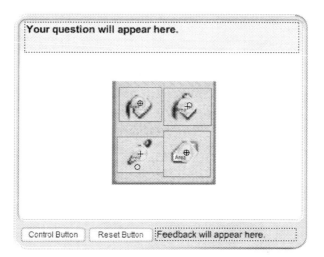

**14** Test the movie (Control → Test Movie).

You should notice that the hot spots are not complete invisible; they show up when you click them. Since you don't want the hot spot to be visible in this interaction, you have two options:

- Select all four hot spots and move them behind the main image (Modify → Arrange → Send Backward). This places the hot spot images behind the button image so they are no longer visible. The interaction still function correctly.
- Add ActionScript to the movie that will set the alpha (transparency) of the hot spots to 0. We will use this technique in the steps that follow.

**Note:** The Hot Spot interaction in Flash MX provided a setting on the Interaction tab that let you set the alpha level for the hot spots. If you set the alpha level to 0, the hot spots were invisible.

**15** Select the Hot Spot component (the instructions) and give it an instance name of *hotspot1* in the Properties Inspector.

This instance name is used in the ActionScript code we will add.

**16** Add an Actions layer to the Flash document.

**17**  Select the frame in the Actions layer. Open the Actions panel (Window →
Development Panels → Actions) and enter this code:

```
hotspot1.UPalpha = 0;
hotspot1.DNalpha = 0;
```

The interaction comes with an alpha setting for both the up state and down
state of the hot spot. This code sets the alpha level for both to 0 so the hotspot
is invisible. This accomplishes the same thing that settings did in the Flash MX
version of the Hot Spot interaction.

**18**  Test the interaction (Control → Test Movie) and make sure things are working
correctly.

# Creating a Hot Object Interaction

The steps for creating a Hot Object interaction are similar to the steps you use for
creating a Hot Spot interaction. However, you will need to create the objects (such
as buttons or movie clips) that you want to use in the interaction and swap them
with those provided in the default interaction. This step-by-step tutorial takes you
through the process of adding Flash's pre-built Hot Object learning interaction to
your movie. You will then configure and test it.

**More Information:** This tutorial builds on the basic process of creating an interaction that
was covered in Chapter 6: An Introduction to Flash Learning Interactions.

## Viewing the Finished Interaction

Before creating this interaction, take a moment to explore the finished product.

**On CD:** Open samples/chapter10/sample_10-2.swf on the CD-ROM to see an
example of the hot spot interaction.

## Creating the Interaction

In this interaction the learner is presented with a question and must select the
correct answer by clicking on an image.

**Use these steps to create a Hot Object learning interaction:**

**1**   Create a new file.

**2**   Access the Learning Interactions library (Window → Other Panels → Common
Libraries → Learning Interactions).

**3**   Drag the Hot Object interaction from the library to the Stage.

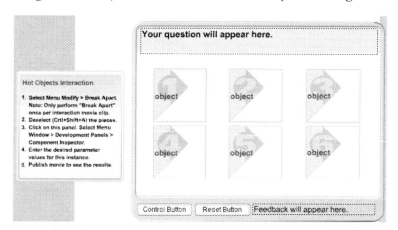

**4**   Break apart the movie clip elements (Modify → Break Apart) so that you can
edit them.

**Caution:** You should only break the interaction apart once.  If you break apart the learning
interactionitself, you will lose the scripts that are associated with this interaction.

The next step is to set up the hot objects for the question. There are several
ways that you can set up each of the objects in the interaction:

- Edit the each of hot object movie clips and use the drawing tools to
  modify the look of the symbol.

- Edit each of hot object movie clips and use imported graphics to modify
  the look of the symbol.

- Create your own movie clip symbol (Insert → New Symbol) for each
  object that you want to appear in the interaction. Then swap out the
  interaction's placeholder symbols with your newly created symbols.

The best method is to create your own movie clip symbols. That way if you
add another Hot Object to the same course you don't take a chance of
replacing the movie clips you have changed.

**5**   Create a new movie clip symbol (Insert → New Symbol).

**6**   Name the symbol *apple* and choice movie clip as the behavior.

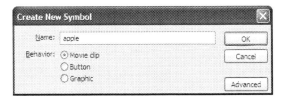

**7**   Click OK.

**8**   Import **images/apple.gif** to the Stage of the movie clip (File → Import → Import to Stage).

**9**   Use the Properties Inspector to position the image at 0,0.

**10**   Click **Scene 1** to return to the main timeline.

**11**   Repeat steps 5 – 10, creating a new symbol for each image using the images indicated in this table:

| Symbol Name | Image |
| --- | --- |
| Banana | Images/bananas.gif |
| Pear | Images/pear.gif |
| Watermelon | Images/watermelon.gif |
| Strawberry | Images/strawberry.gif |
| Nut | Images/nut.gif |

**12**   Return to the main timeline and select the *HotObject1* movie clip.

**13** In the Properties Inspector, click the **Swap** button and select *Pear* as the new movie clip.

Notice that the *HotObject1* retains the instance name.

**14** Repeat steps 12 and 13 for each hot object movie clip on the Stage. Swap in the new movie clips according to this table:

| Movie Clip | Symbol to Swap |
|------------|----------------|
| HotObject2 | Watermelon |
| HotObject3 | Strawberry |
| HotObject4 | Nut |
| HotObject5 | Banana |
| HotObject6 | Apple |

**15** Use the Properties Inspector or the Scale tool (Modify → Transform → Scale) to resize and arrange each movie clip until they are neatly organized on the Stage.

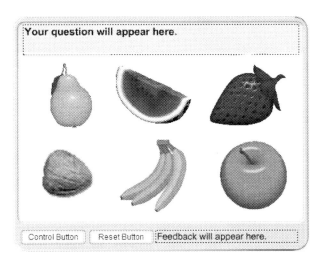

Now you are ready to set up the learning interaction component.

**16** Select the learning interaction component and open the Component Inspector panel (Window → Other Panels → Common Libraries → Learning Interactions).

**17** Enter *Which of the following is not a fruit?* as the question.

**18**  Make sure *HotObject4* is the correct response.

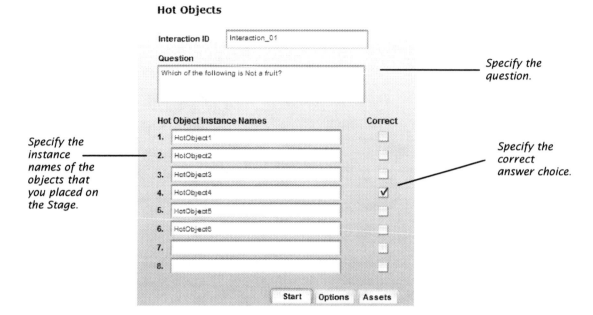

Specify the
question.

Specify the
instance
names of the
objects that
you placed on
the Stage.

Specify the
correct
answer choice.

**19**  Close the Component Inspector.

**20**  Test your movie (Control → Test Movie). Make changes as necessary.

# Adding and Deleting Hot Spots and Hot Objects

With a Hot Spot or Hot Object interaction, you may need to add or delete Hot Spots (Hot Objects) in order to have the appropriate number in your interaction. Adding requires you to create a movie clip symbol and register it as an asset.

**Use these steps to add a Hot Spot (or Hot Object):**

**1**  In the library, duplicate the symbol for one of the existing Hot Spots. You can duplicate a movie clip by right-clicking (CONTROL-clicking on a Macintosh) on the desired Hot Spot (or Hot Object) and selecting Duplicate Symbol from the pop-up menu.

**2**  Provide an appropriate name for the new symbol.

**3** In the timeline, select the frame (and layer) where the learning interaction resides and drag the symbol for the new Hot Spot or Hot Object from the library to the Stage.

**4** In the Properties Inspector, give the symbol a unique instance name.

**5** Select the learning interaction component and open the Component Inspector (Window → Development Panels → Component Inspector).

**6** Add the new Hot Spot's (or Hot Object's) instance name to the list on the Start tab.

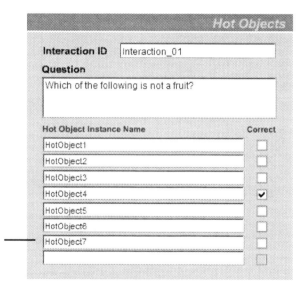

*Use the exact instance name as specified in the Properties Inspector.*

**Use these steps to remove a Hot Spot (or Hot Object):**

**1** On the Stage, select the hot spot(s) that you want to remove and press the DELETE key.

**2** Select the learning interaction component and open the Component Inspector (Window → Development Panels → Component Inspector).

**3** Remove the deleted object's instance name from the list on the Start tab.

**Note:** If you remove a hot spot from the Stage, be sure to remove the references to that Hot Spot in the Component Inspector as well.

# Summary

In this chapter you learned how to create Hot Spot and Hot Object interactions. You also learned how to add additional Hot Spots or Hot Objects if the interaction requires it.

In the next chapter, you will learn about how to further customize the Flash learning interactions.

# Customizing Learning Interactions **11**

Flash Learning Interactions enable you to add interactivity and assessment to your courses. While these learning interactions cut down on the amount of setup and coding that you need to do, you may need to customize them to better suit your needs.

In this chapter you will learn:

- About the types of customization that you can make to Flash Learning Interactions.
- About the assets that make up learning interactions and how those assets are organized in the library.
- How to customize some of the interaction assets.
- How to view and customize the Flash Learning Interaction scripts.
- How to access the Session Array to retrieve information about interactions.

# What Can You Customize?

In the previous chapters in this section, we showed some simple customization that you can perform on specific Flash learning interactions. In this chapter we will discuss methods of customization that apply to more than one interaction type.

As you have already learned, there are several ways to customize Flash learning interactions. Here are some additional ways to customize the learning interactions:

- **Change the text fields.** This will make the text fit or add visual appeal.
- **Change the graphics.** You may want to make the graphics more appropriate for the course or to add visual information to the interaction. Some graphic changes are merely cosmetic, such as changing the background or the style of the buttons. Other graphic changes provide important information to the learner. For example, in Drag and Drop interactions, you change the graphics for the drag and target elements to be relevant to the interaction.
- **Change how the interaction behaves to better meet your needs.** For example, you might want to change a Multiple Choice interaction to give the learner immediate feedback, rather than wait for the learner to click the Submit button.
- **Create custom interactions to create a variation on one of the existing interactions.** For example, you might want to have a variation on the Drag and Drop question where the drag objects can also serve as targets. Or, you might want to create a slider interaction where the learner can drag a pointer across a number line in order to make a selection. Since there is no existing slider interaction, you would need to create a custom interaction.

These examples fall into one of the following categories:

| Change Type | Description |
| --- | --- |
| Modify the properties of a learning interaction element | You can make modifications in the same manner as you would for any Flash object. For example, use the Properties Inspector to change a text field's width or font. Modifying the properties only affects the *instance* of a component or symbol. |

| Change Type | Description |
|---|---|
| Add static elements to the interaction | You can add static elements, such as a screen shot or a diagram, to provide additional information to the learner.<br><br>To do this, simply create the graphic in Flash (or import it into Flash) and then place it on the Stage at the appropriate location. |
| Modify the interaction's assets in the library | Each type of learning interaction contains elements (also known as *assets*). These are stored in the library. In previous chapters, we showed you how to create your own Drag and Drop objects and Hot Objects in the library and then swap them for the placeholder objects that appear by default.<br><br>Later in this chapter we will also show you how to modify the general style of the interaction. |
| Changing an interaction's behavior | This requires a solid understanding of ActionScript as well as how the assets and scripts in the existing interaction are organized.<br><br>At the end of this chapter, we will show you how to view learning interaction scripts and how to make simple changes to those scripts. |
| Creating a custom interaction | If you want to make a variation on an interaction that you can reuse or if you want to create an entirely new interaction, you will need a solid understanding of ActionScript. It's a good idea to turn those interactions into Flash components so that you can reuse them and further customize them. |

**More Information:** To learn more about Flash components, see Section V: Unlocking the Power of Components for e-Learning.

**Tip:** If you want to use complex interactions but you don't want to write code, consider using Flash for the course content and CourseBuilder (which is an extension available for Dreamweaver) for the quizzes. Both can run from within an HTML page. CourseBuilder provides an extensive set of interaction types and options. You can find more information about CourseBuilder in the book: Using Dreamweaver MX to Create e-Learning, by Garin Hess and Steven Hancock.

In this chapter we will first discuss how assets are organized for a learning interaction. Then we will look at a few general ways to customize interactions. Finally, we will examine the code associated with an interaction and look at possible changes in functionality.

# Organization of Interaction Assets

Assets are the elements that make up the interaction. When you drag a Learning Interaction from the Common Library to the Stage, a copy of the learning interaction's assets is placed into the library of your current Flash document. It is important to understand how these assets are organized so that you can find them when you want to make modifications.

Here is an example of what the current document's library will look like after the Hot Object interaction is dragged from the common library to the Stage:

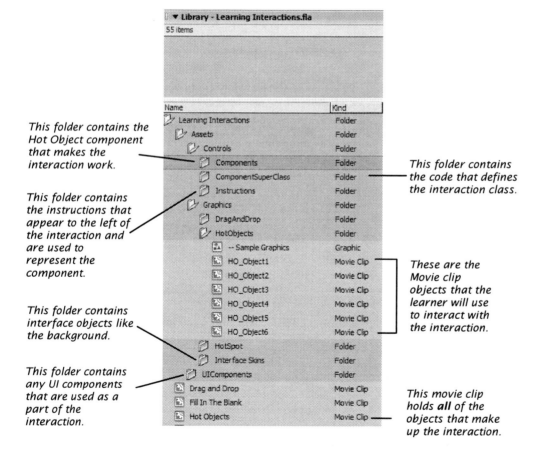

*This folder contains the Hot Object component that makes the interaction work.*

*This folder contains the instructions that appear to the left of the interaction and are used to represent the component.*

*This folder contains interface objects like the background.*

*This folder contains any UI components that are used as a part of the interaction.*

*This folder contains the code that defines the interaction class.*

*These are the Movie clip objects that the learner will use to interact with the interaction.*

*This movie clip holds **all** of the objects that make up the interaction.*

**Tip:** You are not restricted to this organization in your current document's library. You can organize your assets in any way that makes sense to you. For example, if you have a Flash document that has several learning interactions, you may want to consider creating one folder for each learning interaction and then place all the folders and objects that make up a given learning interaction within it.

## Learning Interaction Assets

As you use learning interactions in a course, it is helpful to understand the purpose of different assets as well as rules for naming those assets. When you use multiple interactions of the same type in a movie, several of the assets must use unique names or the interaction may not function as intended.

**Caution:** When using multiple interactions of the same type (for example, more than one multiple choice question), then certain assets require unique names in order for them to function correctly.

This table provides some of that information:

| Asset | Description | Instance Naming Rules |
|---|---|---|
| Learning Interaction Component | Stores the interaction's scripts. | No instance name is required but may be assigned as was done in the Hot Spot example in Chapter 10. |
| Dynamic Text fields | Displays the question and the feedback. | Instance names can be the same across multiple interactions. The default names are *Template_Question* for the question text field and *Template_Feedback* for the feedback text field. |

| Asset | Description | Instance Naming Rules |
|---|---|---|
| Answer Choices | The correct answer and the distracters that are presented to the learner. | Instance names of all graphic answer choices (for example, Drag Objects, Target Objects, Hot Spots, and Hot Objects) must be unique within a single interaction and across multiple interactions of the same type. If not problems may occur with subsequent interactions.<br><br>UI components (for example, Checkboxes and PushButtons) require unique names if multiple interactions of the same type are used in a single course. For example, if you have two Multiple Choice interactions. In many situations this may not cause a problem, but it is better to rename the assets to be safe. |
| Push Button UI Component | The Submit button enters the learner's answer. Hot Spot, Hot Object, and Drag and Drop interactions also have a Reset button to clear the learner's selection prior to submission. | Names must be unique when you use that interaction type multiple times in a movie. Default names are: *Template_ControlButton* for the submit button and *Template_ResetButton* for the reset button. |
| Interface Skins | Contains the container (the border graphic) for the question. | Interface skins don't have any naming restrictions. |

**Note:** Instance naming rules are important if you intend to include multiple interactions in the same Flash document or if you want to make modifications to those assets. You will need to reference these instance names in the Component Parameters panel.

In addition to the standard assets, each interaction has assets that are specific to that type of interaction:

| Interaction Type | Description of Assets |
|---|---|
| Multiple Choice | Check boxes for the learner's selections. These are Flash UI Checkbox components and should have unique names if more than one interaction is used in the same movie. |
| True/False | Radio buttons for the learner's selections. These are Flash UI RadioButton components and should have unique names if more than one interaction is used in the same movie. |
| Drag and Drop | Movie clip symbols for the Drag objects and the Target objects (up to 8 of each). These should have unique names if more than one interaction is used in the same movie. |
| Fill-in-the-blank | Input text field where the learner will supply the answer. This text field is named *Template_UserEntry* by default. |
| Hot Spot and Hot Object | Movie clip symbols for the answer and each of the distractors. These should have unique names if more than one interaction is used in the same movie. |

**More Information:** See Section V: Unlocking the Power of Components for e–Learning, to learn more about the Flash User Interface (UI) Components such as Checkboxes, Buttons, and RadioButtons.

# Modifying Assets

To change the *graphical appearance* of an asset, you will need to edit it. There are two methods that you can use to do this:

- On the Stage, right-click on the object (CONTROL-click for Macintosh) that you want to edit and select Edit (or Edit in Place) from the pop-up menu.
- In the library, right-click on the object (CONTROL-click for Macintosh) that you want to edit and select Edit from the pop-up menu.

**Note:** If you change the graphical appearance of an asset in the library, all instances of that asset change across the document. The reason for this is that these assets are symbols. Keep in mind that the assets of learning interactions are copied from the common library. The assets in the common library are not affected by this type of change, only the assets in the current library will be affected.

## Swapping Assets

Another way to modify the assets of an interaction is to create new assets and swap them in for the default assets. In Chapter 8: *Drag-and-Drop Interactions* and in Chapter 10: *Hot Spot and Hot Object Interactions*, we used this technique to provide objects that were specific to the question. You can also use this technique to change the look of the default background (also known as the Interface Skin).

 **Note:** If you are swapping an asset that is controlled by scripts, such as a drag object or a feedback field, then you need to provide an instance name for the new asset in the Properties Inspector and then list that new instance name in the Component Inspector for the given learning interaction.

 **Tip:** Assets specific to the interaction type reside on the Start tab. However, the Question Field, Feedback Field, Control button and Reset button reside on the Assets tab. Here you can provide the instance name for these types of objects if you have created custom versions of them.

## Changing the Background Graphic

To change the look of the container for the question you must change the background graphic. To make this type of change you must replace the existing background image with a new image.

**Use the following steps to replace an interaction's default background:**

**1**　Create a new graphic symbol and place it in the Interface Skins folder.

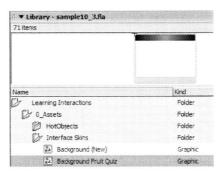

It is not necessary to store the new graphic symbol in the Interface Skins folder, but this way you can keep all assets together.

**2**　On the Stage, select the default background.

**3**　In the Properties Inspector, click Swap and select your new graphic from the list.

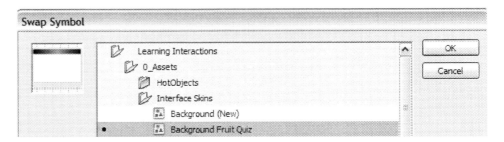

**4**　Click **OK**.

You can continue using this new background symbol for other interactions as well.

## Resizing or Changing the Appearance of Text Fields

Flash learning interactions consist of at least 2 text fields: the question field and the feedback field. These fields come with a preset size, font styles, color, and so forth. You may find that you want to make changes to some of these fields.

To make changes to the question text field or the feedback field, select the field and use the Properties Inspector to change the field's characteristics.

*Make changes to text characteristics.*

*Make changes to the size of the field.*

*Determine how the field displays multiple lines of text.*

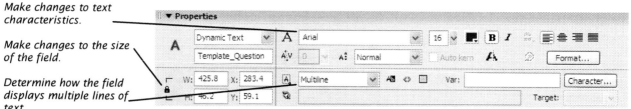

If the feedback text extends beyond a single line, you need to make sure that you change the field to *Multiline*.

**Tip:** To change the text's appearance across multiple questions in a single course, you can use a global style. To learn more about this object, see your Flash online help (Help → Using Flash → Using Components) or refer to Chapter 22: Customizing Flash e-Learning Components.

# Changing a Learning Interaction's Behavior

The way an interaction looks is not the only thing you may want to change. You may also want to change the default functionality. You can affect some of this by the settings you choose in the Component Inspector, but other changes require that you edit the ActionScript code that controls the interaction.

You can make more extensive customizations to your learning interactions behavior if you have a solid command of ActionScript to modify the learning interaction's scripts to meet your needs. For example, you can extend the data tracking features to do more sophisticated tracking of the learner's progress.

## Script Overview

The objects that make up a learning interaction have parameters, which are used by the learning interaction's scripts to make the learning interaction work.

The scripts that control a learning interaction are stored in two different locations in the library:

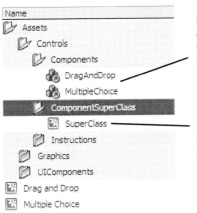

Each interaction type consists of a separate component. Each component contains scripts (specific to that type) that deal with the initialization and event handling for the assets that make up the interaction. These scripts also handle the evaluation of the interaction.

*The SuperClass movie clip contains the interaction class definition and generic scripts that deal with the interaction's data formatting and storage.*

**Note:** In Flash MX the SuperClass movie is called LglobalClass.

Changing code in an interaction component will affect all the components of that interaction type. For example, change the code for Multiple Choice will affect all multiple choice questions. Changing the code in the SuperClass movie clip will affect all components in the movie.

# Viewing Learning Interaction Scripts

Looking at the code that controls learning interactions can help you understand how they work. You may also discover how to make a change that will cause the interaction to function in a different way.

**Use these steps to access the code in the SuperClass movie clip or the learning component:**

**1** Double-click the SuperClass or the learning component.

**2** Select frame 1 of the Actions layer.

**3** Open the Actions panel (Window → Development Panels → Actions).

The top of each script is well documented with comments and describes the purpose of each section in the ActionScript code. Always read through the comments before you start looking at the code. Many times you can find the exact location you need to look to fix a problem.

Here is a list of the main sections contained within the **SuperClass** script:

- Section 1: Start Construction of the Global Class
- Section 2: Graphic Initialization Handling
- Section 3: Feedback Event Handling
- Section 4: Navigation Event Handling
- Section 5: Tracking Toolbox
- Section 6: Common Toolbox

Here is a list of the main sections contained in the Multiple Choice component:

- Section 1: Event Handling Functions
- Section 2: Initialize Objects and Arrays from user parameters
- Section 3: Initialize Session Tracking and Graphic States

Many of these script sections are built within functions to make them modular.

The following is a small excerpt from the **SuperClass** script from section 2. This function initializes the control button:

```
LToolBox.prototype.initControlButton = function (eventHandler) {

    if (this.feedback == true){
            this.label_state = this.buttonLabels[1];
            if (this.navigation == 2) this.navigation = 1;
    }
    else if (this.tracking == true){

            this.label_state = this.buttonLabels[2];
    }
    else if (this.navigation != 0){
            this.label_state = this.buttonLabels[3];
            if (this.navigation == 2) this.navigation = 1;
    }
    else {
            this.label_state = this.buttonLabels[0];
    }

    this.setComponentLabel(this.Assets.ControlButton,
this.label_state);
    this.setComponentState(this.Assets.ControlButton, false);
    this.setComponentListener(this.Assets.ControlButton, eventHandler);
}
```

**Tip:** Use the Find feature  on the Actions panel to search for the particular element that you want to view (or modify).

In the next section we will explore the script in more detail by fixing a problem inherent with the fill-in-the-blank interaction.

# Making Changes to Scripts: Fixing the Limited Response Problem for Fill-in-the-blank

The current fill-in-the-blank interaction only lets you enter three responses in the Component Inspector. In many cases three responses may not enough to account for all the possible variations on the correct answer. You will undoubtedly run into situations where you will want to enter more than three responses.

With a few changes to the fill-in-the-blank component script you can overcome this problem. In this section you will learn how to apply this fix. In the process you will gain a better understanding of the scripts that control a learning interaction.

## Viewing the Finished Interaction

Take a moment to view the modified fill-in-the-blank interaction. The correct answer is True or False. However, there are many different ways to enter this answer. We included a total of five different responses that are considered to be correct. Try these responses when you view this interaction: True or False, True False, TrueFalse, True/False, and True-False.

 **On CD:** Open samples/chapter11/sample_11-1.swf to try the modified fill-in-the-blank interaction. If you would like to view the changes made to the code open sample_11-1.fla.

## Changing the Script of a Fill-in-the-blank Interaction

The initial interaction has already been created for you. In this exercise you will modify the fill-in-the-blank component script to make it possible to add additional responses.

**Use these steps to change the fill-in-the-blank interaction's script:**

**1**   Open samples/chapter11/sample_11-1start.fla.

This file already includes a fill-in-the-blank interaction. The question asks: *Which question type uses radio button components?* So far three responses have been entered as correct: True or False, True False, and TrueFalse. We need to add two more. We can't do that in the Component Inspector because there are only three fields. Therefore, we need to do it with ActionScript. In order to use ActionScript to modify the component, you need to first name the component instance.

**2**   Select the component (the text instructions) and use the Properties Inspector to enter *fillintheblank1* as the name.

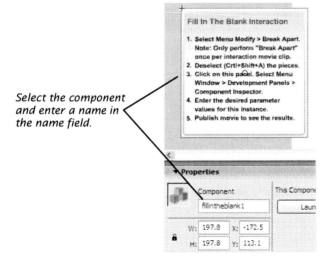

*Select the component and enter a name in the name field.*

Now you are ready to add the code that will assign new responses to the component.

**3**   Create an Actions layer in the main timeline, select the first frame and open the Actions panel.

**4**   Enter this code in the Actions panel.

```
_root.fillintheblank1.Response4 = "True/False";
_root.fillintheblank1.Response5 = "True-False";
_root.fillintheblank1.Response_Value4 = true;
_root.fillintheblank1.Response_Value5 = true;
```

Response4 and Response5 are the new responses added to the component. Response_Value4 and Response_Value5 indicate whether or not these responses are correct. This is equivalent to checking the correct checkbox next to the response in the Component Inspector. Enter false if you want these responses recorded as incorrect.

Now you are ready to change the interaction so it will work with these additions.

**5** Open the library (Window → Library), find the FillInTheBlank component and double-click it to begin making changes.

*The FillInTheBlank component is located inside the Assets/Controls/Components folder.*

**6** Select the first frame of the Actions layer and open the Actions panel (Window → Development Panels → Actions).

For the most part the fill-in-the-blank code was written to handle more than three responses. However, there are a few sections that need changing. One section that needs changing is the section that checks to see if the learner entered the correct answer. It is hard-coded to check only three responses.

The first change you need to make is to add additional else statements to account for two more responses. (You can add as many as you would like to account for more responses.)

**7** Find line 214; it is the line right after a break statement.

*The if/else statements that needs to be changed to account for additional responses.*

```
207    else if(getText[t].toLowerCase() == rValueRef[1].toLowerCase()){
208        response_results[1] = true;
209        break;
210    }
211    else if (getText[t].toLowerCase() == rValueRef[2].toLowerCase()){
212        response_results[2] = true;
213        break;
214    }
```

**Tip:** If the line numbers are not visible in your Actions panel, click the View Options button and select View Line Numbers.

**8**   Add these lines of code immediately after the curly brace in line 214:

```
else if(getText[t].toLowerCase() == rValueRef[3].toLowerCase()){
    response_results[3] = true;
    break;
}
else if (getText[t].toLowerCase() == rValueRef[4].toLowerCase()){
    response_results[4] = true;
    break;
}
```

**Caution:** Remember that ActionScript 2.0 is case sensitive, so make sure you enter the statements using the correct case for each letter.

These new if statements are exactly the same as the previous if statements except the number used in the rValueRef[4] and reponse_results[4] arrays. These new lines check to see if the new response values (rValueRef[3] and rValueRef[4]) match the response entered by the learner (getText[t]). If the response is correct, the response_results is set to true.

We are not quite finished changing this section of the code. The next if statement in the code needs to be changed as well.

**9**   Modify the if statement that is now on line 228 (**if (response_results[0] == "No Match" && response_results[1] == "No Match" && response_results[2] == "No Match")** {) so that it checks the results for the new responses:

```
if (response_results[0] == "No Match" && response_results[1] == "No
Match" && response_results[2] == "No Match" && response_results[3]
== "No Match" && response_results[4] == "No Match") {
```

This code will now check to find out if there was a match for the two new responses.

**10**  We also need to make a similar change to what is now lines 237-241. The resulting script should look like this:

```
else if (response_results[0] == true || response_results[1] == true
||response_results[2] == true ||response_results[3] == true
||response_results[4] == true) {
        router.result = "C";
}
else if (response_results[0] == false || response_results[1] ==
false || response_results[2] == false || response_results[3] ==
false || response_results[4] == false) {
        router.result = "W";
```

The change made to this code is similar to the change made in step 6. This new code is now checking the results for the new responses and seeing if they are correct or incorrect and then recording the results into the result variable.

The final change that needs to be made is the addition of a few lines of code that initialize the two new response. These changes are made at about line 254.

**11** Immediately after line 253 (**Response.Response3 = Response3;**) add these two lines of code to initialize the two new response:

```
Response.Response4 = Response4;
Response.Response5 = Response5;
```

**12** Immediately after line 260 (**Response_Value.response_value3 = toBoolean(Response_Value3);**) add these two lines of code to indicate whether or not these responses are correct if entered by the learner.

```
Response_Value.response_value4 = toBoolean(Response_Value4);
Response_Value.response_value5 = toBoolean(Response_Value5);
```

You have now made all the necessary changes to the component code.

**13** Close the Actions panel and click **Scene 1** to return to the main timeline.

**14** Save and test the movie (Control → Test Movie).

You can now include additional fill-in-the-blank interactions to this movie and each of them will support 5 responses. The only steps you need to repeat are steps 11-13 for each new interaction that you add.

If you would like to use this modified interaction in separate Flash document, open this movie as an external library (File → Import → Open External Library) and you will be able to drag it to the Stage.

**More Information:** See Chapter 21: Customizing Flash Components for another example of how you can change a Flash learning interaction.

# Using the Session Array

You may find occasion while developing an e-learning course when you want to display information recorded by Flash learning interactions. Certain information is recorded and stored in an array named *SessionArray*.

All the information for the first interaction displayed in a movie is stored in **SessionArray[0]**. All the information for the second interaction is stored in **SessionArray[1]** and so forth for each interaction that is used.

To access the properties of an interaction, use dot syntax with the session array to identify the property. For example, to access the result of the second interaction displayed in a movie enter **_root.SessionArray[1].result**.

There are ten properties that track information about each interaction. Here is a list of those properties:

| Property | Description |
| --- | --- |
| interaction_id | Contains the unique interaction id entered into the Component Inspector. |
| interaction_type | Contains code that identifies the type of interaction: Fill-in-the-blank = F, Drag and Drop = M, True/False = T, Multiple Choice, and Hot Object and Hot Spot = C. |
| objective_id | Contains the objective id entered in the Component Inspector. |
| weighting | Contains the weight entered in the Component Inspector. |
| correct_response | A value that identifies the correct response to the question. |
| student_response | A value that identifies the learner's response to the question. |
| result | Contains a code that indicates whether or not the response was correct (C = correct, W = incorrect). |
| latency | Contains the amount of time the learner spent on the question. |
| dateStamp | Contains the date that the learner answered the question. |
| timestamp | Contains the time that the learner answered the question. |

To be able to retrieve these properties, you must know which index of the Session Array stores which interaction. If you are just trying to retrieve the information for every interaction in the movie, then you can cycle through the entire length of the interaction (**_root.SessionArray.length** identifies how many total interactions have been recorded).

To access the interaction that is on the current frame of the movie you can use the session variable (**_root.SessionArray[_root.session].interaction_id**).

With a little practice you can easily extract the information you would like from the Session Array.

 **Note:** The paths used in the examples in this section assume that the interactions were placed on the main timeline (**_root.SessionArray[0]**). If the interaction is loaded inside another movie clip you will need to change the target path accordingly (**_root.movieClipName.SessionArray[0]**).

# Summary

In this chapter you learned how the assets of the interactions are organized and named so that you can customize them. You learned a few specific customizations that you can perform.

You also learned about the code that controls each interaction. As an example of how to change this code you learned how to add additional responses to a Fill-in-the-blank interaction. You also learned how to use the Session Array to access interaction properties.

In the next section, you will learn to put together all of the elements of an e-learning course—content, interactions, and assessments—into one cohesive and well-designed course.

# Section III:
# Creating Course
# Architecture with Flash

Now that you have learned how to create custom interactions and use the Flash learning interactions, you are ready to put a course together.

# Understanding Architecture 12

Up to this point, we have looked at the individual components that make up an e-learning course. In this section, we will show you how to combine these elements into an effective e-learning experience and how to create the underlying course structure that enables you to easily maintain your courses.

To get you started this chapter will provide you with an overview of the various aspects of course design that you will need to consider.

In this chapter you will learn:

- The reasons for having a course architecture.
- The difference between page-level design and an underlying course architecture.
- The main elements of course architecture.

# What is Course Architecture?

When an architect designs a home, he or she takes many elements into consideration. While the underlying structure is the focus, the architect also needs to consider the layout, functionality, style, and comfort for the people who will live in the home. Likewise, course architecture focuses on the underlying structure of the course without losing site of the content, layout, functionality, style, and comfort of the learner.

 **More Information:** The chapters in this section will detail several options for structuring the course. There are several excellent resources for learning about interface design and content design.

## Benefits of a Course Architecture

You need to focus on the high-level course design in the early Stages of an e-learning project. This initial investment in design will pay off in more effective development. The following are some of the benefits of a well thought-out, solid course architecture:

- Streamlined movie development and maintenance.
- Fewer inadvertent errors.
- Easier integration of independent project elements. This is a big time saver on complex projects or projects where there are several developers working together.
- Completed courses that are more modular and flexible. This makes it easier to adapt the course (or parts within the course) to meet a variety of needs.

## Finding a Starting Point

There are endless possibilities for designing course architecture, ranging from the simple to the sophisticated. Before you determine the architecture, you need to ask yourself some key questions:

- Will the course stand by itself or will it need to be integrated with other applications (for example, HTML, external authoring tools, databases, or learning management systems)?

- Will the course be developed by an individual developer or a team of developers?
- What is the technical skill set of the developer(s)?
- How often will the course content need to be updated? Who is responsible for the maintenance?
- How much content will be included in the course? Will the course be included as part of a larger curriculum?
- How much media will be included in the course?
- Are there any design or delivery constraints (i.e., bandwidth, audience, systems, existing design or development standards, etc.)?

The answers to these questions will help guide you as you determine an appropriate course architecture.

# The Role that Flash SWF Files Play in Architecture

While you create, edit, and test Flash movie in a file that has an FLA extension, this is not the file that you will deliver to your learners. You need to publish the file, which generates a SWF (pronounced "swiff") file. The SWF file becomes part of the package that you use to deliver the e-learning course content. There are different ways that you can package the SWF file. The one that you choose will become an important part of the architecture.

| Use | Description |
| --- | --- |
| Embed Flash movies in HTML pages | Use an HTML file as a container for one or more Flash files. Flash can generate an HTML file when you publish your movie. Or, you can create a custom HTML file using an HTML editing tool, such as Dreamweaver. |
| Embed Flash movies in External Applications | Use the file in a course created in another e-learning authoring tool such as Authorware or Toolbook. Another option is to use the file in the Flash ActiveX control (in Microsoft Office and other applications that support ActiveX controls) or as part of a QuickTime movie. |

| Use | Description |
|-----|-------------|
| Play Flash SWF as a stand-alone movie | Use the file as a stand-alone movie. In other words, the learner can just launch the SWF file. Using a SWF file in this manner is known as a projector. |

# Architecture Types Overview

In this book, we will focus on architectures that primarily use Flash movies. Let's look at a high-level overview of some of the available options. You will learn how to implement each option in the chapters that follow.

## Using a Simple Architecture

If you want to create something very basic, you could create an architecture where each page in the course is its own Flash movie. Each Flash movie is a part of an HTML page. The learner has the option of stepping through the pages in a linear fashion or selecting a particular page from a central Table of Contents:

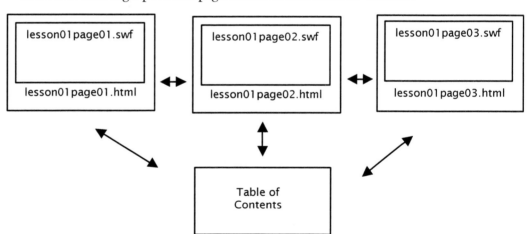

**Note:** In this scenario, the Table of Contents can be an HTML page that just contains links to the other course pages. Or it can be a Flash movie that contains those links.

**More Information:** To learn how to set up the navigation that makes this architecture work, see Chapter 14: Making Effective Use of Navigation:

# Using Flash Pre-Built Templates

If you need to create a course quickly and you don't have time to build a custom architecture, then Flash MX templates are the way to go. Flash MX provides two types of templates that you can use to create a structure for your e-learning course:

- **Presentation Templates** provide a way for you to create a series of pages which have the navigation buttons in already in place.
- **Quiz Templates** provide a way for you to track quiz data using Shareable Content Object Reference Model (SCORM) standards or Aviation Industry Computer-Based Training Committee (AICC) standards.

These templates use an architecture in which each frame of the Flash movie represents an individual screen in the finished e-Learning course.

**More Information:** To learn how to set up the navigation that makes this architecture work, see Chapter 15: Using Flash Templates for Course Architecture.

# Using the Slide Presentation Document Type

Flash Professional comes with another method to create courses quickly. It is called the slide presentation document type. With the slide presentation document type, you develop the course using a series of screens instead of using the frames of a timeline. Each time you need a new screen, you add it to the course. This method of developing an e-learning course uses a metaphor that is similar to other e-learning authoring tools and therefore may be a little easier to adapt to.

The Slide Presentation document type also comes with several features that make the development of navigation much easier. Although only available in Flash Professional, this method of e-learning development offers a lot of promise.

**More Information:** To learn how to create a course using the slide presentation document type, see Chapter 16: Using Slide Presentations for Course Architecture.

# Using a Movie Clip-Based Architecture

This type of architecture is similar to the type of architecture that Flash uses in its Presentation Template. Each frame correlates with a learning page. Background images and functionality, such as the navigation, are placed on a layer that spans all frames that make up the course. The main difference is that most of the content resides outside of the course in bite-size pieces. Each content piece is loaded into a presentation movie-clip symbol when the playback head reaches that frame. By creating the content in separate Flash movies, you can easily edit and maintain content pieces without having to touch the underlying architecture.

 **More Information:** To learn how to set up the navigation that makes this architecture work, see Chapter 16: Creating a Custom Flash Based Architecture.

## Using a Sophisticated Architecture

While a simple architecture is adequate in many cases, you may need to use a more sophisticated architecture to meet more complex needs and provide greater flexibility. A complex project may contain any (or all) of the following:

- Use symbols, movie clips, and components to dynamically load content as appropriate.

- Communicate with external Learning Management Systems, databases, or web applications. This enables you to take advantage of the power of XML, JavaScript, ColdFusion MX, .ASP, .JSP, .PHP, .NET, and Java Application Servers to access data and functionality from other web programming environments.

- Use media elements (for example, external graphics, text, sound, or video) either as externally linked files or as embedded symbols within the Flash movie's library. External elements can be updated easily without republishing the Flash movie.

The following diagram shows you an architecture that has the Flash application at its core. This Flash application can communicate with a variety of sources including: other Flash applications, web applications, databases, external media, text files, and XML Files as appropriate.

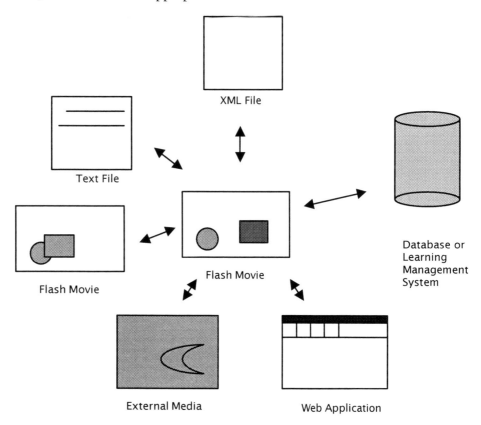

 **More Information:** Creating an architecture that includes all of these components requires a strong understanding of ActionScript programming. Chapter 17: Advanced Architecture Using XML introduces you to XML, which is a key ingredient to this type of architecture.

# Summary

The time that you spend up front researching the project's needs and designing architecture to meet those needs is a worthwhile investment. It will enable you to work more efficiently during the project and reduce the effort that it takes to maintain the course. You should also take the time to document your architecture to ensure that the design is implemented consistently.

In the following chapters of this section you will not only learn about the different ways to create the underlying structure of the course, you will also learn ways to efficiently organize your course elements and how to create the navigation system that enables the learner to fluidly move through the course.

# Getting Organized 13

When you import, build, and publish Flash movies to use as part of an e-learning course, you may notice that you are dealing with a lot of files. Therefore, it is essential that you setup a good organization scheme so that you can efficiently create and maintain your courses. This becomes even more important for complex projects or projects where there are several developers working together.

Later in this section, we will cover various architectures that you can use to structure a complete e-learning course. Before you can do that, it is important to make sure that you have a solid oragnization of your elements both within Flash and external to your Flash movies.

In this chapter, we will look at various techniques for getting organized. You will likely adapt these techniques to best meet the needs of each of your projects.

In this chapter you will learn to:

- Organize your course elements so that you can easily find and edit them.
- Work with libraries so that you can reuse elements.
- Organize your course directories and files to increase efficiency.

# Organizing Your Flash FLA File

To work effectively inside of Flash, it is important to employ a consistent method for naming and locating objects. This saves you time, and if you are working with multiple developers on the project, a consistent naming scheme helps the whole team.

There are many possible ways that you can organize your layers, scenes, and libraries. In this section, we will present you with a starting point, which you can adapt to meet your own needs and preferences.

## Organizing Layers

You should start by creating layers based upon the type of objects that you want to include in your movie (Insert → Layer). You will want to consider including the following layers in your movie as appropriate:

| Layer | Description |
|-------|-------------|
| Actions | Place any actions that are associated with frames on the timeline. You may also want to put any frame labels on this layer. |
| Buttons | Place any buttons such as movie controls, navigation, interactions, or hot spots on this layer. Depending upon the complexity of the movie, you may want to separate these layers based upon their usage. For example, you can create a hot spot layer, a navigation layer, a button layer, etc. |
| Cursor | Shows the mouse cursor movement if you are creating a demonstration. |
| Highlights | Place highlights or annotations to screen shots or graphics. |
| Feedback | Provides text feedback to the learner in response to an interaction (i.e., question, simulation task, mouse over, mouse click, etc.) |

| Layer | Description |
|---|---|
| Text Entry | Displays the text entry that is typed. This can be used in demonstrations or in interactions such as simulations. |
| Text | Displays any text information or directions. If you are animating multiple pieces of text, you will need multiple text layers. |
| Graphics or Screen Captures | Displays the visuals for the course. If you have layers of graphics or graphical animation, you will need multiple graphics layers. |
| Audio | Plays the audio. |
| Background | Displays any background text or graphics that will display throughout the movie. |

**Note:** Keep in mind that for the visual components of the movie, the order of the layers matters. The layer on top will appear in front of lower layers.

## Using Folders to Aid in Layer Organization

You can put layers into folders, which enables you to group layers by function. For example, you can have a folder for each animation and then have the graphics that make up the animation in individual layers. This enables you to manipulate the graphics in each layer individually.

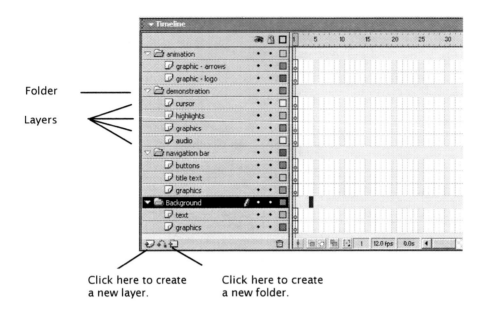

Folder —————

Layers

Click here to create
a new layer.

Click here to create
a new folder.

 **Note:** It is possible to create folders within folders for tidy organization.

 **Tip:** You can expand and collapse folders without affecting what appears on the Stage. You can also hide or lock layers so that you can manipulate particular layers without making other modifications inadvertently.

 **Caution:** There is nothing that prevents you from giving the same name to more than one layer (or folder). This can be useful, for instance you can have a layer named graphic in the background folder and a layer named graphic in the demonstration folder. Just be sure that you don't inadvertently make changes to the wrong layer.

## Using Scenes to Organize Larger Movies

If you have a particularly long or complex movie, you might want to break it up into scenes to help you keep track of the elements contained in each part of the movie. For example, if you have more than one demonstration in a movie, you could use one scene for each demonstration.

By default you work in a single scene, **Scene 1**. You can add scenes as needed (Insert → Scene). Scenes play back in the order that they appear in the Scene panel. To change the order, open the Scene panel (Window → Design Panels → Scene) and drag the scene names to reflect the correct order.

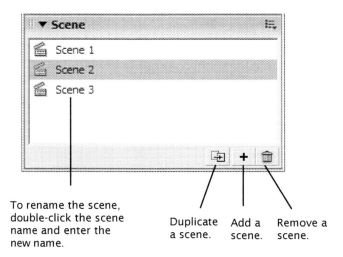

To rename the scene, double-click the scene name and enter the new name.

Duplicate a scene.

Add a scene.

Remove a scene.

Once you have created the scenes, you can easily switch between them using the Edit Scene pop-up menu.

Current scene

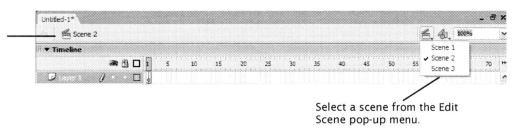

Select a scene from the Edit Scene pop-up menu.

**Tip:** While scenes can help organize your movie, more often you'll use movie clips instead as they are both more flexible and more powerful. You will learn more about using movie clips as part of the overall course architecture later in this section. To learn more about using movie clips in the organization of your courses see Chapter 17: Creating a Custom Flash-based Architecture.

**Caution:** The overuse of scenes can lead you to create very large movies if you do not plan well. For example, it might be tempting to create one scene for each lesson page. The number of objects required to support an entire lesson could result in a large movie and complicate your ability to deliver it effectively.

# Using Library Objects

Any object that you import into your movie, as well as any symbol that you create, is stored in the library. There are many benefits for creating and using library symbols. For example, you can:

- Create the object once and reuse it multiple times (even in other Flash movies).

- Reduce the file size of your movie by storing the item only once.

- Change all instances of an object by modifying the symbol. This can be a real time saver.

- Add effects to objects. There are many types of effects that you can only achieve through the use of symbols. For example, using the alpha property to make a symbol appear to fade in and out.

**Note:** There are some properties that you can change for just a single instance of a symbol. For example, you can rotate, resize, move, and use color effects on the instance without affecting the symbol itself.

## Organizing Libraries

Just as you can use folders in layers to group related objects, you can use folders in libraries to help organize your objects. For example, you can create one folder for imported audio clips, one for navigation buttons, and one for screen captures.

You should come up with a consistent naming scheme that you will use for your folders and your symbols across all of your Flash files. If you are working on a team, then all team members should use the same naming scheme.

**Tip:** Symbol and folder names should be concise, yet descriptive enough so that you can find them easily.

Here is an sample library panel:

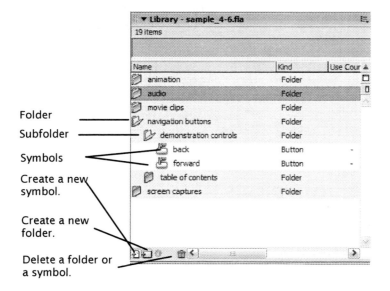

### Naming Symbols for Use with ActionScript

If you plan to use ActionScript to control the symbols you have created, there is a naming scheme you can use to identify the type of symbol. This can aid you when examining code, but it will also provide code hints for the symbol type:

A code hint for a movie clip symbol lists all properties and methods available to that symbol type.

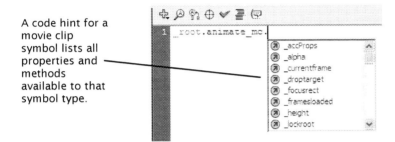

In the example above, the code hints display because the name of the movie clip ends with _mc. This suffix triggers the code hints. There are numerous suffixes available that will trigger code hints. But the three most common are: _btn for a button, _mc for a movie clip, and _txt for a text field.

 **More Information:** For more information about other suffixes that are available, see Writing Code that Triggers Code Hints in the Flash help.

 **Tip:** In ActionScript 2.0 you can also use strict data typing to trigger code hints. For more information on strict data typing, refer to your favorite ActionScript 2.0 reference or Flash help.

# Using Shared Libraries

One way to gain efficiencies in your Flash development is to create an object once as a library symbol and reuse it multiple times in your movie. You can also share library symbols across Flash movies. This can be a great time saver when you have multiple developers on a project. Shared libraries enable you to leverage the work done by each developer. They also enable you to have a centralized method for making modifications to objects.

There are two ways that you can work with shared libraries. You can share library assets at author time (while you are developing the movie) or at runtime (while you are playing the movie). Sharing assets at author time seems the most practical for e-learning development.

When you are authoring a movie in Flash you can update (or replace) the contents of any symbol with any other symbol that resides in an FLA file on your local network. If the source symbol is made up of multiple assets, all of its assets will be copied to the current movie.

**Note:** The symbol in the current movie retains its original name and properties; only its contents change.

**Use these steps to update or replace a symbol:**

**1**   In the library, select the object that you want to replace (or update).

**2**   From the library's options menu, select Properties.

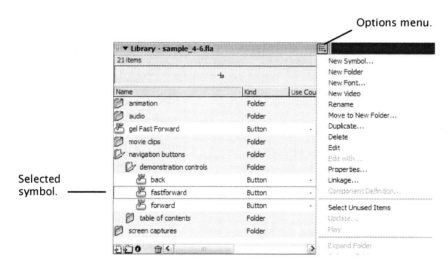

The Symbol Properties dialog displays.

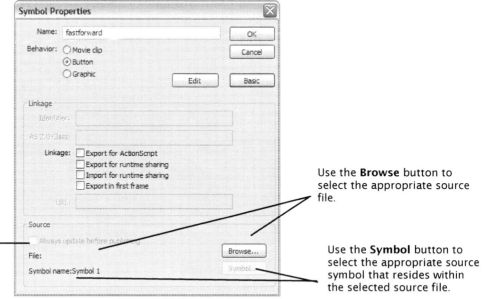

Check here if you want the symbol to be updated with its most current version whenever you publish the movie.

Use the **Browse** button to select the appropriate source file.

Use the **Symbol** button to select the appropriate source symbol that resides within the selected source file.

If the Symbol Properties dialog does not contain the linkage and source information as shown above, click the **Advanced** button to expand it. The **Advanced** button becomes the **Basic** button when linkage and source are displayed.

**3**  In the Source section of Symbol Properties dialog box, click the **Browse** button and select the FLA file that contains the symbol you want to use.

**4**  Click the **Symbol** button and select source symbol.

**5**  Click **OK**.

Note: If you try to share an asset from a source file that has the same name as an asset in the destination file, Flash will give you an opportunity to resolve the conflict. In this situation, Flash will display the Resolve Library Items dialog box. You can then choose whether or not to replace the existing item with the new item. To avoid naming conflicts, place your assets inside library folders.

# Adding to the Common Libraries

Flash ships with some commonly used items such as buttons, sounds, and learning interactions stored in the Common Library. You can also add your own files of things you frequently use to the Common Library. For example, you could create a library that contains commonly used items for demonstrations.

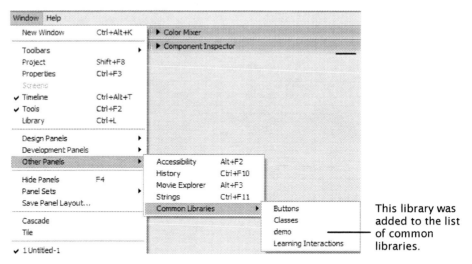

This library was added to the list of common libraries.

**Use these steps to create a common library:**

**1**  Create a Flash file.  For example, create a file named *demo.fla.*

**2**  Place all of the elements that you want included in the library in the FLA file.

**3**  Copy the FLA file to the Libraries subdirectory of the Flash program (for example, C:/**Program Files/Macromedia/Flash MX 2004/en/First Run/libraries**).

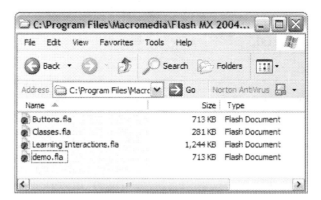

**4**  The next time you open Flash, the new common library will appear on the menu under Window→ Other Panels→ Common Libraries.

# Organizing Your Directories and Files

You will use many kinds of files when preparing your courses. The number and types of files that you will have will vary based on the size and complexity of your course design. However, you will likely have lots of graphic files, perhaps some audio files, and your Flash project files. For a complex course, you may have many more file types. It will be important to design a consistent directory structure and file-naming scheme so that you (and other developers on your project) can easily find the files that make up a course.

## Setting Up a Directory Structure

There are many good ways to set up project directory structures. You will want to include at a minimum the following directories in your project's directory:

- **Admin:** Stores the administrative documents from your course such as project plans, schedules, and correspondence.
- **Design:** Stores your e-learning design document such as outlines and storyboards.
- **Develop:** Stores all of the elements that you will use to create the course. This includes the base files that you will import into Flash, your Flash files, and any other files needed to support your course.
- **Test:** Stores a copy of the actual files, so that you can test the course delivery. For each revision of the course, you should create an individual subdirectory (for example  /test/version1, /test/version2, etc.).

Tip: When you are working with multiple developers you should consider using source control tools, such as PVCS® or Microsoft's Visual SourceSafe®, to help keep track of your files and changes that you (and other developers) make to those files.

## Organizing the Develop Directory

Since most of your development time will be spent working within the Develop directory, it is important to put some thought into its structure.

It's a good idea to separate the base elements from the files that actually make up the course. This makes it easier to know which files need to end up in the final package for delivery to the learner.

| Directory | Description |
|---|---|
| Basefiles | Contains the imported elements of a course, such as bitmap graphics, audio, or video clips. It is likely that you will be using external tools to edit these files.<br><br>It's a good idea to keep both the original and edited version of your files. For example, if you create screen shots and crop them, you should keep both the uncropped and cropped versions. Likewise, you would want to store the original audio (or video) file as well as the final audio file after you have made any edits in 3rd party tools. This gives you a lot more flexibility with your elements.<br><br>You can also use this directory to store any common Flash elements that you will use throughout the course such as buttons, animations, standard demos, and components.<br><br>When packaging a course, the base files generally do not need to be included in the course package. These files are already included when they are imported into the Flash movies. |
| Course | The actual files that will be tested, loaded onto the server, and accessed by the learner. You will need to determine the structure for this directory based upon the architecture that you have designed for your course. |

The following is a sample **Develop** directory structure:

```
📂 basefiles
   📂 audio
   📂 flashelements
      📂 buttons
      📂 demos
      📂 menus
   📂 images
      📂 screenshots
      📂 conceptual
   📂 video
📂 course
   📂 lesson1  -- include both .html and .swf file for each page
   📂 lesson2
   📂 lesson3
   📂 resources -- reference pages used by the course as a whole
   📂 start.html -- file the learner clicks to start the course
```

 **Tip:** If you have a lot of standard elements that you are likely to reuse from course to course, you might want to consider using image cataloging software such as ACDSee (http://www.acdsystems.com/English/index.htm). Cataloging software enables you to associate key words with your media elements so that you can find relevant media items to include in your course.

## File Naming Conventions

Using an effective file-naming scheme not only helps you find your files effectively, it will also help make the creation of your course navigation easier (as you will see in Chapter 14: *Making Effective Use of Navigation*)

For example, if you're using the simple architecture described in Chapter 13: *Understanding Architecture*, then each page in the course would have its own HTML file with a corresponding SWF file. In this architecture, you should name the file according to the lesson number (lesson01, lesson02, etc.) and the page number (page01, page2, etc.). For example, Lesson 1 would contain:

```
lesson01page01.html
lesson01page01.SWf
lesson01page02.html
lesson01page03.swf
```

Using numeric file names can make setting up the Next and Previous navigation buttons as well as the Table of Contents easier. It is easier to write the code to deal with pages that follow a numeric sequence. However, this type of naming scheme can sometimes be difficult to maintain. For example, if you have to create a new page 2 late in the project, you will need to rename multiple files.

**Tip:** Any number less than 10 should be preceded with a 0. So lesson 1 is written out as lesson01. This makes it easier to sort the pages when looking at the files in Windows Explorer or the Finder on Macintosh.

**Note:** There are times when using descriptive names can be very helpful, such as when you have graphics files that you will reuse across courses (glossary.html, hint_button.swf, or login_screen.gif). If you use descriptive names, you should come up with standards. For example, decide if file names will use only lowercase letters, a combination of upper and lower case letters, underscores, prefixes (or suffixes) to indicate how the file will be used or the files location.

# Using the Projects Panel

In the Flash Professional version you have the option of using the Project panel to manage multiple documents in a single project. You can also use version control with the Project panel. Once you create a Flash project, you can add or remove files from the project. Those files may be Flash files or other types of files.

**Use these steps to create a Flash project:**

**1**　Open the Project panel (Window → Project).

**2**　Click the **New Project** link in the Project panel.

**3**　Assign the project file a name and find a location to save it.

　　Generally you want to save the project file with the other files in the project. A project file is an XML document with an FLP extension. The XML document keeps track of all files associated with a project.

**4**　Click Save.

Once you have created the project file, you can add files to that project. You can add folders to help organize all files. You can also assign a file as the default file. When you click the Test Project button the default file is launched as the initial document in the e-learning course. The file may be an SWF or HTML document.

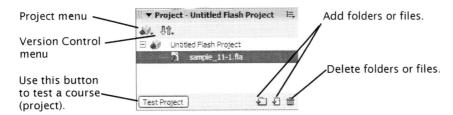

Project menu

Version Control menu

Use this button to test a course (project).

Add folders or files.

Delete folders or files.

In order to use the version control features you must first create a site. A site defines a location for all files associated with a project. You can also place these files on a remote server for central access and version control.

Use these steps to create a site:

**1** Open the Edit Sites window (File → Edit Sites).

If you also use Dreamweaver, you will notice that those sites show up in the Edit Sites window.

**2** Click **New**.

The Site Definition window displays:

Site name, site location and check out information.

Connection information if the files are placed on a remote server.

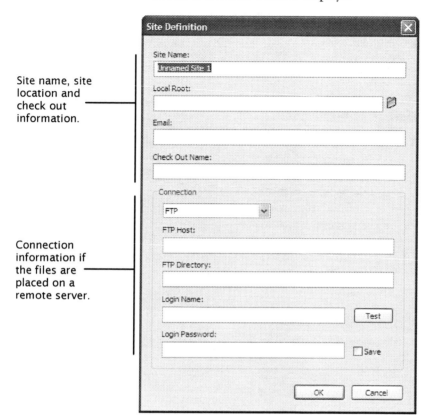

**3**   Fill in the necessary information and click **OK**.

Once the site is created, you can use the check in and check out feature available on the Project panel. This way multiple people can work on a single project and not accidentally work on the same file. If a file is checked out, you cannot work on that file without being notified that it is already being worked on. You cannot check it out until it has been checked in.

# Summary

It's important to use a consistent structure within your Flash movies and in the directories where you store the elements that make up your e-learning course. This will save you a lot of time when you find elements to reuse or modify your course. If you are working with a team of e-learning developers, you should document this structure so that all of the members of the team can follow it. If you are using Flash professional, you may also want to set up a project file.

This chapter focused on how to organize the course elements in a coherent manner. The following chapters in this section will focus on how create an effective architecture for your course.

# Making Effective Use of Navigation  **14**

In any e-learning course, it is important for the learner to have an intuitive way to interact with the elements on a page as well as an intuitive way to navigate between topics. In this chapter, we will focus on the design of course structure from the learner's perspective. In particular, we will look at how to create basic navigation to facilitate the learner's movement through a course.

In this chapter you will learn:

- About basic guidelines for structuring course pages.
- When to use secondary pages to display supplementary content.
- How to create a flipbook to display supplementary content.
- How to set up basic course navigation.
- How to create a Table of Contents.

# Overall Course Flow

Content flow in each course, lesson, and topic is vital to the success of an e-learning product. Both content and navigational elements need to help the learner work within a topic and then transition form one topic to the next.

Topics should have a general flow to them. They should include: a motivational introduction, basic concepts, applications/examples, assessments, a summary, and a transition to the next topic.

**Note:** Different instructional designers may use different terminology to describe how the content is chunked. For example, they may refer to chapters and sections or they may have lessons with topics, or some other scheme. For the purpose of this discussion, courses will contain lessons that are made up of pages. Each page is a small topic.

We will begin by looking at different elements that you can use within a page.

# Page Structure

In the previous chapters of this book, you learned about the types of content that you can include on a page:

- Static content (such as text and graphics).
- Interactive content (and simulations) that react to learner actions (such as mouse overs, button clicks, or key presses).
- Multimedia (such as animation, audio, and video).

## Reducing Text Information

You need to combine content elements in an intuitive way that does not overwhelm the learner with too much information at any given point. You should include only essential information on the page and enable the learner to reveal additional information, as he or she is ready for it. There are many techniques that you can use to reveal additional information. The following are some common techniques:

- **Rollovers:** Display additional information when the learner moves the cursor over items in a bulleted list or over hot spots in a graphic.

- **Buttons:** Display sidebar information such as tips and notes when a button is clicked.

- **Links:** Link to other parts of the course, secondary reference pages, or other sites as appropriate.

- **Flipbooks:** Enable the learner to step through a concept or a task in a sequential manner by displaying a series of images and text. It's like a mini-lesson within the current page of the course. You can use a flipbook to step a learner through the tasks in a process, show before and after (cause-and-effect), compare items, or walk through the different parts of a whole. The following is an example of a flipbook:

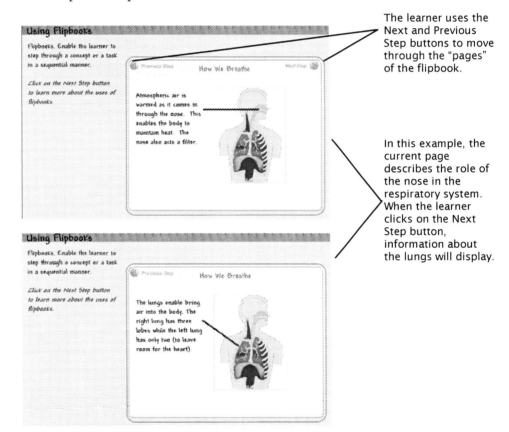

The learner uses the Next and Previous Step buttons to move through the "pages" of the flipbook.

In this example, the current page describes the role of the nose in the respiratory system. When the learner clicks on the Next Step button, information about the lungs will display.

**Tip:** You can use two flipbooks on a page to enable a student to compare two processes.

# Creating Flipbooks

This step-by-step tutorial takes you through the process of creating a flipbook. This flipbook will show how the parts of the respiratory system work. In this example, a flipbook is a good alternative to a multimedia demonstration because there is no audio available.

## Viewing the Finished Interaction

Before you begin creating this flipbook, take a moment to view what the finished file will look like.

**On CD**: Take a moment and try out the finished interaction: **samples/chapter14/sample_14-3.swf.** Take note of which items change and which remain the same as you step through the interaction.

## Setting Up the Flipbook

Flipbooks are primarily made up of a background graphic and two navigation buttons (Next Step and Previous Step). You will start by placing these elements on the Stage and then adding your content to each frame (for example, text, graphics, interactions, etc.).

**Use these steps to set up a flipbook:**

**1**   Open the file **samples/chapter14/sample_14-3start.fla.**

Notice that the library folder **Flipbook Elements** contains the background graphic and the navigation buttons for the flipbook.

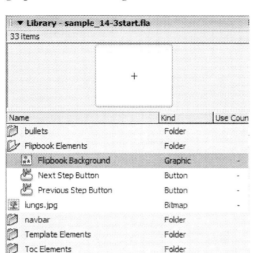

**2**    Create a Flipbook layer in the timeline (Insert → Layer).

**3**    In this Flipbook layer, drag all of the **Flipbook Elements** from the library onto the Stage. This includes the Flipbook Background, Next Step Button, and Previous Step Button.

**4**    Use the Text tool to create a Static text field at the top of the background. Enter *How We Breathe* as a title. Use a **12 point Comic Sans MS** font.

*The Flipbook Background symbol provides the container for the flipbook.*

*Use the Text tool to create a title for the Flipbook. Be sure that the title is located in front of the Flipbook Background (Modify → Arrange → Bring to Front).*

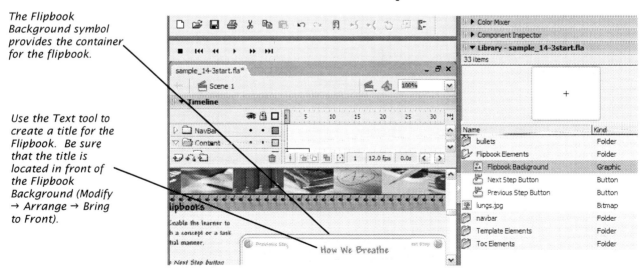

**5**   Extend all of the layers in the movie to include 3 frames. Insert a frame (Insert → Timeline → Frame) at frame 3 to make this happen.

**6**   Create a Flipbook Text layer(Insert → Timeline → Layer) to place the descriptive text for each of the individual frames of the flipbook.

Make sure that this layer is above the Flipbook layer.

**7**   In the Flipbook Text layer, insert keyframes (Insert → Timeline →Keyframe) at frames 1, 2, and 3.

**8**   Insert a static text field and place the following text in the corresponding frame on the Stage. Use a 12 point Comic Sans MS font.

| Frame | Text |
|-------|------|
| 1 | You can use a flipbook to show a show the parts of a whole. For example, you can describe the individual parts that make up the respiratory system. |
| 2 | The nose warms air as it comes into the body, enabling the body to maintain heat. |
| 3 | The lungs also bring air into the body. The right lung has three lobes, but while the left lung has only two (to leave room for the heart). |

Frame 1 does not contain an image, so you can spread the text across the flipbook background. Frames 2 and 3 contain images, so the text must be placed on the left side of the background.

**Note: Make sure that the text fits within the borders of the flipbook.**

**9**   In the Graphics layer, drag the graphic *lungs.jpg* to the Stage and place it next to the text. The graphic should appear in both frames 2 and 3. (Insert a keyframe at frame 2 in the Graphics layer and then drag the graphic to that frame.)

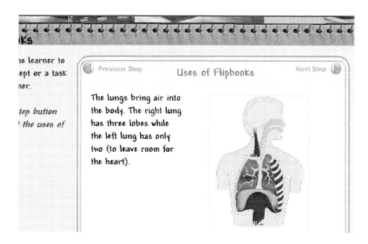

**10** Resize the image so that it fits inside the background image.

## Making the Flipbook Work

Now you need to add the navigation to the flipbook so that the learner can move forwards and backwards.

**Use these steps to add the navigation to the flipbook:**

**1** In the Flipbook layer insert a keyframe at frames 2 and 3.

Placing a keyframe will allows us to make changes to first and last frame. Because the **Previous Step** button is not used on the first frame and the **Next Step** button is not used on the last frame, we will delete them.

**2** Delete the **Previous Step** button from frame 1 and the **Next Step** button from frame 3.

**3** Add the following actions to the movie:

| Action | Location |
| --- | --- |
| on(release){<br>　nextFrame( );<br>} | Each instance of the **Next Step** Button. |
| on(release){<br>　prevFrame( )<br>} | Each instance of the **Previous Step** Button. |

You will notice that a **stop( )** action has already been added to the Action layer.

**4**  Test the movie (Control → Test Movie).

# Using Secondary Windows

In the examples used thus far, all content (both static and interactive) was displayed in the current window.  In general, keeping the learner contained within one window at a time is good idea because the learner can focus on the content without getting lost in a sea of windows. However, there are times when you will want the information to appear in a separate window:

| Application | Description |
|---|---|
| Large quantities of supplemental information | Information that supplements the contents of the page, but is too dense for the learner to absorb all at once.  A secondary page is a particularly good choice when there is enough information to require scrolling or that the learner may want to print out and reserve for later. |
| Links to supporting sites, applications, or job aids | Information that resides external to the course but can be used as reference by the learner later on. You can also give the learner the option of adding these pages to their Favorites menu on their browser. |
| Need more screen real estate | There may be times when your multimedia demonstration or simulation is difficult to fit within the context of the course due to a lack of space. In these cases you may want to pop up a larger secondary window for the demonstration or simulation. |

**Caution:** Make sure that you provide clear directions on secondary pages so that learners know how to return to the primary page.

**Tip:** It's a good idea to tell learners to bookmark important reference pages (such as job aids), so that they can be easily accessed later on. You may also want to give the learner the option to print job aids.

Sometimes additional information can be displayed as sidebar information and doesn't require a secondary screen. However, that is not always the case.

The following is an example of sidebar information that the user clicks on the **Tip** button to reveal additional information. Since the information is concise and immediately applicable to the learner, it is displayed within the context of the current page as a sidebar.

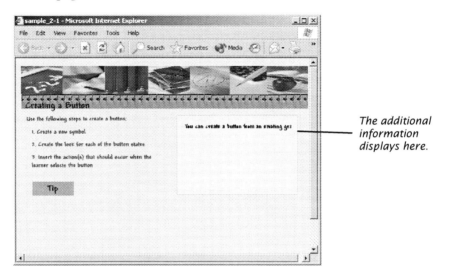

*The additional information displays here.*

In the next example, the learner clicks on a button to access the course glossary. The glossary contains a lot of information—spanning several pages—and can be accessed at any point during the course. (The learner may even want to use it after he or she has completed the course.) In this situation, a secondary window is a good choice.

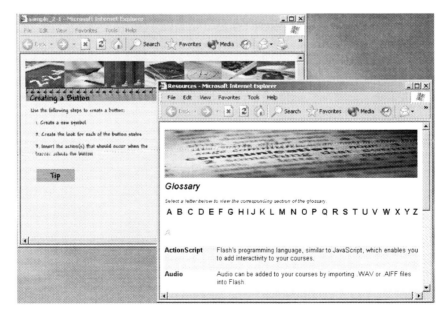

If you'll recall from Chapter 2: *Adding Interactivity to a Course*, you can link to another course page using the getURL( ) action (or you can create a link from the Property panel of a text object). If you want to create a secondary window for the glossary, you would need to have a button on the course page that contains the following action:

```
on(release) {
    getURL("glossary.html", "_blank");
}
```

This getURL action contains two parameters. The first parameter is a URL to the page that you want to open. The second parameter indicates which window should be used to display this page. The entry *_blank* indicates that a new window should be opened to display the page.

# Setting Up Simple Course Navigation

All courses need some form of navigation system to enable the learner to move from topic-to-topic or to access course features. For most courses, you will want to provide the learner with the option to:

- Step through the course in a linear fashion
- Navigate to specific topics
- Navigate to reference information

If you are using a simple architecture as described in Chapter 12: *Understanding Architecture*, then there will be one SWF document and a corresponding HTML file for each topic (for example, **lesson01page01.swf** and **lesson01page01.html**).

With this type of architecture, you will primarily be using the **getURL( )** function to navigate to the various course pages and reference information.

In the next section we will look at setting up the navigation for this type of architecture.

# Creating Linear Navigation Buttons

This step-by-step tutorial takes you through the process of adding Forward and Back buttons to navigate through several course pages. This is similar to Creating a Flipbook except you will be navigating to a new HTML file rather than within a single SWF file.

**Use these steps to create the linear navigation:**

**1**    Open the file *samples/chapter14/sample_14-4start.fla*.

**2**    In the NavBar folder of the timeline, add a layer named *Buttons* (Insert →
Timeline →Layer). Make this the top layer in the folder.

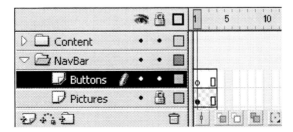

**3**    In the Buttons layer, drag the **Next Page** button to the Stage. It can be found
in the **navbar/NextandPrevious** folder of the library. Position it towards the
upper, right-hand corner of the green area.

**4**    In the library create a copy of the **Next Page** button (select Duplicate from the
popup menu). Name the copy *PreviousPage*.

**5**    Edit the button and change its orientation to point to the left. (Modify →
Transform → Flip Horizontal).

**Note:** When you flip this button, make sure that all the different graphic elements are
selected.

**6**    Drag this button to the Stage and position it by the **Next Page** button.

Now you have buttons that the learners can use to navigate to the next page
and to the previous page in the course.

**7**    Add these actions to the buttons:

| Button | Action |
|--------|--------|
| | ```on(release) {     getURL("lesson01page03.html","_self"); }``` |
| | ```on(release) {     getURL("lesson01page01.html","_self"); }``` |

Using the **_self** parameter in the **getURL( )** action causes the new lesson page to load into the current window, replacing the existing contents of the window.

**8**  Save the movie as *lesson01page02.fla*.

**9**  Publish the current movie as *lesson01page02.swf*. When you publish, be sure to include an HTML file with the same name (File → Publish Settings or File → Publish).

## Adding the Navigation to All of the Lesson Pages

In the previous section you added the forward and backward navigation for a single page. Now you will repeat this process for other pages in the lesson.

**Use these steps to add the navigation to pages 1 and 3:**

**1**  Open **samples/chapter14/lesson01page01.fla** and add the **Next Page** navigation button. The navigation button is already included in the library.

When adding navigation buttons to multiple pages, you want to make sure that the buttons are positioned in the same location on all pages. If you don't do this, the navigation buttons appear to move from one page to the next. This can be distracting to the learner. Use the Properties Inspector to make sure that the X and Y settings for the navigation buttons are the same.

**2**  Add this script to the **Next Page** button:

```
on(release) {
    getURL("lesson01page02.html","_self");
}
```

**3**  Publish the current movie as *lesson01page01.swf*. When you publish, be sure to include an HTML file with the same name.

**4** Open samples/chapter14/lesson01page03.fla and add the **Previous Page** button. Position it at the correct X and Y coordinates.

**5** Add this script to the **Previous Page** button:

```
on(release) {
    getURL("lesson01page02.html","_self");
}
```

**6** Publish the current movie as **lesson01page03.swf**. When you publish, be sure to include an HTML file with the same name.

**7** Open lesson01page01.html and test the navigation between the pages. Make any adjustments as needed.

 Tip: It's a good idea to add some text to each of the pages that orients the learner as to where he or she is in the course (for example, Page 1 of 3, Page 2 of 3, and so forth).

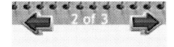

# Navigating to Specific Topics

One of the benefits of e-learning is that the learner is able to control the order of the content. Therefore, you should provide the learner with the ability to select the desired topic from some type of list. You could create a Table of Contents page that provides links to each of the course topics, or you can create some type of a menu to enable the learner to select the desired topic without leaving the current page.

 Note: This is especially helpful in a long course or in situations where the learners will not be able to finish the course in a single sitting. This makes it easier for the learner to start where he or she left off.

 ## Creating the Table of Contents

This step-by-step tutorial takes you through the process of creating a simple Table of Contents using movie clips. The Table of Contents movie clip contains buttons (one for each lesson and one for each topic). When the learner clicks any lesson, the corresponding topics display. When the learner selects a topic, the course navigates to the corresponding page using the **GetURL( )** function.

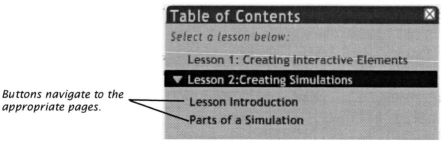

*Buttons navigate to the appropriate pages.*

**More Information:** There are other more sophisticated techniques that you can use to create menus. For example, you can use a Menu template in conjunction with XML to build the Table of Contents dynamically. To learn more about this technique, see Chapter 17: Creating an Advanced Architecture Using XML.

## Viewing the Finished Interaction

Before creating the Table of Contents take a moment to see how it will function. This will help act as a guide while you are creating the new Table of Contents.

**On CD:** Take a moment and try out the finished interaction:
**samples/chapter14/lesson02page01.html.** Click on the Get Table of Contents button and try selecting a topic from the menu that appears. You can also try clicking on the Get Table of Contents button and then closing the Table of Contents without making a selection.

*Get Table of Contents button*

## Setting Up the Table of Contents

The Table of Contents is a movie clip that contains multiple buttons. Each topic on the Table of Contents is a button. The first step is to create the Toc movie clip. Then you will add buttons to the movie clip for each individual lessons. All of the buttons have been created for and are stored in the Toc Elements folder.

**Use these steps to create the movie clip:**

**1** Open the file samples/chapter14/lesson02page01_start.fla.

If you open the library you will notice that a number of buttons have already been created.

**2** In the NavBar folder, add a Table of Contents layer (Insert → Timeline → Layer). This should be the top layer in the folder.

**3** Create a new symbol (Insert → New Symbol). Name it *Toc* and assign it a movie clip behavior.

**4** Rename the initial layer to *Background*.

**5** In frame 1 of the background layer, draw a green rectangle (#66CC99) that is about 280 pixels wide and 180 pixels high. Position the rectangle at 0,0.

**6** At the top of the green rectangle, draw a blue rectangle (#003366) that is 280 by 18 pixels. Position it at the top of the green rectangle as shown here:

**7** Create a new layer above the background layer and name it *Text*.

**8** In frame 1 of the Text layer, add a static text field to the top left corner and enter *Table of Contents* in yellow text (#FFCC00).

**9** Just below Table of Contents, add another text field and enter *Select a lesson below:*. Make the font size smaller and the color black (#000000).

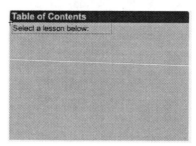

**10** Create a new layer above the text layer and name it *Buttons*.

**11** In frame 1 of the Buttons layer add the Close Button movie clip from the library. Position it in the upper right hand corner.

*Close Button movie clip*

**12** In the Buttons layer, place the Course Overview, Lesson 1 Button and Lesson 2 Button buttons on the Stage and position them as shown here:

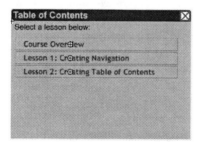

To make sure things line up correctly you will want to set the X property of each button to 9.5. This is the setting that is required for the Opened version of this button that you will add later. Each of these buttons already have a rollover state created.

## Adding Buttons for Each Course Topic

Now that you have the starting state for the Table of Contents, you need to add the elements that cause the lesson topics to display when the learner selects a lesson. Opening a lesson to display the sub-topics is accomplished by advancing to another frame in the movie clip.

**Use these steps to display the lesson topics:**

**1**   Extend the timeline for each of the layers to include 4 frames.

**2**   Since you want the Table of Contents to be invisible until the learner clicks on
the **Table of Content** button, create a blank keyframe in the first frame of
each layer. To do this hold down the CONTROL key and drag the keyframe
from frame 1 to frame 2.

**3**   Create an Actions layer (Insert → Timeline → Layer). In frame 1 enter a stop(
) action.

**4**   Insert a keyframe at frame 3 and frame 4 of the Buttons layer (Insert →
Timeline → Keyframe).

**5**   Select frame 3 of the Buttons layer and move the button for lesson 2 down so
that you can add the topics for lesson 1.

**6**   Select the Lesson 1 button and click the **Swap** button in the Properties
Inspector. Select **Lesson 1 Open Button** from the library.

This button shows an open lesson category.

**7**   Beneath the Lesson 1 button, place the 3 topic buttons: **L1 Topic 1 Button,
L1 Topic 2 Button**, and **L1 Topic 3 Button**.

The buttons already exist in the TOC Elements folder in the library.  When
finished, frame three should look similar to this:

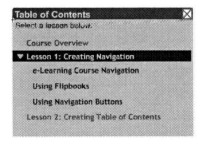

**8**   In frame 4 of the Buttons layer select the Lesson 2 button and click the Swap button in the Properties Inspector. Select **Lesson 2 Open Button** from the library.

**9**   Beneath the Lesson 2 button, place the 2 topic buttons: **L2 Topic 1 Button** and **L2 Topic 2 Button**.

The final results should look similar to this:

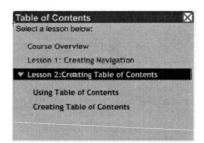

**10**  For each button in frame 3, enter the corresponding ActionScript in the Actions panel (Window → Development Panels → Actions):

| Button | Actions |
|--------|---------|
| Lesson 1 Open button | ```on (release) {    gotoAndStop(2); }``` |
| Lesson 1 Topic 1 button | ```on (release) {    getURL("lesson01page01.html", "_self"); }``` |
| Lesson 1 Topic 2 button | ```on (release) {    getURL("lesson01page02.html", "_self"); }``` |
| Lesson 1 Topic 3 button | ```on (release) {    getURL("lesson01page03.html", "_self"); }``` |
| Lesson 2 button | ```on (release) {    gotoAndStop(4); }``` |

The ActionScript assigned to each button does one of two things. The code either moves to a different frame in the movie clip to give the illusion that the menu is opening up to show sub-topics or displays a new page in the current browser window.

We need to add the same type of ActionScript for frame 4.

**11** For each of the buttons in frame 4, enter the corresponding ActionScript in the Actions panel:

| Button | Actions |
|--------|---------|
| Lesson 1 button | `on (release) {`<br>`    gotoAndStop(3);`<br>`}` |
| Lesson 2 Open button. | `on (release) {`<br>`    gotoAndStop(2);`<br>`}` |
| Lesson Introduction button | `on (release) {`<br>`    getURL("lesson02page01.html", "_self");`<br>`}` |
| Lesson 2 Topic 2 button | `on (release) {`<br>`    getURL("lesson02page02.html", "_self");`<br>`}` |

**12** For each button in frame 2, add the corresponding ActionScript to the Actions panel:

| Button | Actions |
|--------|---------|
| Lesson 1   button | `on (release) {`<br>`    gotoAndStop(3);`<br>`}` |
| Lesson 2   button | `on (release) {`<br>`    gotoAndStop(4);`<br>`}` |

Note: In this particular example the Course Overview is not active. You can easily make it active by using a getURL action to open another page or use the techniques already shown to provide sub-topics.

Now the Table of Contents is active, we just need to add one more bit of ActionScript code to make the Table of Contents hide when the **Close** button is clicked. To make it hide we just have the movie clip advance to frame 1. Remember, nothing shows on the first frame.

**13**   Select the **Close** button and add the following ActionScript in the Actions panel:

```
on(release){
    gotoAndStop(1);
}
```

Now we are ready to add a button that will show the Table of Contents when the learner is ready.

**Tip:** The method shown in this exercise for hiding and showing the Table of Contents is only one way to accomplish this. Another common method is to use the loadMovie or attachMovie commands to dynamically load the movie clip. For more information on these commands see the ActionScript reference in Flash help.

## Adding Actions to Open the Table of Contents

The Table of Contents itself is complete. Now you can add the actions that enable the learner to open it.

**Use these steps to add actions for opening the Table of Contents:**

**1**   Click Scene 1 to return to the main timeline. Select the Table of Contents layer and drag the Toc movie clip from the library and position it on the Stage where you would like it to appear.

The movie clip will appear as a small circle with a cross because the first frame of the movie clip has nothing to display.

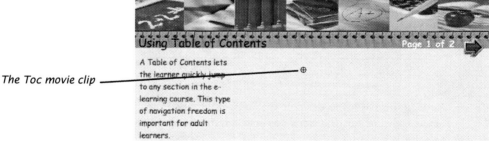

*The Toc movie clip*

**2**   In the Properties Inspector, give the movie clip an instance name of *toc*.

You will refer to this instance name in the actions that call the movie clip.

**3**   Drag the **Get Table of Contents** button from the library to the Stage and position it to the left of the navigation buttons.

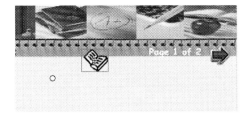

**4**    Add this ActionScript code to the **Get Table of Contents** button.

```
on (release) {
    _root.toc.gotoAndStop(2);
}
```

**5**    Save and publish the movie as lesson02page01.swf. Make sure to publish the HTML file.

**6**    Open **lesson02page01.html** and test the Table of Contents.

The **Table of Contents** button has not been added to any of the movies in the first lesson. You can make that change if you like. The FLA file for each of those movies contains the Toc movie clip.

## Tips for Effective Use of Navigation

It is important to provide methods for the learner to navigate through the course. It is equally important to ensure that the learner does not get lost. The following are some basic tips for ensuring effective navigation.

- Use page titles that match the topics listed on the Table of Contents. Page titles should be clear, yet concise.
- Create and use standard page titling conventions to ensure that page titles are consistent across the course.
- Use links within your titles to enable the learner to backtrack through the hierarchy of the course if it has multiple levels of content (e.g, Lessons, Topics, Pages). This technique (known as breadcrumbs) is frequently used on the Web.

*If the learner clicks on this link, he or she will be taken to the Lesson 1 overview.*

- Put the course name in the title bar of the HTML page so that the learner can easily find the course even when it is minimized. Likewise, put appropriate page titles on all secondary pages (for example, glossary, reference, and so forth).

*You can add a title to the HTML page in Dreamweaver.*

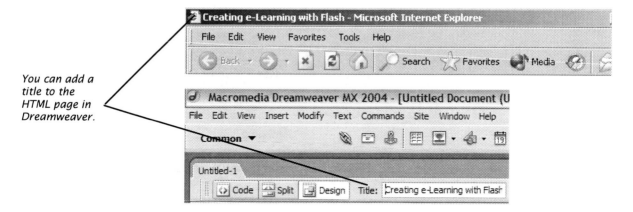

# Summary

This chapter focused on how to organize your course content in a coherent manner. You learned how to create inner course navigation, called flipbooks, as well as basic navigation techniques for a course delivered with HTML page. You also learned one method to create a Table of Contents. The Table of Contents is valuable because it lets the learner move through a course at his or her own pace.

# Using Flash Templates for Course Architecture 15

If you need to create a course quickly and you don't have time to build a custom architecture, then Flash templates are the way to go. In this chapter we will discuss how to use both Quiz templates and Presentation templates for creating courses and quizzes.

In this chapter you will learn:

- About advantages and disadvantages of using Quiz and Presentation templates.
- How to create a course using a Presentation template.
- How to add pages and make changes to a Presentation template.
- How to add Flash interactions to a Presentation template.
- How to create a quiz using a Quiz template.
- How to make changes to a Quiz template.
- How to add pages to a Quiz template.
- How to publish Quiz templates.
- How to connect a course created using Presentation templates to a Quiz created using Quiz templates.

# Using Templates for Architecture

Flash provides two types of templates that you can use to create a structure for your e-learning course: Presentation and Quiz. There are four different Presentation templates and three different Quiz templates.

**Note:** Different versions of Flash contain different template designs. However, the basic structure and methods for working with these templates, as presented in this chapter, have changed very little.

The main difference between these two template types is that Quiz templates were built to help you track quiz data using Shareable Content Object Reference Model (SCORM) or Aviation Industry Computer-Based Training Committee (AICC) standards. Presentation templates were created to provide an easy way to build presentations, similar to what you can do in Microsoft PowerPoint®. However, Presentation templates come with navigation buttons, so you can use them for e-learning if you aren't interested in tracking learner data.

**More Information:** For more information on SCORM, AICC, and data tracking using a Quiz template, see Section IV: Tracking Student Data.

## Using Presentation and Quiz Templates

Quiz templates are great for creating quizzes using Flash learning interactions. However, the interactions are set up to track quiz data and are only meant for quizzes. They are not very flexible for other types of e-learning applications. Therefore, we don't recommend that you use a Quiz template to create an entire e-learning course, which consists of both content and quizzes. Use the Presentation templates or other solutions discussed in this book for this purpose. If you need to add quiz questions to a Presentation template, use the standard Flash learning interactions.

**Note:** If you need the advantages of both a Presentation and a Quiz template, later in this chapter we discuss connecting a course created with a Presentation template to a quiz created with a Quiz template.

In the first part of this chapter, we focus on Presentation templates. In the second part, we discuss Quiz templates. Both templates provide architectural features that let you establish your course structure and navigation.

**Caution:** If you plan to publish the Flash movie using one of the publishing templates, make sure you avoid any arithmetic symbols in the name of the movie. When the movie is published using some of these templates, JavaScript functions are created. These symbols can cause JavaScript errors that are very difficult to debug.

# The Architectural Structure of Templates

Both templates provide these architectural elements:

- Navigation buttons, title fields, and background graphics. The Quiz template navigation is limited to going to the next question only. You cannot navigate back to a previous question.
- Individual frames for each content screen.
- A structure that helps streamline development.

In addition, Quiz templates provide a way to track learner data to a server-side Learning Management System (LMS).

The Quiz and Presentation templates use a simple architecture design that is strictly Flash based. The idea behind these templates is that each frame is a different screen in the e-learning course. ActionScript is added to force the movie to stop at each frame. The movie does not advance to the next frame until a navigation button is clicked. Each time the learner clicks to advance to a new screen in the course, the movie moves to a new frame.

Each frame is a separate screen in the finished e-learning quiz created from a Quiz template.

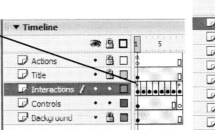

Each frame is a separate screen in the finished e-learning course created from a Presentation template.

This type of architecture makes it easy to add background elements to the entire course (i.e., something that appears on every frame). These elements might include a logo or other background images that you want to appear on every "page" of the course. You can do this by adding elements to the Background layer. You can create this type of architecture on your own, but it is already provided for you in the templates.

**More Information:** See Chapter 17: Custom Flash–based Architecture for more information on creating a similar architecture by yourself.

# Presentation Templates Overview

Presentation templates were created to provide a simple way to create a PowerPoint-like presentation using Flash. However, they also provide the navigation elements that are necessary for an e-learning course.

A course created from a Presentation template does not provide built-in data tracking for quizzes, but you can set up that functionality if you want.

A Presentation template comes with these features:

- Navigation buttons
- A print page button
- A background style
- A section for the company logo that you can use to add a title
- A counter field that identifies the current screen and the number of total screens
- The ability to modify text and graphics and add additional frames

There are four Presentation template styles to choose from:

| Name | Sample | Notes |
| --- | --- | --- |
| Classic Presentation | **My Company.**<br><br>2003 Annual Report<br>Examining the past year of sales at myCompany, Inc. | Because of the placement and style of the navigation buttons, this template is not well suited to e-learning applications. This template comes with multiple background images that you can hide or show to change the background design. |

| Name | Sample | Notes |
|------|--------|-------|
| Retro Presentation |  | This template comes with multiple backgrounds. You can hide one background and show another to change the design of the movie. |
| Sharp Presentation | | Because of the placement of the buttons, this template may not be the best choice for e-learning. |
| Tech Presentation | | The placement of the buttons helps make this template a good choice for e-learning. |

 **Note: The Presentation template styles will differ for different versions of Flash.**

 **Tip:** As we discuss later in the chapter, it is very easy to change the color provided by each Presentation template. It is also possible to change and add background images.

# Using Navigation in a Presentation Template

Navigation buttons are already provided in a Presentation template. The default navigation buttons consist of a previous and a next button. No home button or exit button is provided. The previous button is automatically deactivated on the first page, and the next button is automatically deactivated on the last page.

For the tech and retro styles, the navigation buttons are located on the bottom right-hand side of the screen. On the other two styles, the navigation buttons are located in the middle of the screen.

In addition to the next and previous buttons that are provided, a learner can also navigate through the course one page at a time using the left and right arrow keys on the keyboard. The up arrow will take the learner to the first page of the course, and the down arrow will take the learner to the last page of the course.

# Using a Presentation Template

Using a Presentation template is as simple as creating a new Flash document. Once you have created a new Flash file using a Presentation template, you can then begin to customize the existing functionality.

**Use these steps to open and use a Presentation template:**

**1**   Open a new file (File → New).

You may also use the start window in Flash MX 2004 to select a presentation file.

Flash displays the New Document window:

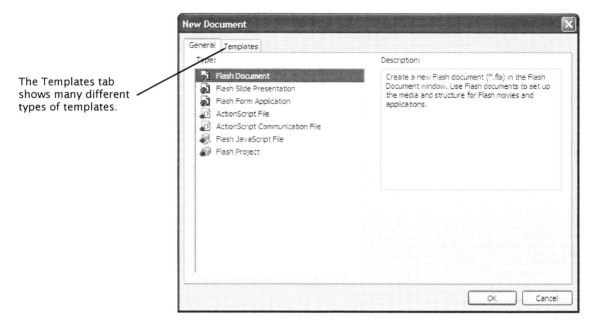

The Templates tab shows many different types of templates.

**2**    Click the Templates tab.

**3**    Select Presentation as the category.

**4**    From the Templates, select one of the four presentation styles.

**5**    Click **OK**.

A new presentation movie loads into the Stage. It consists of multiple frames and layers. Each frame corresponds to a different screen in the e-learning course. The frames come with sample content that you will generally want to delete.

**6**    The first thing you should do before changing the content and adding new frames is to save it as a new file (File → Save As).

The Presentation template comes ready to publish and use. You are not required to make any changes to access the default functionality. Before you use a Presentation template take a moment to view the default behavior provided (Control → Test Movie). Move through each screen using the next button. Use the previous button to move backwards.

# The Presentation Template Layers

Each Presentation template comes with several layers. You will be better able to work with the Presentation template if you understand the contents of some of these layers. Here is a description of the most common layers:

| Layer | Description |
|---|---|
| Headers | In the Presentation templates this layer contains text fields and sometime logos for a company's name. In an e-learning course you may choose to use a company name or Logo for this layer or you may choose to make this the name of the course. In one template this layer is named Page Headers. |
| Content | This layer contains the main content of each frame. The sample content provided by the Presentation templates consists of text and graphics. When creating an e-learning course, use this layer to place content and interactions in the frame. Each frame in this layer will represent a separate screen in the e-learning course. |
| Navigation Buttons | This layer contains the navigation buttons. This layer is generally labeled Buttons, Nav elements, or Navigation elements. |
| Background | This layer contains the artwork that is used as the background for the course. This layer is initially locked to prevent you from accidentally making changes. In most of the templates, there are multiple background layers for the many different background elements. |
| Actions | This layer contains ActionScript that provides the functionality for the course. This ActionScript disables the next and previous buttons at the appropriate time as well as add other functionality. |

# Creating a Course Using a Presentation Template

Now that you know a little bit about the Presentation template, you are ready to create a course. To create a course using a Presentation template, follow these main steps:

**1** Create a new document from a Presentation template and make changes to the template.

**2** Add content and Flash interactions.

**3** Add new pages.

**4** Publish the movie.

These steps may seem a bit simplistic for creating an entire e-learning course and they probably are. However, these basic steps outline the types of tasks that must be completed when using a Presentation template. Each step is described in more detail in the sections that follow.

## Viewing the Finished Course

Take a moment to look through the finished example of the course you will create.

 **On CD:** Open file **samples\chapter15\sample15-1.swf** from the CD and navigate through the course using the buttons provided.

While viewing the finished course, consider these questions:

- How many pages and what types of pages are used in the course?
- How do we add pages that include Flash interactions?
- How is content added to the frames of the course?
- What type of functionality is provided automatically by the Presentation template?

# Creating a New Document from a Presentation Template

The first step in using a Presentation template to create a course is to create a new Flash document from one of the templates provided.

**Use these steps to create a new document from a Presentation template:**

**1**   Create a new document (File → New).

**2**   Click the Templates tab to access it.

**3**   Select the Sharp Presentation template and click **OK**.

Flash displays the new document created from the template:

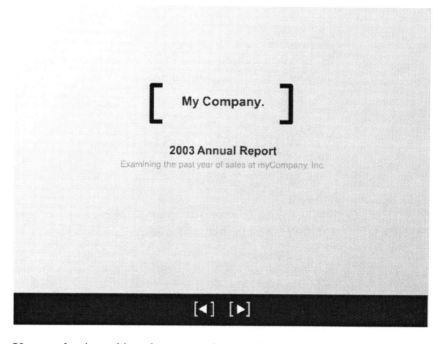

You can begin making changes to the template. There are a number of changes that are possible. Many of the enhancements are covered in a later section of this chapter. In this sample course we will make a change to the headers to add the course name.

**Use these steps to add a course title:**

**1**   Double-click the **My Company** text field in the middle of the screen to begin editing the text.

**2**   Select all the text and type *Flash Software Demos*.

**3**   Set the color of the text to **#FF9900**.

**4**   Select the two square brackets and delete them.

**5**   Select frame 2 in the Headers layer and replace the My Company text with *Flash Software Demos*.

**6**   Change the x and y location of the field to **0**.

**7**   Set the color of the text to **#FF9900**.

**8**   Select the two square brackets and delete them.

You have not set up the course title and opening screen. In the next section you will add content and Flash interactions.

## Adding Content and Flash Interactions

With the document created and the course title changed, we are ready to begin adding content. In this section you will make changes to default pages that come with a Presentation template. You will create four pages as described here:

- The first page of a course is a welcome page with some introductory information.
- The second page consists of a Flash learning interaction that will act as an attention getting exercise.
- The third page contains an alternative for adding content to a course. On this page we will load an external Flash movie to provide the content.
- The forth page is a summary with a list of URLs.

Each page is covered in its own section.

## Adding Basic Content to a Page

The first page of our sample e-learning course consists of some welcome information. When it is completed it will look like this:

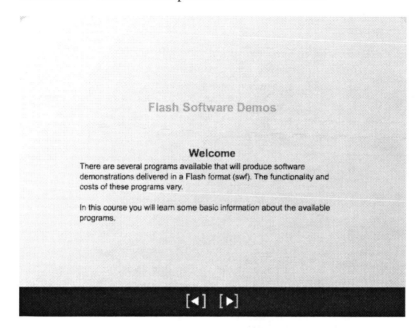

**Use these steps to create the welcome page:**

**1**    To begin making changes to the first screen in the course, select frame 1 of the Headers layer.

To make changes to frames, you can add content using the Flash tools or you can import external images. On this sample screen we will simply edit the text fields that are provided.

**2**    Select the text in the second field on the screen and enter *Welcome*. Make sure that the color of the text is black (#000000).

**3**    Select the text in the third text field and enter this:

*There are several programs available that will produce software demonstrations delivered in a Flash format (swf). The functionality and costs of these programs vary.*

*In this course you will learn some basic information about the available programs.*

**4**    Set the color of the text field to black.

**5**    Make sure the text is left justified. You may need to resize the text field. Also make sure the text is centered on the Stage.

**6**    Save the document.

You have now created the first screen of this sample e-learning course. As you can see one of the nice things about these templates is that you can focus on the content and you don't have to worry as much about course architecture.

## Adding a Flash Interaction to the Sample Course

On the second page of our sample course we will add a Flash learning interaction to the page to create an attention-getting exercise. When completed, the final page will look like this:

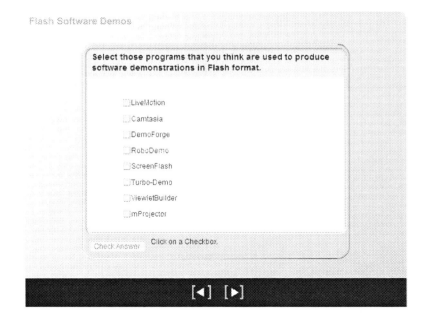

**Use these steps to add a Flash learning interaction to the sample course:**

**1**    To begin editing the second screen of the course, click on frame 2 of the Content layer.

**2**    Delete the objects that have already been added to this frame.

**3**    Open the Learning Interactions common library (Window → Other Panels → Common Libraries → Learning Interactions).

**4**   Drag a Multiple Choice learning interaction to the Stage. Center the interaction on the Stage.

**5**   Choose Break Apart from the modify menu (Modify → Break Apart) and configure the component parameters for this interaction. Establish the interaction settings according to the information in this table:

| Field | Setting |
|---|---|
| Interaction ID | No change. |
| Question | Select the programs that you think are used to produce software demonstrations in Flash format. |
| Instance Label Text | Add a total of 8 responses to the interaction. For the label text enter the following: 1. LiveMotion, 2. Camtasia, 3. DemoForge, 4. RoboDemo, 5. ScreenFlash, 6. Turbo-Demo, 7. ViewletBuilder, and 8. mProjector. |
| Instance Name | Name the instances Checkbox1 through Checkbox8. |
| Correct | The correct responses are: Camtasia, DemoForge, RoboDemo, ScreenFlash, Turbo-Demo, and ViewletBuilder. LiveMotion and mProjector are incorrect responses. |

 **More Information:** Establishing settings for the Multiple Choice learning interaction is covered in Chapter 6: Multiple Choice and True/False Interactions.

**6**   Click **Options** and establish the options settings according to this table, leaving all other settings as they are by default:

| Field | Setting |
|---|---|
| Tries | 2 |
| Correct Feedback | Good, you selected all of the correct programs. |

| Field | Setting |
|---|---|
| Incorrect Feedback | Sorry, LiveMotion and mProjector are incorrect. All others are correct. |
| Additional Tries | Sorry, LiveMotion and mProjector are incorrect. All others are correct. |
| Knowledge Track | Deselect the knowledge track option. |
| Navigation | Off |

**7** Close the Component Inspector.

**8** Select the last checkbox and duplicate it (Edit → Duplicate).

**9** Name the new instance *Checkbox6* and movie it to the correct position below *Checkbox5*.

**10** Duplicate 2 more instances and name them *Checkbox7* and *Checkbox8*. Place them in the correct position.

You may need to move the checkboxes around to get the spacing correct.

**11** Select the Question field and use the Properties Inspector to change the font size to 14.

**12** Select the Feedback field and use the Properties Inspector to change the font size to 12.

**13** Double-click inside the Feedback field to activate it, then resize the field so that it is large enough for two lines of text. You may also need to reposition the field.

**More Information:** Making changes to Flash learning Interactions is covered in more detail in Chapter11: Customizing Learning Interactions.

**14** Save and test your movie (Control → Test Movie).

You have now added a Flash learning interaction to the course.

## Adding an External Flash Movie to the Sample Course

So far we have looked at two methods for adding content to a sample course created with a Presentation template. In this section, we will add content to the course by loading an external Flash movie. This is possible using the **loadMovie** ActionScript command.

Once completed the page should look like this:

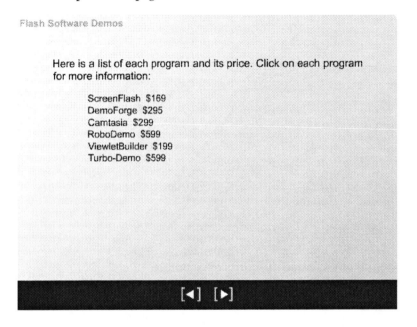

**More Information:** This technique for adding content to an e-learning course is covered in more detail as a part of Chapter 17: Custom Flash-based Architecture.

**Use these steps to load an external movie into the course:**

**1**   To begin editing the third screen of the course, click on the third frame of the Content layer.

**2**   Select the text and graphics that are already on this screen and press DELETE.

Before we can load an external movie into this frame, we must create a movie clip symbol first. This movie clip symbol will become the location where we will load the external movie.

**3**   Create a New Symbol (Insert → New Symbol). Enter *external* as the name and choose **Movie Clip** as the behavior. Then click **OK**.

There is no need to add any content to this symbol because we are simply using it to load an external movie.

**4**    Click **Scene1** directly above the timeline to return to the main timeline.

**5**    In the library (Window → Library), find the symbol you just created and drag it onto the Stage. Position it in the upper left corner of the Stage as shown here:

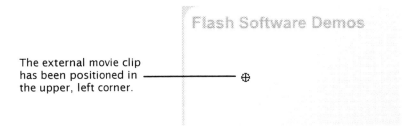

The external movie clip has been positioned in the upper, left corner.

**6**    Use the Properties Inspector (Window → Properties) to name this instance *external_mc*.

**7**    Copy the movie **samples\chapter15\demo_software.swf** from the CD and place it in the current directory. This is the movie we will load.

**Tip:** You can place external movies in different folders; you just need to make sure you enter the correct target path when setting up the **loadMovie** command.

Now that everything is in place you can add the ActionScript that will load the external movie. You will add a line of ActionScript to frame 3 of the Actions layer.

**8**    Select frame 3 in the Actions layer.

**9**    Open the Actions panel (Window → Development Panels → Actions) and enter this line of ActionScript code immediately beneath the **stop( )** command:

```
loadMovie("demo_software.swf","external_mc");
```

The loadMovie method contains two parameters: the name of the file to load and the instance name of the movie clip symbol where you want the movie displayed.

**Note:** You must enter a path to the file you want to load unless it is in the same directory as the movie you are working with.

**10**  Save your changes and test the course thus far.

You have now added content by loading an external Flash movie.

## Adding Content with HTML Links

You may find it necessary to include Flash content that provides links to external Web sites. In this section you will create such a page.

**Use these steps to complete the final screen:**

**1**  Select frame 4 in the Content layer and delete the images and text.

**2**  To complete the fourth screen in the sample course, add a static text field to the frame. Make it Arial, 20 point text. Enter the text shown here:

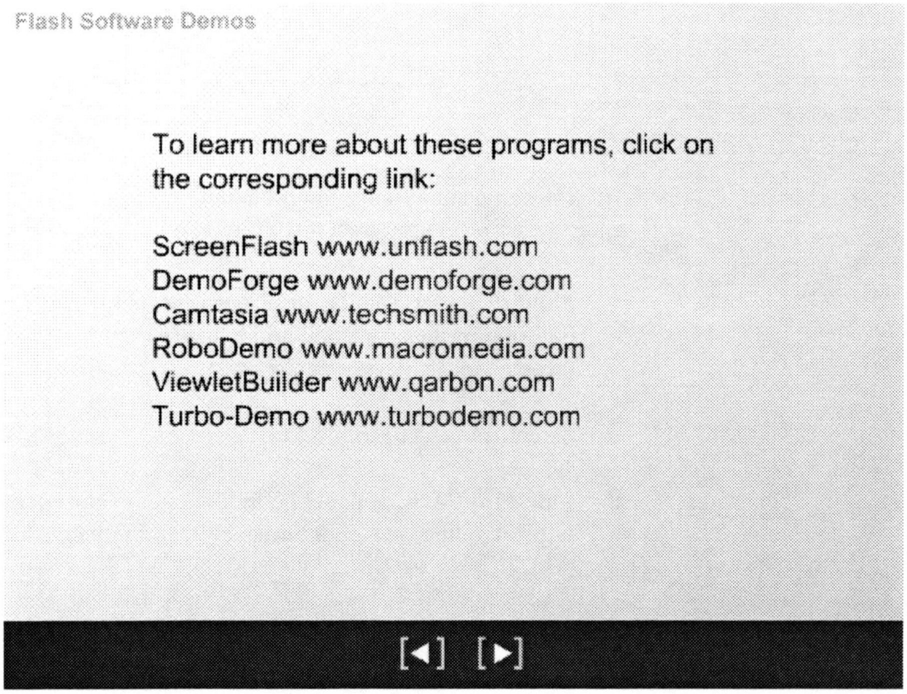

Flash Software Demos

To learn more about these programs, click on
the corresponding link:

ScreenFlash www.unflash.com
DemoForge www.demoforge.com
Camtasia www.techsmith.com
RoboDemo www.macromedia.com
ViewletBuilder www.qarbon.com
Turbo-Demo www.turbodemo.com

[◄] [►]

**3**  Select each URL and change the text color to blue. Activate the link by entering the URL with the *http://* prefix in the **URL Link** field of the Properties Inspector. Also choose **_blank** as the target in the Properties Inspector.

The *_blank* target tells Flash to open a new browser window before going to the URL.

**Tip:** If you are having trouble changing the text color to blue, make sure that the text field is a static text field instead of a dynamic or input.

**4**   Save your course and test it (Control → Test Movie).

Congratulations, you have just created a simple e-learning course in a short amount of time.

# Adding and Deleting Frames

The pages are finished but there is one extra set of frames that you will not be using. Before the course is completed, you will need to delete these frames. You will more likely run into situations where you need to add frames. Both situations are discussed in this section.

**Use these steps to delete extra frames:**

**1**   Select frame 5 in the top layer (Actions layer). While holding down the shift key select the fifth frame in the bottom layer (Background layer).

This will select all the frames as shown here:

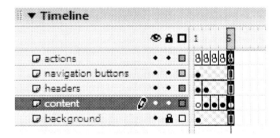

**2**   Right-click (CONTROL-click on a Macintosh) on the select frames and choose **Remove Frames**.

**3**   Save the movie (File → Save).

**Use these steps if you need to add extra frames to a course:**

To add a new screen to the course, you need to add another frame to each layer. Select the last frame of each layer and then choose Insert → Timeline → Frame, or you can insert a frame for each layer one at a time.

**1**    Select the last frame in the top layer. While holding down the shift key, select last frame in the bottom layer.

This will select the last frame in all the layers.

**2**    Insert a new frame (Insert → Timeline → Frame or press F5).

A new frame is inserted in each layer.

**3**    For those layers that require a keyframe (Content), select the frame and insert a blank keyframe (Insert → Timeline → Blank Keyframe).

Now you have a keyframe to which you can add more content. This is the process that is used to add additional frames to your sample course.

# Customizing a Presentation Template

Presentation templates come with a predefined look. However, you are not required to stick with that design. There are several things you can do to provide a different look for any Presentation template. These changes can range from simply changing the color to providing an entirely new background.

As mentioned earlier, the Classic and Retro presentations come with multiple background images. You can change the look of the background for these templates by hiding and showing different background layers.

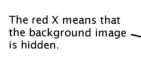

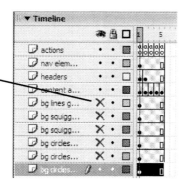

The red X means that the background image is hidden.

In this section you will learn how to make changes to the background, the buttons, and the titles.

# Changing the Background Color

The easiest type of change to make in a Presentation template is to change the background image color. There are two methods you can use to change the color of the background image. The first method is to change the background color of the movie. The second method is to change the color settings for the background image. Both methods are discussed in this section.

**Use these steps to change the background color of the movie:**

**1**   To change the background color of the document, access the document's properties (Modify → Document).

Flash displays the Document Properties window:

Use the **Background Color** setting to change the color.

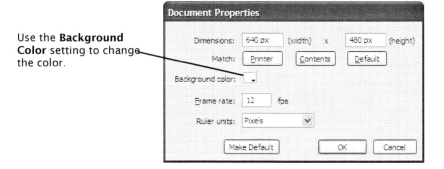

**2**   Click the Background Color palette and select a different color.

**Tip:** The background color will bleed through the background image if the Alpha setting is used on the background image. See the next set of steps to make a change to the Alpha setting of the background image.

**Use these steps to change the color settings for the background image:**

Most of the templates contain images that have been changed to symbols. You can change certain characteristics of the symbols to give them a different appearance. The background images for the Sharp presentation are simple Flash images. Therefore, you will need to change those using regular Flash editing techniques.

Before you can make any changes to the background image, you must first unlock the layer that contains the image.

**1**   Unlock the appropriate background layer by clicking on the padlock to the right of the layer name.

**2**  Select the background image.

**3**  In the Properties Inspector you change any of these settings by selecting it in the Color drop down box:

| Setting | Description |
| --- | --- |
| Brightness | Use this setting to determine the brightness level of the background image. |
| Tint | Using this setting you can provide a different tint to the image. When you choose this setting, you can enter a color using the RGB numbers or you can simply choose a color. You can also determine the intensity. |
| Alpha | Use this setting to determine how transparent the background image is. The more transparent you make it, the more the background color of the movie will show through. |
| Advanced | Use this setting to make percentage changes to the RGB values or to change the alpha setting. |

# Changing the Background Image

If a color change is not adequate, you can design your own background image and use it instead of the images provided by default by removing the current images and adding your own. In this section you will create a new document from a Presentation template and change the background image.

## Viewing the Finished Background Image

Before you modify a Presentation template by changing the background image, you may want to look at the finished result.

**On CD:** Open *samples/chapter15/sample15-2.swf* to view a Presentation template with a different background image.

## Changing the Background Image

To make a background image change, you first create a new movie from a
Presentation template, then delete the background image and import a new image.

**Use these steps to change the background image:**

**1**   Create a new movie using a Presentation template. Choose the **tech
presentation** template.

**2**   Use the Properties Inspector to change the background color to **#CCFFCC**.

**3**   Select frame 1 of each background layer and delete the contents. There are a
total of four background layers and they all start with *bg*.

**Note:** If you choose to you can delete the background layers.

**4**   Create a new layer and name it *bg new*.

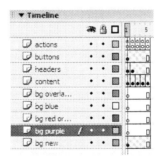

**5**   Select frame 1 of the new layer and import (File → Import → Import to Stage)
**images/pictures.gif**. Position this image so it is centered at the top of the Stage.

**6** With frame 1 still selected, import **images/notebook_bkgnd.gif**. Position this image directly below the **pictures.gif** image.

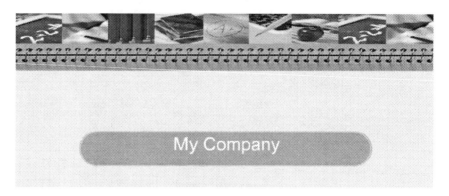

You have just made a change to the background image.

**Note:** To complete the new look, you would need to make changes to the headings like color and perhaps a different image. You may also want to change the color of the navigation buttons.

## Making Additional Changes to the Presentation Template

In addition to changing the backgrounds of a Presentation template, there are numerous other types of changes you can make without much difficulty. These changes only require basic Flash skills:

- **Change the Position of the Headers**: Many of the headers used in Presentation templates are Static Text boxes so you can select them and move them to any position on the Stage.
- **Change the Color of Headers**: Once again, since the headers are Static Text boxes, you can select the entire text box or select a part of the text within the text box and change the color using the Properties Inspector.
- **Change the Navigation Buttons and Fields**: The navigation elements of a template are an instance of a movie clip symbol. Therefore, you can select the navigation elements and make changes using the Color drop down box on the Properties Inspector.

# Making the Navigation Non-linear

Even though the default navigation in a Presentation template is linear, without much difficulty you can make the navigation non-linear.

In order to create non-linear navigation, you need to be able to jump to different frames within the movie. There are two ways you can accomplish this:

- Use ActionScript to move to a specific frame number.
- Use ActionScript to move to a frame label.

In either case you will use the ActionScript command **goToAndStop** for this type of navigation. The **goToAndStop** command lets you include a frame number or frame label:

**goToAndStop(4);**

Or

**goToAndStop("overview");**

The first example causes the movie to go to frame 4 and then stops playing. The second example causes the movie to go to a frame labeled *overview* and then stops playing.

## Using Non-linear Navigation

Non-linear navigation may be used to enhance a course. Here are some ways to use this type of navigation:

- Provide more than one path through the training for different levels of learners. This provides the ability to skip parts the learner is already familiar with.
- Provide access to advanced topics.
- Provide remediation training for learners that are having difficulty mastering the content.
- Provide more freedom on the choice of topics a learner will study by providing a course menu with links to different sections of the course.
- Provide a home button or menu button that lets the learner access a main page at any time.

**Tip:** Usually it is better to use a frame label rather than a frame number. The reason for this is that you can continually add additional frames without messing up these links. Even if the frame number of a label changes, the label will stay the same and the ActionScript will still work as you intended.

**On CD**: Open file *samples/chapter15/sample_15-3.fla* and take a look at the home button to see a simple example of this technique. This sample course uses a template style that was available with Flash MX. Different versions of Flash provide different templates.

In the sample course on the CD you can see an example of how this is implemented. A home button was added to the *_control* layer and scripted to link to the first frame of the course using a frame label. Here is the code attached to the home button:

```
on (release) {
_root.gotoAndStop("#b");
}
```

When the mouse button is released, this code executes. The **gotoAndStop** action executes at the root level of the movie (the main timeline). The #*b* label is a label already added to the first frame.

This is a simple example of this technique. You can adapt this technique for other situations as well.

# Quiz Templates Overview

Quiz templates offer a quick solution for developing quizzes that can track student data on a web server Learning Management System (LMS). The templates are compliant with AICC and SCORM standards.

**Caution:** For AICC or SCORM tracking, Windows users must have Internet Explorer 4.0 or Netscape Navigator 4.0 or higher. Macintosh users must have Netscape 4.5 or higher. Tracking will not work with Internet Explorer on the Macintosh.

The templates were created to incorporate the Flash learning interactions. In fact, each template includes one copy of each of the interactions. You can add and remove interactions to fit your needs.

**More Information:** For more information about Flash learning interactions, see Section II: Using Flash Learning Interactions to Create Assessment and Interactivity.

This list identifies the features that the Quiz templates provide:

- An introduction screen.
- A screen for each of the six different interaction types: Multiple Choice, Drag and Drop, True False, Hot Spot, Fill-in-the-blank, and Hot Objects.

- A results screen that displays the quiz results.
- An interface that lets you navigate between screens.
- The ability to modify text and graphics.

 **More Information:** Macromedia provides a tutorial that takes you through the process of creating and using the Quiz templates. This tutorial is available at http://www.macromedia.com/resources/elearning/tutorials/.

# Using a Quiz Template

Like the Presentation template, getting started with a Quiz template is not difficult. It is as simple as opening a new Flash document. Once you have started with the Quiz template, you can begin customizing the interactions and the quiz.

**Use these steps to open and use a Quiz template:**

**1**   Open a new document template (File → New).

**2**   Access the Templates tab and select Quiz as the category.

Flash displays the possible templates:

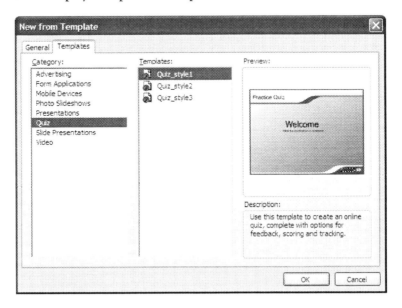

**3**   In Templates, select one of the three quiz styles.

**4**  Click **OK**.

Flash loads a new quiz movie into the Stage. It consists of 8 frames and 5 layers. Each frame corresponds to a different screen in an e-learning quiz. You can click on each frame to see its contents.

**5**  Save the document using a new file name (File → Save As).

The Quiz template comes ready to publish and use because it contains generic content. Before you use a Quiz template, take a moment to view the default behavior and content provided by default as a Quiz template.

**6**  Choose Control → Test Movie to view the quiz movie.

**7**  Move through each screen using the next button. Answer the questions. After you have finished answering the questions, a results screen will give you a score.

You are now ready to begin creating your quiz. But first, let's take a look at the contents of each layer that comes with the template.

## Quiz Template Layers

The Quiz template comes with five layers. You are better able to work with the Quiz template if you understand the contents of each of these layers. Here is a description of what each layer contains:

| Layer | Description |
| --- | --- |
| Actions | This layer contains ActionScript that makes the playhead stop at each frame of the course. This makes it possible to use each frame as a separate screen in the e-learning course. The movie does not change frames until one of the navigation buttons is clicked. Without this ActionScript, the movie would play through each frame continuously without stopping. |
| Title | This layer includes the title text that is intended to appear on every frame of the movie. |
| Interactions | This layer contains content for each screen of the e-learning quiz. The default Quiz template comes with a sample interaction from each of the six learning interactions. |

| Layer | Description |
|-------|-------------|
| Controls | This layer contains the quiz component and the navigation buttons. You must select the quiz component to establish quiz parameters. |
| Background | This layer contains the images that make up the background of the quiz. You can change the background to give the course a different look. |

# Creating a Quiz Using a Quiz Template

Now that you know a little about the Quiz template, you are ready to create a sample quiz. To create a quiz, follow these five main steps:

**1**   Create a new document from a Quiz template.

**2**   Establish the quiz parameters.

**3**   Modify the welcome page.

**4**   Modify, add, or delete learning interactions.

**5**   Modify the Results page.

In this hands-on section you will work through each of these steps to create a sample quiz.

## Viewing the Finished Quiz

Take a moment to look through the finished quiz that you will create.

**On CD**: Open file **samples/chapter15/sample15-4.swf** from the CD and navigate through the course using the buttons provided.

While viewing the finished quiz consider these questions:

▪   How many pages and what types of pages are used in the course?

- What type of functionality is automatically provided by the Quiz template?

# Creating a New Document from a Quiz Template

The first step to using a Quiz template is to create a new Flash document from one of the templates provided.

**Use these steps to create a new document from a Quiz template:**

**1**  Create a new file (File → New).

**2**  Access the Templates tab and select Quiz as the category.

**3**  Select the **Quiz_style3** template and click **OK**.

Flash displays the new document created from the quiz3 template:

Before you begin adding content or making changes, you need to set the quiz parameters.

# Establishing the Quiz Parameters

The quiz parameters control how the entire quiz is presented to users. To display and edit the quiz parameters you must first select the quiz component. As is the case with the Flash interactions, Macromedia has chosen to attach the component in the form of a set of instructions. Here is the component for the quiz:

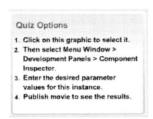

To change the parameters, you need to select the component and access the component parameters.

**Use these steps to establish the quiz parameters:**

**1**   Click on the component (set of instructions) on the left side of the Stage.

**Note:** The component does not show up in a finished course.

**2**   Open the Component Inspector (Window → Development Panels → Component Inspector or click the **Launch Component Inspector** button on the Properties Inspector).

**3**   If the fields on the inspector are too small to read, resize the inspector.

The panel contains 6 parameters:

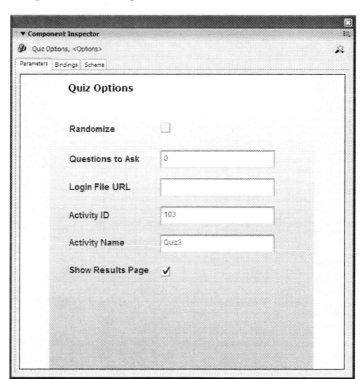

Each parameter is described in this table:

| Parameter | Description |
| --- | --- |
| Randomize | You may choose to have the quiz questions presented in a random order. To do so, check this option. |
| Questions to Ask | If you are using the Quiz template to create a quiz, then you may want to determine how many of the total quiz questions will display to the learner. If you would like all questions displayed, make sure this is set to 0. Otherwise, enter the number you would like to see. You can use this feature with the Randomize option to present a certain number of randomized questions from a larger question pool. |

| Parameter | Description |
|---|---|
| Login File URL | If you want the learner to log in to take the quiz and it is not launched through an AICC compliant LMS, then enter the login file URL in this field. The HTML code will redirect to this file if a login has not occurred. However, the redirect does not occur if you use the SCORM template. For more information see Section IV: *Tracking Student Data*. |
| Activity ID | If you need to identify the course in an LMS, enter an activity ID. |
| Activity Name | If you need to identify the course in an LMS, enter an activity name. |
| Show Results Page | If you would like to display the results page to the learner, check this box. |

**4** Make changes to the parameters on the Component Parameters Panel. For this sample course, make these 2 changes:

- Remove any information from the **Login File URL** field.

- Enter *SampleQuiz* as the course name.

**5** Close the Component Inspector by clicking the **X** button at the top of the window.

## Modifying the Welcome Page

Now that the parameters have been established, you are ready to make a few changes to the welcome page. In this section we will talk about basic changes such as changing the welcome information and the header.

**Use these steps to modify the information on the welcome page:**

**1** Select frame 1 of the Interactions layer.

The welcome information on the welcome page should be selected:

**2**    Change the second text line to read: *To take a quiz click the Next button.*

**3**    Reposition and resize the text box so that it is centered underneath the word *Welcome*.

**Use these steps to modify the header information:**

**1**    Select frame 1 of the Title layer.

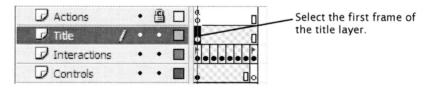

Select the first frame of the title layer.

The two header fields should be selected:

The two header fields
are selected.

**2** Change the word *Interactions* in first header field to read: *Additional Flash Programs*. Delete the text *Section1.1:*.

**3** Change the second header field to read: *Quiz*.

The welcome page should now look like this:

# Adding, Deleting, and Changing Interactions

A Quiz template comes with the six standard interactions. As you build your quiz, you will need to set up existing interactions, add additional interactions, or delete some of the interactions that are provided by default.

The sample quiz will consist of three questions: one Fill-in-the-blank, one Multiple Choice (multiple correct), and one standard Multiple Choice (single correct). First you need to delete the interactions that are not needed.

## Deleting Interactions

When deleting the default interactions that come with a Quiz template, you need to delete not only the frame in the interaction layer but also the corresponding frames in the other layers.

**Caution:** When deleting interactions, be careful not to delete the first or last set of frames in the movie. If you do you will delete the Welcome screen or the Results screen.

In the sample quiz you need to delete frame 2 and frames 4-5 and frame 7.

**Use these steps to delete a single interaction from a Quiz template:**

These steps will show you how to delete the interaction that is associated with frame 2.

**1**   Select frame 2 in the top layer. Hold down the shift key and click on frame 2 in the bottom layer.

This will select the second frame in every layer.

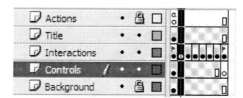

**2**   Right-click one of the frames (CONTROL click on a Macintosh) and choose Remove Frames from context menu.

**Tip:** Pressing DELETE will not give you the same results as choosing remove frames. DELETE will remove the contents of the frame but not the actual frame.

**Use these steps to delete multiple interactions from a Quiz template:**

These steps will show you how to delete the interactions associated with frames 3 and 4 and frame 6.

**1**   Select frame 3 of the top layer. Then hold down the shift key and click on frame 4 of the bottom layer.

This will select frames 3-4 in every layer.

**2**   Remove the frames (right-click (CONTROL-click on a Macintosh) and select Remove Frames from the context menu).

**3**   Select the second to last frame in all of the layers and remove them.

**4**   Save the changes you have made so far.

## Adding a New Interaction

To add a new interaction to the course, you must add a new frame to all five layers. First, determine where you want the new frame inserted. Then select the frames directly ahead of where you want to insert it. Make sure to select that frame in all of the layers.

In this sample quiz you will start by adding a new interaction at frame 4. First you need to add the frame, then you will add the interaction.

**Use these steps to add a new frame:**

**1**   Select frame 3 across all layers. To do this, select frame 3 in the top layer, hold down the shift key, and click on frame 3 in the bottom layer.

The reason we select the third frame is because we want to add a new frame at the fourth position. A new frame is inserted after the selected frame.

**2**   Insert a new frame (Insert → Timeline → Frame).

Flash adds a new frame to each layer.

**Use these steps to add an interaction to the new frame:**

**1**   In the Interactions layer select frame 4—the frame you just added—and insert a blank keyframe (Insert → Timeline → Blank Keyframe).

This creates a keyframe in the interaction layer that you can now add an interaction to.

**2** Open the library (Window → Library).

**3** Find the Multiple Choice interaction and drag it onto the Stage.

**Note:** All of the learning interactions have already been added to the library of this movie. Therefore, you don't want to add an interaction to the frame using the learning interactions common library.

**Tip:** Since the Quiz template comes with 6 learning interactions, you can use those learning interactions for your quiz. You do not need to delete them. You can easily swap learning interactions. For example, if you do not want to use a Hot Spot interaction, select the interaction before it is broken apart and in the Properties Inspector, click the Swap button. Choose the interaction you would rather use.

**Tip:** Another method you could have used to add a Multiple Choice interaction is to insert a keyframe, instead of a blank keyframe. Adding a keyframe would duplicate the previous interaction. You can then use the Swap button in the Properties Inspector to swap interaction types.

## Modifying the Learning Interactions

Now that you have the correct number of interactions in the sample quiz, you are ready to set up those interactions.

**Use these steps to modify the learning interactions in the sample quiz:**

**1** Select frame 2. Break apart the interaction and set it up according to the information shown in this table.

| Parameter | Description |
|---|---|
| Question | How many of the programs discussed produce Flash output? |
| Responses | For response 1, enter *six* and mark it as correct. |
| Case Sensitive and Exact Match | Deselect both of these settings. |

| Parameter | Description |
|---|---|
| Knowledge Track | Deselect the Knowledge Track setting. |

**2** Leave all other settings as they are.

**3** Select frame 3. Break apart the interaction (Window → Library) and set it up according to the information shown in this table.

| Parameter | Description |
|---|---|
| Question | Which three programs are the most inexpensive? |
| Responses | Checkbox1: Camtasia (correct)<br>Checkbox2: Turbo-Demo (incorrect)<br>Checkbox3: RoboDemo (incorrect)<br>Checkbox4: DemoForge (correct)<br>Checkbox5: ScreenFlash (correct) |
| Knowledge Track | Deselect the Knowledge Track setting. |

**4** Leave all other settings as they are.

**5** Select frame 4. Break apart the interaction and set it up according to the information shown in the table.

| Parameter | Description |
|---|---|
| Question | Which product has been around for several years but most recently provided Flash output? |
| Responses | Response1: ScreenFlash (incorrect)<br>Response2: Camtasia (correct)<br>Response3: Turbo-Demo (incorrect)<br>Response4: ViewletBuilder (incorrect)<br>Response5: RoboDemo (incorrect) |

| Parameter | Description |
|-----------|-------------|
| Knowledge Track | Deselect the Knowledge Track setting. |

**6** Leave all other settings as they are.

You have created a simple quiz using a Quiz template.

## Making Changes to the Results Page

The Results page does not contain a lot of content. It mainly consists of text fields that are used to display the results of the quiz. Here are a few changes you can make to the results page if you would like:

- **Change the color of the text fields**. You can use the Properties Inspector to make changes to the color associated with any of the text fields.

- **Rearrange the text fields**. You can change the position of the text fields on the Stage.

- **Add additional elements to the page**. You can add additional images or text fields to the Results page.

# Publishing the Quiz

If you created a quiz that you will use to track student data, it is important that you select the correct publishing settings. As is the case with the sample quiz created in this chapter, we chose not to include data tracking and not require any special publishing settings. You can simply publish the movie (File → Publish) and you are set to go. If you are not tracking data to an LMS make sure you don't use the Flash with AICC Tracking or Flash with SCORM Tracking templates.

If you are planning on including data tracking, then you will need to access the publish settings first.

**Use these steps access the publish settings for a Quiz template:**

**1** Choose File → Publish Settings.

**2**   On the Formats tab make sure that both Flash and HTML are selected.

**3**   On the HTML tab, select the appropriate template, either **Flash with AICC Tracking** or **Flash with SCORM Tracking**.

 **More Information:** For more information on tracking student data using Flash interactions see Section IV: Tracking Student Data.

# Customizing a Quiz Template

As with Presentation templates, Quiz templates come with a predefined look created by the background and colors used. However, you are not required to stick with that design. There are several things you can do to provide a different look. These changes can range from simply changing the color to providing an entirely new background.

In this section you will learn how to make changes to the Quiz template.

## Changing the Background Color

The easiest type of change to make to a Quiz template, is to change the background color. As with a Presentation template there are two methods you can use to change the color of the background image. The first method is to change the background color of the movie. The second method is to change the color settings for the background image. We discuss both methods in this section.

**Use these steps to change the background color of the Quiz template:**

**1**   To change the background color of the document, access the document's properties (Modify → Document).

The Document Properties window displays:

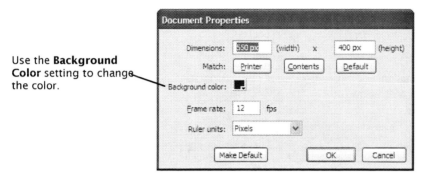

Use the **Background
Color** setting to change
the color.

**2**   Click the Background Color palette and select a new color.

The background color is changed and shows through the background image.

**Tip:** You can also make this change from the Properties Inspector.

**Use these steps to change the color settings for the background image:**

**1**   Unlock the Background layer and then select the image.

**2**   In the Properties Inspector you change any of these settings by selecting it in
the Color drop down box:

| Setting | Description |
|---------|-------------|
| Brightness | This setting lets you determine the brightness level of the background image. |
| Tint | Using this setting you can provide a different tint to the image. When you choose this setting, you can enter a color using the RGB numbers or you can simply choose a color. You can also determine the intensity. |
| Alpha | Use this setting to determine how transparent the background image is. The more transparent you make it, the more the background color of the movie will show through. |
| Advanced | Use this setting to make percentage changes to the RGB values or to change the alpha setting. |

**3**  To remove all settings choose **None**.

# Changing the Background Image

If a color change is not adequate, you can design your own background image and use that instead. To do this, first delete the current image then add yours.

**Use these steps to change the background image:**

**1**  Select the background image and delete it.

**2**  Select frame 1 of the Background layer and import the new image (File → Import → Import to Stage).

**3**  Position the image so it looks correct in the Quiz template.

**4**  You can import additional images until you have the background looking like you want.

# Making Additional Changes to Quiz Templates

In addition to changing the backgrounds of a Quiz template, there are numerous other types of changes you can make without much difficulty. These changes only require basic Flash skills and are outlined here:

- **Change the Position of the Headers**: The headers used in Quiz templates are Static Text boxes so you can select them and move them to any position on the Stage.
- **Change the Color of Headers**: Since the headers are Static Text boxes, you can select the entire text box or a part of the text within the text box and change the color using the Properties Inspector.
- **Change the Navigation Buttons and Fields:** The navigation elements of a template are instances of movie clip symbols. Therefore, you can select the navigation elements and make changes using the Color drop down box on the Properties Inspector.
- **Add Additional UI Components**: You may want to add additional buttons to the Quiz template. For example, you may feel that a **Quit** button is necessary.

You can use one of the Flash components available in Flash MX, or you can create your own movie clip symbol.

# Connecting Presentation Templates to Quiz Templates

Since you can include Flash learning interactions inside a Presentation template, you may not want to connect movies created from these two templates. However, there may be a few reasons to do this. For example, maybe you want to include a quiz, at the end of a course, with questions randomized from a pool. This is one instance where it may be advantageous to make connections between these two types of templates.

**Tip:** You may also find it advantageous to connect multiple Presentation templates together. For example, you may want to break up a large course into sections. Each section is created using a Presentation template and then you connect them together.

## Possible Methods of Connecting to a Quiz

There are two possible ways you could connect a Presentation template to a Quiz template. There are advantages and disadvantages to both methods.

- **Connecting to the quiz HTML page from the Presentation template**: This method is probably the preferred method because it will let you track learner data if you wish. This is also fairly easy to implement—you simply use a getURL behavior or ActionScript command. One disadvantage of this method is it is a little more difficult to return to the original course when you open a quiz in this manner.

- **Loading the quiz movie into a frame of the presentation movie**: Although this method may seem cleaner it has several disadvantages. First, when you load the quiz movie using the loadMovie action, there will be two sets of navigation buttons: one for the quiz and one for the course. Also, you eliminate the ability to track learner data if you load the quiz movie in this manner. The HTML page contains code that is necessary to track learner data.

# Hands On: Connecting the Quiz to the Course

In this section you will connect the simple quiz you created in this chapter to the sample course you created in this chapter. You will use the **getURL** ActionScript command to do this.

**On CD.** To view a finished example of this type of connection, open **samples/chapter15/sample15-5.html** in a browser. Move through the course and then access the quiz by clicking the Take Quiz button on the last page of the course.

**Use these steps to connect the quiz to the course:**

**1** Open the course you completed earlier in the chapter or open **sample/chapter15/sample_15-1.fla** if you did not complete the exercise.

**2** Click on frame 4 of the Slides layer.

**3** Open the Components panel. Open UI Components and drag a **Button** component to the Stage.

**4** In the Properties Inspector, change the label of the button from *Button* to *Take Quiz*.

**5** Position the button towards the bottom of the Stage as shown here:

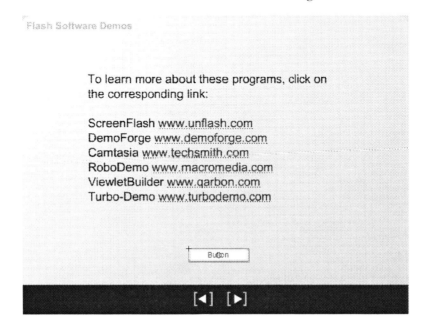

**6**  Select the button and open the Actions panel. Enter these three lines of Action Script for the button:

```
on (release) {
    getURL("sample15-4.html","_top");
}
```

The **getURL** action opens another HTML page in a new window or the current window depending upon the value entered in the second parameter. The parameter **_top** refers to the outer most window.

In order for this command to work, you must publish the quiz (**sample15-4.fla**) so that the file **sample_15-4.html** is generated along with the SWF file.

Because we are not tracking learner data with this quiz, make sure you access the publish settings (File → Publish Settings) and select the **Flash Only** template on the HTML tab.

Tip: If you would like the quiz to display in its own browser window, you can enter _blank instead of _top as the second parameter. Using a second browser window makes it easier for the user to return to the original course after taking the quiz. However, they can also view the course while they are taking the quiz.

**7**  Save the file (File → Save) and publish the movie (File → Publish).

You can test the movie by opening the **sample_15-1.html** file. You need to open the HTML file for it to function properly. The reason for this is that you are connecting to another HTML file using the Take Quiz button. By opening the HTML file to begin with, the course and the quiz remain in the same browser window.

# Summary

In this chapter you have been introduced to both the Presentation template and the Quiz template. The Presentation template is ideal for creating a Flash course. The Quiz template should be use mainly for quizzes.

You learned the process required to set up a basic course and a quiz. You also learned several different ways to make modifications to a Quiz and Presentation template.

Finally, you learned how to connect a Quiz template to a Presentation template.

In Section IV of this book, we will continue to work with Quiz templates as we discuss different methods for tracking student data.

# Using Slide Presentations for Course Architecture

With the release of the professional version of Flash MX 2004 came an exciting feature for e-learning developers: the Slide Presentation document type. Flash Professional comes with three document types: traditional, form, and slide. The Slide Presentation document type is ideal for e-learning development.

There is one downside to this new document type; it is only available if you have Flash MX 2004 Professional. If you do not have Flash Professional you can skip this chapter. However, the features are so exciting it may be worth the upgrade.

In this chapter you will learn how to:

- Use the Slide Presentation document type for creating e-learning.
- Define the parameters and properties associated with a screen.
- Add navigation buttons and other structural features for an e-learning course.
- Add content to the screens.
- Add a Flash learning interaction to a screen.
- Work with the different features available for screens.
- Use ActionScript with a Slide Presentation document.

# Introduction to Slide Presentations

The professional version of Flash MX 2004 offers three types of documents: traditional, form, and slide. A Slide Presentation fits nicely into e-learning development. This document type is available on the Startup screen or when you choose to create a new document.

Click to create a slide presentation document.

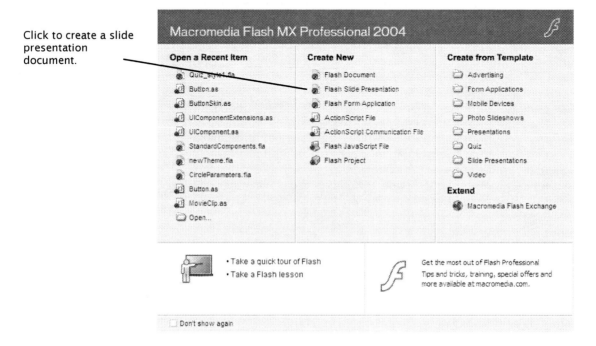

If you choose to create a Slide Presentation document using the file menu (File → New) and then selecting Flash Slide Presentation, you also have the option of choosing a template.

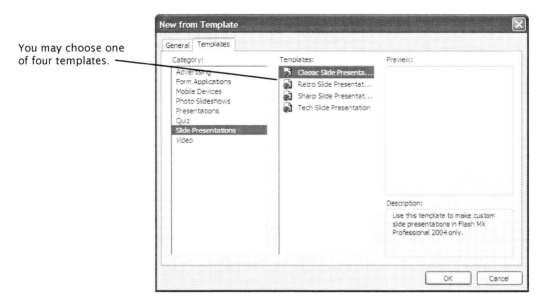

You may choose one of four templates.

There is a total of four templates to choose from. The templates come with default screens and navigation buttons. The default screens are made for presentations not for e-learning. This table shows a sample of each template:

| Template | Sample |
|---|---|
| Tech Slide Presentation | 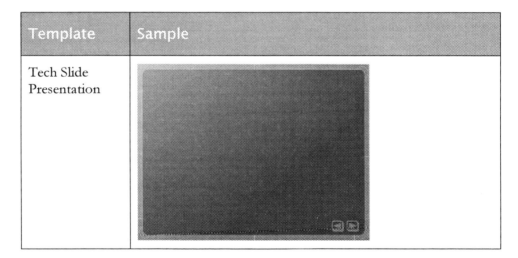 |

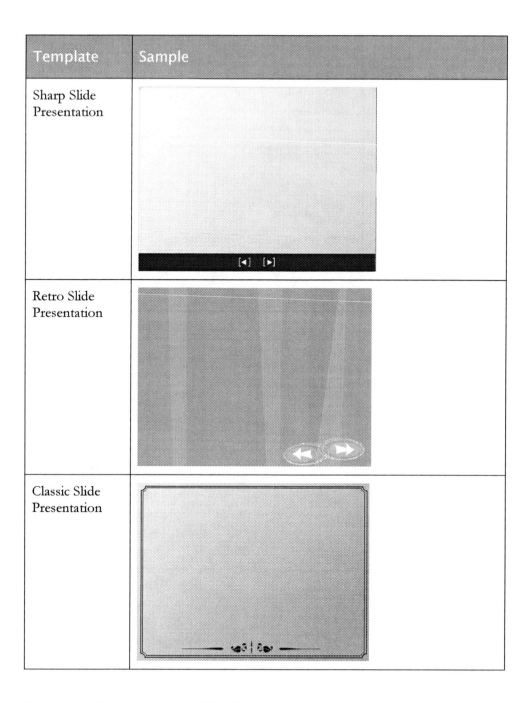

| Template | Sample |
|----------|--------|
| Sharp Slide Presentation | |
| Retro Slide Presentation | |
| Classic Slide Presentation | |

The main difference between a Slide Presentation document and a traditional Flash document is that with a slide presentation document you work with individual screens not frames. When you select a screen, the contents of that screen shows on the Stage. You add content to the screen by adding it to the Stage. You can add or delete screens as needed.

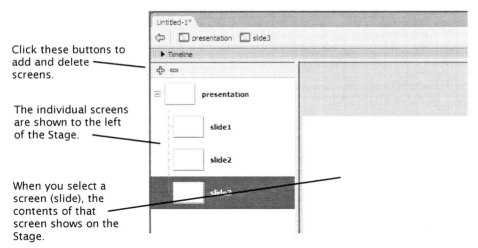

Click these buttons to add and delete screens.

The individual screens are shown to the left of the Stage.

When you select a screen (slide), the contents of that screen shows on the Stage.

One of the nice things about Slide Presentation documents is that it creates a structured framework for your e-learning course. You do not need to spend a lot of time on architectural developments. As you add screens they are placed in a sequential order. You can easily navigate these screens using behaviors and ActionScript. We will cover those topics later in this chapter.

Each screen also comes with properties and parameters that let you determine the exact functionality of that screen. Before we look at creating an e-learning course using a Slide Presentation document, we will look at the properties and parameters associated with a screen.

# Screen Properties and Parameters

Each screen that you create comes with several different properties and parameters. The properties and parameters determine how the screen functions.

## Screen Properties

The properties for a screen are found on the Properties tab of the Properties Inspector:

The most important property is the instance name or screen name. By default Flash assigns each screen a name such as slide1, slide2, and so forth. You can change the name so it is more descriptive of the content. For example you may want to use screen names like overview, objectives, quiz1, and so forth. You can change the screen name on the Properties Inspector or on the Screen Outline pane that appears to the left of the Stage.

**Use one of these methods to change the screen name:**

- Select the name in the Properties Inspector and enter a new name.
- Double-click the name in the Screen Outline pane and enter a new name.

Normally will not need to change any of the other properties.

# Screen Parameters

The parameters for a screen are found on the Parameters tab of the Properties Inspector:

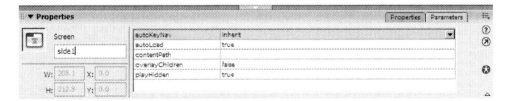

Each parameter is described in this table:

| Parameter | Description |
|---|---|
| autoKeyNav | Determines whether the screen uses default keyboard keys to control navigation. When autoKeyNav is set to true, pressing the Right Arrow key or the Spacebar advances to the next screen, and pressing the Left Arrow key moves to the previous screen. This navigation is not active when it is set to false. If the value is set to inherit, this screen takes on the behavior of its parent screen. |

| Parameter | Description |
|---|---|
| autoLoad | Indicates whether the contents should load automatically (true), or wait until the **Loader.load( )** method is called (false). This parameter is only significant if a path is entered into the contentPath field. |
| contentPath | Enter an absolute or relative URL indicating the file to load into the screen. This content is loaded based upon the setting for the autoLoad parameter. This lets you load external SWF files into a screen. |
| overlayChildren | This parameter is only important if you use child screens. It specifies whether child screens overlay one another on the parent screen during playback. When this is set to true, child screens overlay one another. This means that when a child screen displays, the previous child screen is not removed. |
| playHidden | Specifies whether a screen continues to play if it is hidden after it has been shown. When this parameter is true the screen will continue playing. |

In many cases the defaults will work fine. But you may run into situations where you want to change the functionality. We will look at one example in the next section.

# Creating a Course

In this hands-on exercise you will create the same sample course created in Chapter 15 using the Presentation Template. This will help you see the differences between these two techniques.

To create a course using a slide presentation document, follow these main steps:

**1**   Create a new Slide Presentation document.

**2**   Set up all the background content and navigation buttons.

**3**   Add new screens to the course and add content to the screens.

**4**   Publish the course (File → Publish).

These steps may seem a bit simplistic for creating an entire e-learning course, and they probably are. However, these basic steps outline the types of tasks that must be completed when using a Slide Presentation document. Each step is described in more detail in the sections that follow.

## Viewing the Finished Course

Take a moment to look through an example of the course you will create.

 **On CD**: Open file *samples\chapter16\sample_16-1.swf* from the CD and navigate through the course using the buttons provided.

While viewing the finished course consider these questions:

- How many pages and what types of pages are used in the course?
- What different methods are used to provide content? Can you tell how the different content is added to each screen?
- Can you tell which elements belong to the master screen (the background)?

You may also want to open **sample_16-1.fla** to see how the course was created.

## Creating a New Slide Presentation Document

The first step in using a Slide Presentation document to create a course is to create a new document. You can use one of the templates provided if you choose to. We won't use a template for this exercise so we can demonstrate how to add buttons and other background elements.

**Use these steps to create a new slide presentation document:**

**1**   Create a new slide presentation document by selecting File → New, choosing the Flash Slide Presentation on the General tab and clicking **OK**.

Flash displays the new document created:

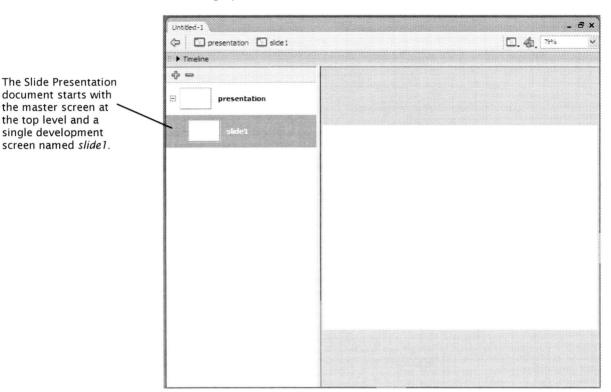

The Slide Presentation document starts with the master screen at the top level and a single development screen named *slide1*.

**2**   Change the dimensions of the Flash document to 700 x 520 (Modify →
Document). This will give us a little more space to work with.

**3**   Also change the background color of the document to #9DCEA7 (Modify →
Document).

The first thing you will want to do is establish background elements on the
master screen. Anything added to the master screen will show up on all
development screens (children screens of the master screen).

The name of the master screen is *presentation* by default. You can rename the
master screen to reflect the name of your course if you want.

**4**   Enter f*lash_alternatives* as the new master screen name by double-clicking
*presentation* in the Screen Outline pane or by selecting the master screen and
making the change in the Properties Inspector.

**5**   Save the movie as *Flash Sample Course* (File → Save).

Now you are ready to establish the background elements.

# Adding Background Elements to the Master Screen

Anything that you add to the master screen will show on all of the screens. Therefore you can consider the master screen as the background to the entire course. In this section you will add some graphic elements and navigation buttons to the master screen.

**Use these steps to add graphic elements to the master screen:**

**1**   Select the master screen.

**2**   Import *images/pictures.gif* (File → Import → Import to Stage) and position it towards the top of the Stage.

**3**   Set the width of the image to 700 so it covers the entire width of the Stage.

**4**   Import *images/notebook_bkgnd.gif* (File → Import → Import to Stage) and position it underneath the *pictures.gif* image.

**5**   Set the width of the image to 700 so it covers the entire width of the Stage.

You have now added the background images that will be used on all screens.

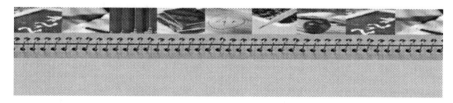

The next step is to add the navigation buttons.

**Use these steps to add navigation buttons to the master screen:**

**1**   Make sure the master screen is selected.

**2**   Open an external library and select the file *samples\chapter16\ button.fla* (File → Import → Open External Library).

**3** Drag the previous, next, and home buttons to the Stage and position them in the bottom right as shown here.

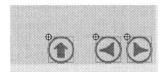

Now that the navigation buttons have been added to the master screen, you can add behaviors to make them functional.

**Tip:** The previous, next, and home buttons are just button symbols we created to make this exercise progress smoother.

**4** Select the next button and open the Behaviors panel (Window → Development Panels → Behaviors).

**5** Click on the behavior menu (+ symbol) and select **Go to Next Slide** from the Screen submenu (✥ → Screen → Go to Next Slide). Make sure that the event is **On Release**.

Add the go to next slide behavior to the next button.

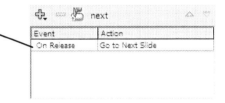

**6** Select the previous button and add the **Go to Previous Slide** behavior. Make sure the event is **On Release**.

**7** Select the home button and add the **Go to First Slide** behavior. Make sure the event is **On Release**.

The behaviors you have added to the buttons now make them functional so they will work on every screen in the course. There are some additional things we can do with these buttons such as disable them using ActionScript.

**More Information:** For more information on disabling buttons, see the section Using ActionScript with a Slide Presentation Document.

**Note:** When you add a behavior to an object or a screen, ActionScript code is added. You can see the ActionScript that is added if you select the object or screen and open the Actions panel.

The final element to add is a heading.

**Use these steps to add a heading to the master screen:**

**1**　Make sure the master screen is selected.

**2**　Add the text *Flash Software Demos* to the upper left area as shown here.

**3**　Set the font to _sans, the font size to 24 point and the color to black (#000000).

You have now added all the elements to the master screen and you are ready to add additional screens.

# Adding Content and New Screens

With the document created and the background elements added, we are ready to begin adding content. In this section you will add the content screens to the Slide Presentation document. There will be a total of four pages. The four pages are described here:

- The first page of the course is a welcome page with some introductory information.
- The second page consists of a Flash learning interaction that will act as an attention getting exercise.
- The third page contains an alternative for adding content to a course. On this page you will load an external Flash movie to provide the content.
- The last page will list the products discussed in this short course and provide a link to the respective web sites.

Each pages is covered in its own section.

### Adding Basic Content to a Page

The first page of our sample e-learning course consists of some welcome information. When it is completed it will look like this:

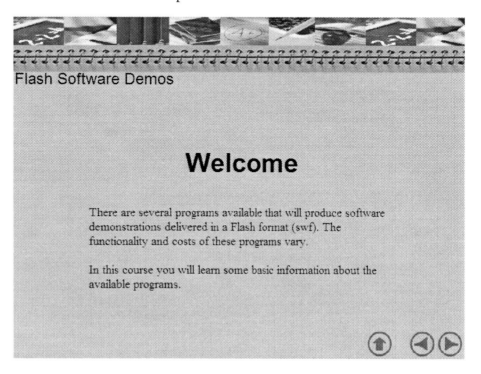

In this section you will learn how to add content to the different screens of the course by creating this welcome page.

**Use these steps to create the welcome page:**

**1**  Use the Properties Inspector or the Screen Outline pane to enter *welcome* as a new name for the first screen in the course.

**2**  To begin making changes to the first screen select it in the Screen Outline pane.

   You will notice that as you are working on content screens, the background elements placed on the master screen are dimmed.

   To make changes to any screen you can add content using Flash tools or importing external images as you would for any regular Flash movie. On this sample screen you will simply add text.

**3**   Add a text field to the screen and enter *Welcome*. Set the color of the text to black (#000000), the font to _sans, the style bold, and the size to 40 point.

**4**   Select the Welcome text field and center it on the Stage. (If the size of the text box fits the size of the text you can choose Modify → Align → To Stage, then select Modify → Align → Horizontal Center to center the text.)

**5**   Add a second text field with this text:

*There are several programs available that will produce software demonstrations delivered in a Flash format (swf). The functionality and costs of these programs vary.*

*In this course you will learn some basic information about the available programs.*

**6**   Make sure the text is 18 point _serif, black (#000000), and left justified. Make sure the text is centered on the Stage.

**7**   Save the document (File → Save).

You have now created the first screen of this sample e-learning course.

## Adding a Flash Learning Interaction to the Sample Course

On the second page of our sample course we will add a Flash learning interaction to create an attention-getting exercise. When completed, the final page will look like this:

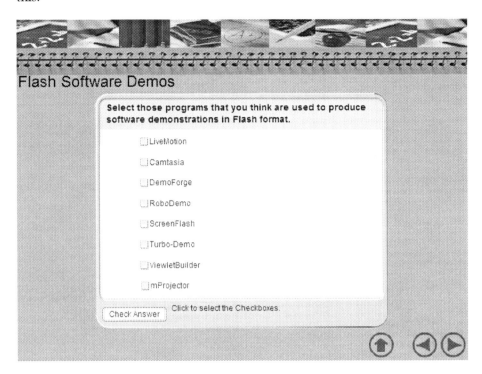

Before you can add the Flash learning interaction, you must add a new screen.

**Use these steps to add a new screen:**

**1**  Select the welcome screen.

**2**  Insert a new screen by right clicking (CONTROL-clicking on a Macintosh) the welcome screen and selecting Insert Screen from the context menu or use the Insert menu (Insert → Screen).

**3**  Enter *attention* as the name of this screen.

You are now ready to add the Flash learning interaction.

**Use these steps to add a Flash learning interaction to the sample course:**

**1**  Select the second screen of the course if it is not already selected.

**2**  Open the learning interactions common library (Window → Other Panels → Common Libraries → Learning Interactions).

**3**  Drag a Multiple Choice learning interaction to the Stage. Center the interaction on the Stage.

**4**  Choose Break Apart from the Modify menu (Modify → Break Apart) and configure the component parameters for this interaction. Establish the interaction settings according to the information in this table:

| Field | Setting |
|---|---|
| Interaction ID | No change. |
| Question | Select those programs that you think are used to produce software demonstrations in Flash format. |
| Instance Label Text | Add a total of 8 responses to the interaction. For the label text enter the following: A. LiveMotion, B. Camtasia, C. DemoForge, D. RoboDemo, E. ScreenFlash, F. Turbo-Demo, G. ViewletBuilder, and H. mProjector. |
| Instance Name | Name the instances Checkbox1 through Checkbox8. |
| Correct | The correct responses are: Camtasia, DemoForge, RoboDemo, ScreenFlash, Turbo-Demo, and ViewletBuilder. LiveMotion and mProjector are incorrect responses. |

**More Information:** Establishing settings for the Multiple Choice learning interaction is covered in more detail in Chapter 6: Multiple Choice and True/False Interactions.

**5** Click **Options** and establish the options settings according to this table, leaving all other settings to the default:

| Field | Setting |
|---|---|
| Initial Feedback | Click to select the checkboxes. |
| Correct Feedback | Good, you selected all the correct programs. |
| Incorrect Feedback | Sorry, LiveMotion and mProjector are incorrect. All others are correct. |
| Tries Feedback | Sorry, LiveMotion and mProjector are incorrect. All others are correct. |
| Tries | 3 |
| Knowledge Track | Deselect the knowledge track option. |
| Navigation | Off |

**6** Close the component parameters.

**7** Select the fifth checkbox and duplicate it (Edit → Duplicate).

**8** Name the new instance *Checkbox6* and move it to the correct position below *Checkbox5*.

**9** Duplicate 2 more instances and name them *Checkbox7* and *Checkbox8*. Place them in the correct position. You will need to adjust the position of the checkboxes to make them fit.

**10** Select the Question field and use the Properties Inspector to change the font size to 14.

**11** Select the Feedback field and use the Properties Inspector to change the font size to 12.

**12** Double-click inside the Feedback field to activate it. Resize the field so that it is large enough for two lines of text. Reposition the field if necessary.

**More Information:** Making changes to Flash learning Interactions is covered in more detail in Chapter11: Customizing Learning Interactions.

**13** Save and test the course.

At this point, you can make sure the navigation buttons you added are working correctly. You can also test the Flash learning interaction. If something is not functioning properly, double check your work.

**Tip:** If you would like the color of the learning interaction to fit more closely with the background color, select the learning interaction border and choose Alpha from the Color drop down box in the Properties Inspector. Set the percentage to 50. This will allow some of the background color to bleed through the graphic.

## Adding an External Flash Movie to the Sample Course

So far we have looked at two methods for adding content to a sample course created with a Slide Presentation document. In this section, we will add content to the course by loading an external Flash movie. This is made possible using the contentPath parameter.

Once completed the page should look like this:

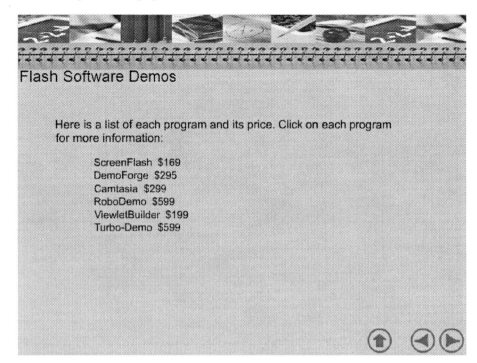

**More Information:** Chapter 16: Custom Flash–based Architecture teaches another technique for adding external Flash files to an e-learning course.

**Use these steps to load an external movie into the course:**

**1**  Select the second screen and insert a new screen (Insert → Screen). Enter *price* as the screen name.

**2**  Copy the movie **demo_software2.swf** from the CD and place it in the current directory. This is the movie we will load.

**Tip:** You can place external movies in different folders; you just need to make sure you enter the correct path in the contentPath parameter.

**3**  Select the new screen and click the Parameters tab in the Properties Inspector.

**4**  In the contentPath parameter enter *demo_software2.swf*.

You must enter a path to the file you want to load. Since you placed this movie in the same directory as the course, the path just consists of the movie name.

To prevent the external movie from loading until the screen is shown, you must change the autoLoad parameter.

**5**   Change the autoLoad parameter to false to prevent the movie clip from loading prematurely.

Now the movie clip will not load prematurely. However, you still need to add code to the screen so that the movie clip will load when the screen displays.

**6**   Make sure the screen is selected, open the Actions panel and enter this code:

```
on(reveal){
    this.load();
}
```

The on(reveal) event occurs when the screen is displayed. The load action causes the external movie clip to load.

**7**   Save your changes (File → Save) and test the course thus far (Control → Test Movie).

**Note:** The main difference between this external movie and the one used for the Presentation template in Chapter 15 is where we positioned the content. Since a Slide Presentation document has the background elements at the top of the movie, we don't want to display the external movie on top of those. So when this external movie was created, we left a space of about 150 pixels at the top of the movie.

## Adding the Final Screen to the Course

In this section you will add one more screen to the sample course to make it complete.

**Use these steps to complete the forth screen:**

**1**   Select the third screen and insert a new screen (Insert → Screen). Enter *websites* as the screen name.

**2**   To complete the forth screen in the sample course, add a static text field to the screen. Set the font to 18 point, _serif, black (#000000), and enter the text shown here:

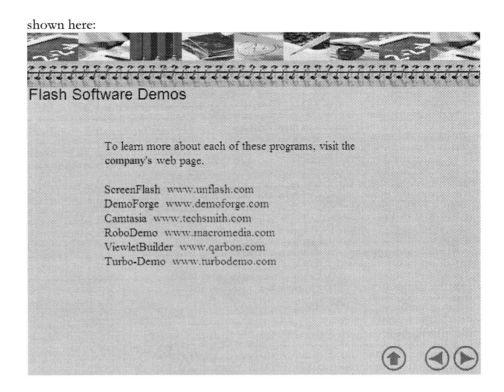

**3** Select each URL and change the text color to blue (#0000FF). Activate the link by entering the URL with the *http://* prefix in the **URL Link** field of the Properties Inspector. Also choose **_blank** as the target in the Properties Inspector.

The *_blank* target tells Flash to open a new browser window before displaying the URL.

**4** Save your course (File → Save) and test it (Control → Test Movie).

Congratulations! You have just created a simple e-learning course using a Slide Presentation document.

# Additional Features of the Slide Presentation Document

Now that you have created a basic course, you may be interested to learn some of the additional features available. In this section we will look at how you can add transition effects, access a screens timeline, move screens around within the Screen Outline pane, and use the right-click menu to work with screens.

## Adding Transition Effects

Flash comes with several predefined transition effects. You can use these transitions as the learner moves from one screen to the next. For example, you may want to fade in the next screen when the learner clicks a navigation button.

Adding a transition is as easy as adding a behavior to a screen.

**Use these steps to add a transition to a screen:**

**1**　Select the screen you want to add the transition to.

**2**　In the Behaviors panel menu select the transition behavior from the Screen submenu.

　　　Flash displays the transitions window.

Select a transition.

Establish the settings for the transition.

View a sample of the transition here.

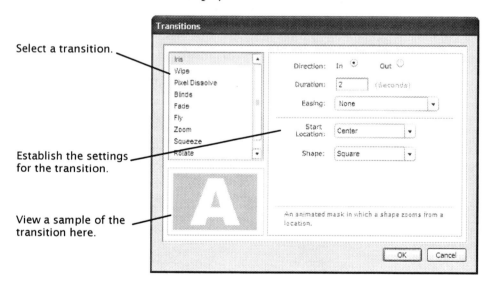

**3**　Select a transition.

**4**　Make any changes to the transition settings that you would like.

**5**　Click **OK**.

The transition is added to the screen.

## Accessing a Screen's Timeline

To this point in the chapter we really haven't dealt with the Flash timeline at all. That is because the timeline isn't necessary with a Slide Presentation document. However, you can use the timeline if you want.

For example, each screen has its own timeline. When a screen appears you may want the timeline to run. To do so you simply develop a Flash movie on the screen timeline just as you would on any other Flash movie.

When you first create a Slide Presentation document, the Timeline panel is closed. To open the panel, click the timeline arrow.

Click here to open the timeline.

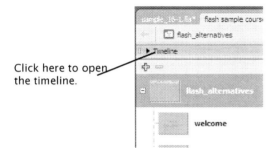

Once the timeline is opened, you can begin working in it.

## Working with Screens

The Screen Outline pane shows you all of the screens that are a part of the course. You can open or collapse groups of screens by clicking the plus or minus buttons next to root screens. This makes it easier to work with numerous screens in the course.

Click to close and open a group of screens.

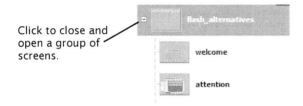

You can also change the order of screens by dragging a screen to a new place. When you click a screen and start dragging it, a line will appear to show you where the screen will move to if you drop it.

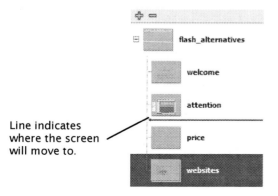

Line indicates where the screen will move to.

As you change the order of screens, they still retain the name you assigned them.

## Using the Right-click Menu

To enable you to work quickly with slides, a right-click menu has been added to each screen.

This right-click menu makes it easier to insert a screen or a nested screen. You can also cut, copy, paste, or delete the screen.

**Note:** To access the right-click menu on a Macintosh, hold down the CONTROL key and click.

# Using ActionScript with a Slide Presentation Document

Screens that are created as a part of Slide Presentation document are actually instances of the Slide class. This class comes with methods and properties that lets you interact with each screen using ActionScript. You have seen some examples of this as you have made changes to parameters or added behaviors. When you add a behavior, actual ActionScript code is added to the screen.

Behaviors may not always be flexible enough for your needs, so you may need to use ActionScript. In this section we provide some guidelines for using ActionScript with a Slide Presentation document.

## Inserting ActionScript

You can use ActionScript in a Slide Presentation document just as you would in a normal Flash movie. The one difference is that you can add ActionScript code to a screen. This is similar to adding ActionScript to a movie clip.

Here are common locations for attaching ActionScript when developing e-learning using a Slide Presentation document:

- A frame that is part of the screen timeline
- The screen itself
- A component on the screen
- Any symbol placed on the screen

## Using ActionScript

The slide class that is used to create each screen comes with methods and properties that you can use in your ActionScript code. A full list of everything that is available can be found in the online help. In this table we provide a description of a few of the methods to give you an idea of how to use them. As your course becomes more advanced you will want to refer to the online help for more examples.

**More Information:** For more information about methods, properties, and events available for the Slide Presentation document, refer to the Screen Class API and Slide Class API in the Using Components help.

| Method | Description |
|---|---|
| gotoFirstSlide( ) | Activates the top screen in a hierarchy. If all the screens are on the same level, this is the first screen. If the current screen is in a sub group of screens, this is the top screen in that sub group. |
| gotoLastSlide( ) | Activates the last screen in a hierarchy. If all the screens are on the same level, this is the last slide. If the current screen is in a sub group of screens, this is the bottom screen of that sub group. |
| gotoNextSlide( ) | Navigates to the next screen that is on the same level as the current screen. |
| gotoPreviousSlide( ) | Navigates to the previous screen that is on the same level as the current screen. |
| gotoSlide(*slidename*) | Navigates to the screen you indicate using the *slidename* parameter. |

When using the methods and properties from the slide class, you need to make sure you use the correct path to the object. There are a couple of ways this can be done.

For example, one of the methods described in the online help is **gotoNextSlide( )**. If you were to place a button on the master screen, how would you script that button to go to the next slide? This example will not work:

```
on(press) {
  gotoNextSlide();
}
```

The problem with this code is that it doesn't reference the object (instance), which is the screen. We need to somehow reference the current screen. There are a couple of ways to do this.

In this first method we use a couple of properties: **rootSlide** and **currentSlide**. **RootSlide** is a property that always returns the root slide of a slide hierarchy. The root slide may be the master screen if you have a bunch of slides all on the same level. Or it may be the top most slide for a sub group. The **currentSlide** property returns the currently active slide. You can script the button to work using both of these properties:

```
on(press) {
  rootSlide.currentSlide.gotoNextSlide();
}
```

Another way to reference the current slide when calling the gotoNextSlide method is to enter an absolute path. If the name of the master screen is flash_alternatives as it is with the current movie, you can script the button like this:

```
on(press) {
  _root.flash_alternatives.currentSlide.gotoNextSlide();
}
```

You can use the same technique to access any method or property provided by the slide class. This basic information will help you get started using ActionScript in a Slide Presentation document.

# ActionScript Example: Disabling Buttons

You may have noticed in the sample course created earlier that on the first screen of the course, the previous button is not disabled. The next button is also active on the last screen of the course. We can fix this problem using ActionScript.

A great way to learn ActionScript is to view scripts created by others. For example, the Slide Presentation templates come with a good deal of ActionScript that you may find useful. The ActionScript code used in this example is borrowed from one of the templates. In this example you will add ActionScript code to disable the previous and next buttons at the appropriate time. You will continue to work on the example course you created earlier in this chapter.

**On CD**: If you did not complete the sample course earlier in this chapter, you can open **samples\chapter16\sample_16-2.fla** and use this file as a starting point.

**Use these steps to add the code necessary to disable the previous and next buttons on the first and last screen:**

**1** Select the master screen.

**2** Select the previous button and assign it an instance name of *prevBtn*.

**3** Select the next button and assign it an instance name of *nextBtn*.

We will use these instance names in the ActionScript code that we will add.

**4**   Open the timeline for the master screen, add a new layer and name it *Actions*.
Select the first frame of the new layer.

We will add the ActionScript code to the first frame of the master screen
timeline. This will ensure that it will execute when the course is opened. We
first need to add the ActionScript code that will enable and disable the buttons
at the appropriate time.

**5**   Open the Actions panel (Window → Development Panels → Actions) and
enter this code:

```
function updateButtons() {
    if (this.firstSlide  == this.currentSlide) {
          prevBtn.enabled = false;
          prevBtn._alpha = 50;
    } else {
          prevBtn.enabled = true;
          prevBtn._alpha = 100;
    }
    if (this.lastSlide  == this.currentSlide) {
          nextBtn.enabled = false;
          nextBtn._alpha = 50;
    } else {
          nextBtn.enabled = true;
          nextBtn._alpha = 100;
    }
}
```

This function is the first step in setting up a *listener* for the screen. A listener is
some code that "listens" for a particular event and when that event occurs, the
code executes. The updateButtons function will execute once the event occurs.

This function contains two **if** statements. Using the firstSlide property and the
currentSlide property we check to see if the current slide is also the first slide of
the course. If it is the first slide we disable the previous button and set its alpha
property to 50 percent. By setting the alpha to 50 percent, it causes the button
to take on a disabled look. If it is not the first slide then we enable the previous
button and set the alpha to 100 percent.

The second if statement does the same type of comparison but uses the
lastSlide property. It then enables or disables the next button.

We have created the function that we want to execute, but before anything will
occur we must add an event listener that will execute this function whenever a
certain event occurs. The event we will use is *revealChild*. The revealChild event
occurs anytime a new screen is displayed.

**6** Press return after the last line of the updateButton function and enter this code.

```
this.addEventListener("revealChild", updateButtons);
```

This code adds a listener. The this keyword refers to the screen object. The listener is added to that object. The addEventListener function has two parameters. The first parameter is the event: revealChild. The second parameter is the function that should be called when the event occurs.

**7** Save the course (File → Save) and test it (Control → Test Movie).

Now you have added some sample ActionScript code to your course.

# Summary

In this chapter you have learned about the Slide Presentation document type and how you can take advantage of this document type for e-learning. This document type is only available with Flash MX 2004 Professional or later.

You learned which properties and parameters are available for screens and how they affect the functionality of the screen. As you built the sample course in this chapter, you learned to add elements to the master screen and build each individual screen using different techniques.

You can also add transitions to screens, use a screens timeline to add additional functionality, move screens around and group them if necessary, quickly work with screens using a right-click menu, and control screens using ActionScript.

# Creating a Custom Flash-based Architecture 17

In previous chapters you learned some architecture basics. While those concepts are important and are appropriate for certain situations, some aspects of a simple architecture can be hard to maintain. In this chapter you'll learn how to create a Flash-based architecture that is easy to maintain because of its modular organization.

In this chapter you learn how to:

- Create visual and interactive objects that apply to all *pages* of the course, such as background images and navigation buttons.
- Use ActionScript to make navigation buttons active.
- Create content in external modular chunks that are easier to maintain.
- Load external content into a presentation area movie clip.

# Introduction

In Chapter 14 you learned how to create an architecture mainly housed by linked HTML pages, each loading a different Flash movie. In this chapter you'll create the architecture in Flash, thus eliminating multiple HTML pages. There is just one HTML page with one Flash movie on the page. All of the navigation and organization takes place within the Flash movie.

With this approach, each piece of content is an external SWF file and is loaded as needed into the main architecture. Because each piece of content is a separate Flash movie, to change the content for a specific topic you only need to modify the content movie. You never need to touch the architecture. With this architecture, multiple developers can work on different pieces of the content at the same time.

Using this approach can also make adding additional content *pages* easier. Each frame within the Flash movie represents a different page so adding a *page* is as simple as adding another frame in the main timeline and telling it which external movie to load into the presentation area when the playback head reaches that frame. This approach to architecture, in which each frame contains completely new content, has sometimes been called a *pseudo-scene* approach.

# How the Pseudo-scene Architecture Works

In this section you will learn some fundamental concepts about designing a custom Flash-based architecture.

## Main Steps

Follow these steps when creating a custom Flash-based architecture. You'll learn more about these steps later in this chapter.

**1**  Create the layer(s) on the main timeline that will hold your background elements, such as a background image.

**2**  Add as many frames to the timeline as there will be topics. (Frames correlate with *pages* in other e-learning authoring tools).

**3**  Add elements such as navigation buttons and background images to a Background layer.

**4**  Add a layer to hold the ActionScript for each frame.

**5**  Create content pieces as separate Flash movies and publish them as separate SWF files.

**6**  Label each frame that will contain a piece of content. By labeling the frame you can more easily create links to the content from other parts of the course.

**7**  Add a Presentation layer. Create an empty movie clip symbol and add it to that layer. Make sure to use the Properties Inspector to give it an instance name so you can reference it later using ActionScript.

**8**  Add the **loadMovie** action to each frame to load the external content into the presentation area.

You will follow these steps in more detail later in the hands-on exercise.

## Using Movie Clips vs. Scenes

You might be wondering, *Why not just use Flash's built-in Scenes architecture to hold all of the different content? You could build the content pieces in different scenes, then you could just use the nextScene and prevScene actions to move between scenes.*

That approach is a valid way to design a custom Flash-based architecture. However, we think there are some definite advantages to using movie clip symbols and frames as *pseudo-scenes* instead of the actual scene functionality:

- **Maintaining background elements is more efficient.** By keeping all of your content in one scene it is easier to implement and maintain background images and navigation elements—modifying background elements requires making changes in just one location.

- **Modifying the presentation area properties is more efficient.** Suppose you wanted to change the position of the presentation area. If you used scenes you would need to change the position of the *presentation* movie clip in every scene. By using just one scene and one *presentation* movie clip you could make that change with just one edit, and it would affect the entire course.

- **Navigating during authoring is easier.** Because all of your content is in one scene you never have to switch scenes to find the content you are looking for.

- **Maintaining content pieces is easier.** When you need to make a change to a piece of content, instead of having to open what would be a large course file, navigate to the appropriate scene, and make the changes, you can simply open the smaller external source file for that piece of content and make the change. The change will appear in the course because that content gets loaded into the course when the navigation calls it.

**Tip:** You may want to consider using an alternative SWF authoring tool, such as SWISHMax, to create some of the content pieces. For underlying architecture, nothing beats Flash in its power and flexibility. However, we think SWISH is easier to use than Flash when it comes to creating animations (which cuts down on the time it takes to make the content pieces). SWISH contains hoards of awesome built-in effects and is reasonably priced (around $99). If you prefer to stick with just one authoring environment, you can add many of these effects to Flash using the SWISHPowerFX extensions (around $50). If you're doing software demonstrations, take a look at Camtasia for the content. Its SWF export is small and it is easy to use.

**More Information:** See the appendices on the CD-ROM for more information about alternative Flash authoring tools.

# Creating Your First Custom Flash-based Pseudo-scene Architecture

In this section you will create a custom Flash-based architecture.

## Viewing the Finished Exercise

Before you begin, take a moment to view the completed exercise on the CD-ROM.

**On CD:** Explore a custom Flash-based architecture by opening **sample_flash_arch_complete.fla** on the CD-ROM. You may also want to look at **sample_flash_arch_complete.swf** to experiment with it in action.

When viewing the source file, here are some things to look for:

- How are the layers organized and named?
- Can you find the background layer?
- Can you find the presentation layer and the presentation movie clip symbol?

- What changes do you see, or do you not see, as you move from frame to frame?

- Can you find the ActionScript code that tells the architecture what content to load and when?

## Creating the Architecture

In this exercise we'll create a custom Flash-based architecture that uses a separate frame for each e-learning *page* and dynamically loads external content pieces using the **loadMovie** action.

**To create a custom Flash-based architecture, follow these steps:**

**1** Open **samples/chapter17/sample_flash_arch_start.fla** on the CD-ROM.

**2** Name the existing layer *background*.

**3** Extend the keyframe of the Background layer to frame number 10. (Insert a frame at frame 10.)

Now that we've added the Background layer, we're ready to add elements to that layer that we want to appear on all pages of this mini-course.

**4** Open the library (Window → Library) and drag the button labeled *Next* (from the Buttons folder) onto the lower right-hand corner of the Stage.

**5**  From the library, drag the button labeled *Back* to the Stage and place it next to the **Next** button. You may want to align these buttons using the Properties Inspector or the Align panel.

**6**  Import the image (File→Import→Import to Stage) named **images/background.jpg** and place it at the top of the Stage.

 **Tip:** A quick way to move the image to the top of the Stage is to set the Y pixel position to 0.0. You can do this in the Properties Inspector.

**7**  Add a layer named *scripts*.

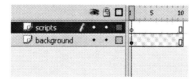

This layer will hold the scripts that we want to execute every time the learner advances the course one frame.

**8**　Add a layer called *labels*.

We will use this layer to label each frame so that in later exercises we can easily navigate to a specific topic (the label) even if the relative location (frame number) of that frame changes. During the process of developing a course, you may change the location of a frame several times.

**Note**: There are, of course, many ways you can organize this kind of layout. You could, for example, simply label each of the frames on the Scripts layer, removing the necessity for an extra layer called Labels. However, by having the labels on a separate layer it is easier to keep straight where your labels and scripts are.

**9**　In the Labels layer create one blank keyframe (Insert → Timeline → Keyframe) for each of the ten frames and label them (using the Properties Inspector) according to this table:

| Frame | Label |
|-------|-------|
| 1 | Objectives |
| 2 | Step1 |
| 3 | Step2 |
| 4 | Step3 |
| 5 | Step4 |
| 6 | Step5 |
| 7 | Step6 |
| 8 | Step7 |
| 9 | Step8 |
| 10 | Review |

When you are finished with this step, the timeline for that layer should look like this:

**9**　Add a layer called *presentationLayer* at the top of the timeline.

**10**　Create an empty movie clip symbol and name it *presentationMovieClip* (Insert → Symbol).

Name the symbol *presentationMovieClip* and select **Movie Clip** as the Behavior.

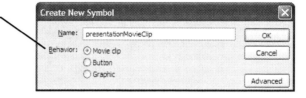

**11**　When the movie clip appears on the Stage, don't add anything to it. Just click **Scene 1** to return to the main timeline.

Click Scene 1 to return to the main timeline.

**12**　Drag the presentationMovieClip symbol from the library to the Stage in the PresentationLayer layer. Position the movie clip at the far left of the Stage, just under the background image.

Whenever you load an external Flash movie into a movie clip, Flash loads the movie at the center of the crosshair images shown in the empty movie clip symbol. This means that you need to place the crosshair image at the top left of wherever you want the loaded clip to display.

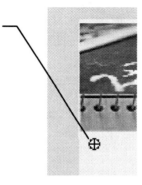

**13** Using the Properties Inspector, give the movie clip symbol an instance name of *presentation*.

**Note**: You must use an instance name in the ActionScript code to reference the movie clip symbol. You will later load external Flash movies into this movie clip.

We have already created the external Flash movies needed for this exercise. They are stored in the **samples/chapter17/sample_files** subfolder.

**14** Add the following ActionScript code to the frame 1 of the Scripts layer.

```
loadMovie("sample_files/objectives.swf","presentation");
stop();
```

In this code, the first parameter (*sample_file/objectives.swf*) refers to the external movie to be loaded into the movie clip. The second parameter (*presentation*) refers to the name of the movie clip instance into which the external movie will be loaded.

In short, we are telling Flash to load the external Flash movie called *objectives.swf* into the movie clip instance called *presentation*. By attaching this script to the frame itself, we are telling Flash to execute this script when the playback head reaches this frame. The **stop( )** command prevents the playback head from moving to the next frame until the user clicks the **Next** button.

**Note**: In order for the target path **sample_files/objectives.swf** used in this ActionScript to work, you must copy the **samples/chapter17/sample_files** folder to the same location where you have saved this movie.

**15** Add the following ActionScript code to the following frames, according to this table. You will need to insert a blank key frame for each frame before adding the ActionScript (Insert → Timeline → Blank Keyframe). Then select the frame and open the Actions panel (Window → Development Panels → Actions).

| Frame | Code |
|-------|------|
| 1 | loadMovie("sample_files/objectives.swf","presentation"); <br> stop(); |
| 2 | loadMovie("sample_files/step1.swf","presentation"); <br> stop(); |
| 3 | loadMovie("sample_files/step2.swf","presentation"); <br> stop(); |
| 4 | loadMovie("sample_files/step3.swf","presentation"); <br> stop(); |
| 5 | loadMovie("sample_files/step4.swf","presentation"); <br> stop(); |
| 6 | loadMovie("sample_files/step5.swf","presentation"); <br> stop(); |
| 7 | loadMovie("sample_files/step6.swf","presentation"); <br> stop(); |
| 8 | loadMovie("sample_files/step7.swf","presentation"); <br> stop(); |
| 9 | loadMovie("sample_files/step8.swf","presentation"); <br> stop(); |
| 10 | loadMovie("sample_files/review.swf","presentation"); <br> stop(); |

Now we are ready to add the code to the **Next** and **Back** buttons to control the sequential navigation. Because the navigation buttons are on a layer that spans all ten frames we only need to add this code to the buttons once.

**16** Select the **Next** button, open the Actions panel and add this code:

```
on (release) {
    nextFrame();
}
```

**17** Select the **Back** button, open the Actions panel and add this code:

```
on (release) {
    prevFrame();
}
```

**Note:** By creating Next and Back buttons that move from frame to frame, inserting a page in this architecture becomes a breeze. Simply insert the frame and point to its associated content. Assuming you insert the new frame in the right location, there is no need to tell the Next and Back buttons where go when clicked.

**18** Save your work (File → Save) and test your movie (Control → Test Movie).

You have successfully created a simple, custom architecture in which each frame acts as a *pseudo-scene*. In review, by using a *pseudo-scene* navigation:

- You can create a *background* that can be used across multiple pseudo-scenes (where each frame is a *scene*).
- You can easily insert a frame anywhere in the sequence and there is no need to update the navigational controls.
- You can modify *scene* content by modifying the external Flash movie—creating a modular approach to content creation and maintenance.
- You can easily navigate between *scenes* by moving from frame to frame.

# Enhancements to a Pseudo-scene Architecture

So far in this chapter you have learned how to create linear navigation using a pseudo-scene approach, in which every frame contains different content. The **Next** and **Back** buttons navigate from frame to frame creating the sense of multiple *pages*, or content pieces, for the learner.

However, sequential topic navigation is only one part of most course navigation systems. In this section of the chapter, you'll learn how to add these additional features:

- A course map that allows learners to jump immediately to any topic within the lesson (as well as to other lessons).
- A Back button that is disabled on the first page of the lesson and a Next button that is disabled on the last page (thereby letting the learners know they are at the beginning or end of the lesson).
- A link to a pop-up glossary.
- A graphical progress meter that shows learners how far they have progressed within the lesson.

# Using a Course Map to Add Non-sequential Navigation

Many learners want to be able to jump from topic to topic without being forced to complete the current topic. They may even want to jump from lesson to lesson. In this section you will learn how to create navigation using a Course Map that is accessible from any content pseudo-scene (frame).

First, let's take a look at the two high-level steps that you need to complete.

**1**    Create the Course Map as a separate SWF. Ideally it should be small enough to pop-up over the top of the current topic. The links in the Course Map will point to the frame labels of each pseudo-scene.

**2**    Add a navigational control to the background layer of the architecture that displays the external Course Map SWF on top of the other layers. One way to accomplish this is to create an empty movie clip container and use the *loadMovie* action to load the external Course Map SWF into the container.

## Step 1: Creating the Course Map as a Separate SWF

You can design the Course Map in a number of ways depending on your individual preference. For the purposes of this book, we have created an external SWF that simply lists the title of the lesson and also lists the subtopics.

**On CD:** Open and explore the file
**samples/chapter17/sample_files/coursemap/coursemap.fla.**

In this file we have three layers: Scripts, Links, and Background.

### The Scripts Layer

The Scripts layer contains a function associated with this timeline that handles what happens when the learner clicks a topic on the course map.

```
function goToTopic(framename) {
    _parent.courseMapClip.loadMovie("sample_files/coursemap/blank.swf");
    _parent.gotoAndStop(framename);
}
```

This function accepts one parameter: the label name of the frame in the parent movie clip (the original course). In the second line we use the **gotoAndStop** method of the **_parent** movie clip to move the playback head to whatever frame is specified by the **framename** parameter.

The **loadMovie** command is used again to load a blank movie. This essentially *hides* the course map. The **unloadMovie** command is also available but we have chose to load a blank movie because the **unloadMovie** command sometimes causes load errors.

### The Links Layer

The Links layer contains several button symbols. The first is the Course Map title. The others are button symbols to which we attach some code that gets executed when the learner clicks that button. Here is the code for the link that points to Step 7:

```
on (release) {
    goToTopic("step7");
}
```

As you can see, when they click the link, we simply call the **goToTopic** function that is located on the Scripts layer and pass the label of the frame we want the playback head to move to. Because the **goToTopic** function is located in the first frame, it is placed in memory when the course map is opened. Therefore, it is available to execute whenever the learner clicks a topic.

### The Background Layer

The Background layer contains a simple colored rectangle. When this movie is loaded into the Course Map movie clip container, the text has an opaque background that sets it apart from the content in the presentation Stage.

While this is a very simple course map, hopefully you can see the potential for having more lessons and more subtopics.

**Note:** Again, as with the other content in this chapter, we've created the Course Map as an external SWF file. That way we can modify it as needed without running the risk of disturbing our architecture. A modular approach to content pieces and other elements like this can also help when you have multiple developers working on the same course. One developer can be modifying the course map, another can be modifying a content piece, and they can be published independently, yet appear seamlessly connected to the learner.

## Step 2: Adding Navigation to Access the Course Map

**On CD:** Open and explore the file titled **sample_flash_arch_wCourseMap.fla**.

We've added an empty movie clip container called *courseMapClip* into which we load the external Course Map SWF.

This empty movie clip symbol indicates the top-left position where the course map movie is going to appear. Remember to give the movie clip an instance name. In this case we named it *courseMapClip*.

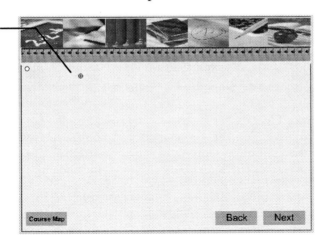

We placed this movie container in a separate layer on top of all other layers so that when the container loads the movie, it appears on top of all other content.

The CourseMap layer is at the top, so it will appear above other content.

We have also added a **Course Map** button.

This code, attached to the **Course Map** button, causes the course map movie to load in the movie clip container:

```
on (press) {
    loadMovie("sample_files/coursemap/coursemap.swf","courseMapClip");
}
```

Remember, in order for this target path to work in your own movie you must copy this folder and file to the location of your course.

In summary, when the learner clicks the Course Map button, the code attached to that button loads the *coursemap.swf* movie into the *courseMapClip* instance of the *courseMapObj* movie clip symbol.

The learner then clicks one of the buttons in that movie clip which sends the frame label name to a function that causes the playback head to move to the frame with that label. The function also hides the *coursemap.swf* movie by loading a blank movie.

## Hiding the Next and Back Buttons

To make the sequential navigation more user-friendly, you may want to hide the Next button on the last page of a topic sequence. Likewise, you may want to hide the Back button on the first page of a topic sequence.

**On CD:** Open and explore the file titled *samples/chapter17/sample_flash_arch_disableNextBack.swf*. When you are finished exploring the finished sample, open the associated FLA file.

In this sample file, we hide the **Next** button on the last frame by adding some code to the Scripts layer for that frame:

```
nextButton._visible = false;
```

This does the job of hiding the button every time the playback head reaches that frame. However, if the learner clicks the **Back** button, the **Next** button is still hidden. So, we need to add some code to the **Back** button to make sure that whenever the learner clicks it, Flash displays the **Next** button:

```
nextButton._visible = true;
```

**Tip:** You might be asking yourself, why don't we just add this code to the next-to-the-last frame? This will work, of course, assuming you know the next-to-the-last frame is always going to be the next-to-the-last frame. In other words, you might want to insert a frame at some point down the road for some additional content. If you do, you might forget to add this line of code to that new frame. By adding it to the Back button, you are making sure that no matter how many frames of content you add before the last frame, Flash will always display the Next button when the learner navigates from the last frame. This is a simple example, but it is always a good idea to be thinking of maintenance during architectural design.

We take a similar approach to the hiding the **Back** button. We place some code on the first frame—to hide the **Back** button. Then we add some code to the **Next** button to show the **Back** button on any subsequent frame.

While this method works, since the learner can use the Course Map as an optional way to navigate to any frame in the sequence, they could feasibly jump to the last page (which would hide the **Next** button) and then jump directly to the first page (which would hide the **Back** button) and be stuck with no **Next** or **Back** buttons at all. To accommodate that possibility, let's take a look at another example.

**On CD:** Open and explore
**samples/chapters17/sample_flash_arch_disableNextBack_onEnterFrame.swf.** You can see that regardless of how you get to the last frame or the first frame the correct buttons appear or hide. When you are ready, take a look at the associated FLA file.

In this example, we show and hide the **Next** and **Back** buttons using one piece of code in just one location. We like this approach the best because not only does it handle the various ways a learner might navigate to a particular frame, but it's also easy to maintain because all of the code is in one place.

You can find the code on the Background layer:

```
this.onEnterFrame = function() {
    if (_currentframe == _totalframes) {
        nextButton._visible = false;
    } else {
        nextButton._visible = true;
    }
    if (_currentframe == 1) {
        backButton._visible = false;
    } else {
        backButton._visible = true;
    }
    //trace(_currentframe);
}
```

To hide the **Next** button, we determine if the current frame of the playback head is also the last frame. There are two properties of movie clips that come in handy:

**_currentframe** and **_totalframes**. Each of these properties return a number, so our code essentially asks the question, "Is the current frame number the same as the total number of frames?" If so, then we have reached the last frame.

To hide the **Back** button we determine if the current frame is also frame 1, which means we are at the beginning of the topic sequence.

Let's briefly discuss the **onEnterFrame** method of the MovieClip object used in this script. The name is somewhat misleading. The term "frame" does not refer to the frame the playback head is on, but rather the frame rate of the movie. If the movie's frames per second (FPS) is set at 12, then this code will execute 12 times per second once it starts. Since we've placed it on frame 1 of the timeline, it starts as soon as that frame loads and will continue to execute throughout the length of the movie, regardless of where the playback head is currently located. You can see this demonstrated if you remove the comment marks before the trace command in the next-to-the-last line.

Tip: Think of code associated with the **onEnterFrame** method as a continuously repeating script running in the background (which is why we put it on the Background layer). This can be powerful because you can use it to check the states of different objects in your movie at any time during the movie and take appropriate action. And because it runs continuously once it is started, you only need to start it once.

Tip: Though it is not helpful in this example, if you ever need to stop code started by **onEnterFrame**, you can use this line of code: **this.onEnterFrame = null;**

Note: Remember to give the Next and Back button instance names. In this case we've given them names of nextButton and backButton.

That's it! Adding touches like this to your architecture can go a long ways to making the user feel comfortable with your course.

# Adding a Visual Progress Meter

Many learners appreciate a visual indicator of how far they have progressed within the course or lesson. In this section we'll look at how to add a progress meter that includes a horizontal rectangle that grows in length as the learner progresses through the topic sequence.

Visual Progress Meter

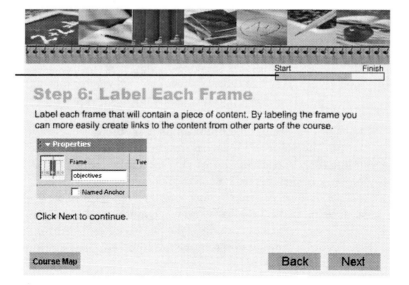

On CD: Open and explore **samples/chapter17/sample_flash_arch_progMeter.swf**. Once you are ready to look at the source file, open its associated FLA file.

To create this progress meter we first added three items to the Background layer: the text *Start*, the text *Finish*, and a transparent rectangle with black borders.

Next, we added a layer called ProgMeter and placed it beneath the Background layer.

On the first frame, the ProgMeter layer contains a short solid orange rectangle with without any borders. We duplicated the rectangle in the last frame and then made it longer and added a shape tween so that in playback mode, the rectangle grows with every frame advance the learner makes. Placing the ProgMeter layer beneath the Backgrounds layer causes the appearance that the expanding rectangle is filling the transparent rectangle.

Note: You could also create a progress meter by creating a movie clip symbol with a small rectangle in it and modifying the **_xscale** property using ActionScript. (This is similar to the rectangles used in many preloaders).

## Adding a Pop-up Glossary

Adding a pop-up glossary to this architecture follows many of the same steps we describe in the section titled *Using a Course Map to Add Non-Sequential Navigation*.

To add any kind of pop-up content in this architecture, first create the content as a separate SWF or movie clip. We recommend separate SWF files because of the ease of modular maintenance. Then simply create an empty movie clip container and add a button to the background that loads that external movie SWF file into the movie clip container.

To do this for a glossary, create the glossary as an external SWF. Then create a movie container into which your glossary button loads that external SWF. Remember to add code to hide the glossary when the learner "closes" the glossary. See the section on adding a Course Map for more details.

# Summary

In this chapter you have learned how to create a custom Flash-based architecture that uses a pseudo-scene approach in which each frame of the main timeline represents a "scene" or "topic". You create the actual content for the course as modular external SWF files.

You also learned some basic enhancements to this architectural approach. You learned how to add non-sequential navigation by creating a Course Map that pops-up over the content. You learned how to show and hide the **Next** and **Back** buttons at the appropriate locations in the sequence. You learned how to add a visual progress meter. And finally, we had a brief discussion about how to add a pop-up glossary.

# Advanced Architecture Using XML 18

In the previous chapter you learned how to make a more flexible architecture using one movie clip as a container or a "shell" for other movie clips. You can use XML to take that architecture one step further, separating some of the structural framework of the course from the content. If done well, you can reuse this structure for many courses even if the course has a different look to the interface. While there are many ways to store external data, we will focus on using XML as the storage mechanism in this chapter.

This chapter is intended for more advanced users of Flash who want to learn some techniques that can make their course design more powerful and flexible. It assumes a high-degree of proficiency with ActionScript.

In this chapter you will learn:

- About the benefits of building course objects dynamically.
- About the types of data storage methods that you could use when building course objects dynamically.
- How to use XML to create a framework that you can use to build courses dynamically.

# Static vs. Dynamic Courses

Up until this point, much of your content was built in a *static* fashion—meaning that you provided the specifics about the object, such as the text or graphic to display, in Flash. In this chapter, you will learn how to create e-learning elements *dynamically* (as the application runs). This enables you to make changes without needing to touch the FLA file.

You can build objects based upon user input, or in this case, you will build objects based upon data that you store externally from Flash. While there are many ways to store external data, we will focus on using XML as the storage mechanism in this chapter.

# Creating a Flexible Course Architecture

Even if you have content that you feel is reasonably stable, there will be times that you want to modify it. For example, you might want to:

- Modify the Table of Contents to reflect changes in the course—such as the addition, deletion, or modification of pages.
- Build quizzes based upon questions stored externally to Flash. This enables you to develop a bank of questions and pull in a subset of those questions into Flash to generate a quiz.
- Build course pages, which are tailored to the needs of a specific audience. By building course pages dynamically, you can change the content of the course to meet the needs of a given learner. For example, you can store a user profile, which determines the type of content that will display.
- Build courses which can be easily localized (i.e different languages). Store the content for each language that you plan to make available in a separate file. When the learner selects a language, pull in the content that corresponds to that language.

## Storing Information Externally

In order to get this type of flexibility, you will need to store information about the pages (such as titles, text, and navigation) externally from Flash. The basic process is described here:

**1** You can store the information in a text file, an XML file, or a database.

**2** When the course begins, your Flash application will load the external data and build objects based upon that data.

**3** The assembled Flash course is then presented to the learner.

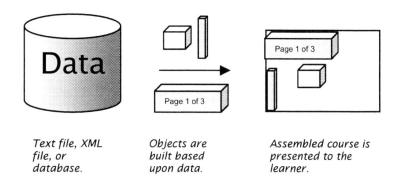

Text file, XML file, or database.

Objects are built based upon data.

Assembled course is presented to the learner.

## Using Stored Data to Create Flash Objects

If you think about it, the objects of a course are really made up of pieces of data. These pieces of data are generally specified in the Properties Inspector. For example, a Table of Contents is merely a movie clip that contains several buttons. Each button contains some text and a link to a specified page.

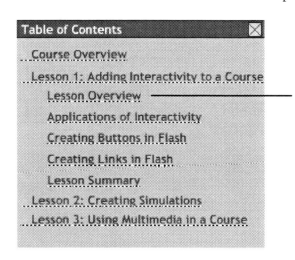

In this button, the *text* property is *Lesson Overview*. There is a link associated with the text that navigates to the Lesson Overview page.

There are many ways to store data externally from Flash. This table describes some of your options:

| Storage Method | Description |
| --- | --- |
| Text file | A simple, but limited method. It does not require specialized knowledge of databases or XML, but it is not as flexible and is less secure than other storage methods. Use text files if you have small amounts of information, and a structure that is unlikely to change. |
| Database | A powerful, secure storage method. It requires that you own and know how to use a Database Management System (DBMS) such as SQL Server or Oracle. |
| XML file | XML (eXtensible Markup Language) uses tags, similar to HTML. However, XML describes the structure of the data, rather than the structure of the page. XML has become a standard method for importing and exporting data from different applications.<br><br>The main benefit of XML is that Flash can read it—without knowing the exact structure of the data beforehand—and then create objects that will enable you to manipulate the data. You can also export data from XML and Flash to an external application. |
| Flash Remoting MX | A product that provides a channel to communicate between Flash movies and remote services across multiple platforms and devices. This means that you can communicate with application server technologies like JavaBeans, ColdFusion (components or pages), ASP.NET pages, or web services. This lets you build sophisticated e-learning courses that include features such as message boards.<br><br>Flash Remoting MX is sold separately from Flash. For more information about Flash Remoting MX, go to www.macromedia.com. |

In this chapter, we will focus on using data that is stored in an XML file to dynamically generate objects in Flash.

# XML Examples

Before we create objects based on the contents of an XML file, let's take a brief look at some of the things that you can do with XML in an e-learning course. In this section we will show you some simple XML examples to give you a feel for the kinds of information you can store externally from a Flash movie.

 **More Information:** This section is not intended to be a tutorial on XML, rather it will provide you with some ideas for how you can apply XML in an e-learning course. To find out more about using XML refer to one of many popular books available on the subject.

## Example 1: Specifying the Elements in a Table of Contents

This example shows a way that you could specify Table of Contents entries in an XML file. For each topic, **text** refers to the text that will display on the Table of Contents, while **page** refers to the name of the corresponding HTML page that is linked to that topic.

```
<toc_lesson_elements>
    <topic text="Lesson Overview" page="L01P01.html"/>
    <topic text="Applications of Interactivity" page="L01P02.html"/>
    <topic text="Creating Buttons in Flash" page="L01P03.html"/>
</toc_lesson_elements>
```

## Example 2: Specifying Page Elements

This example shows some options for specifying page content such as the text, navigation buttons, graphics, and audio in an XML file. For each element (also known as a node) we specify additional attributes, such as the size or location, for the object that will be generated.

```
<page_elements>
    //information about the page title text
    <title text="Overview" font="_sans" size="14" align="center" />
    //information about the navigation buttons
    <navigation button="Next" x="10" y="50" page="L01P03.html" />
    <navigation button="Previous" x="20" y="50" page="L01P01.html" />
    //files that will be used for the content
    <content graphic="screenshot.jpg" />
    <content audio="endmusic.mp3" />
</page_elements>
```

This example takes Example 2 one step further. The term **type** in this example refers to a previously created SWF file that you can tailor to specific situations (using it like a template). If you create SWF templates for the different types of pages in the course, such as an overview page or a quiz page, you would then be able to use XML to provide the specific details for a given page.

```
<page_elements>
    <page type="overview.swf" />
    <title text="Overview" font="_sans" size="14" align="center" />
    <navigation button="btnNext" x="10" y="50" page="L01P03.html" />
    <navigation button="btnPrev" x="20" y="50" page="L01P01.html" />
    <content graphic="screenshot.jpg" />
    <content audio="endmusic.mp3"/>
</page_elements>
```

**Tip:** You can use this same technique to tailor the look and feel of a course to specific audiences. For example, you can specify different background graphics and buttons for different audiences by creating SWF files tailored meet those needs.

## Example 3: Quiz Questions

You can also use XML to provide a modular way of creating quiz questions. In the XML file you would specify the question type, question stem, distractors, correct answer choice, and feedback.

```
<question>
    <tracking ID="Interaction_01" />
    <content type="Multiple Choice" />
    <content stem="How many drag objects you use in quiz question?" />
    <content choice1="1" />
    <content choice2="8" />
    <content choice3="20" />
    <content choice4="64" />
    <learner answer="choice2" />
    <feedback correct="You're right!" />
    <feedback incorrect="Sorry. That's incorrect." />
</question>
```

**Tip:** You can store XML data in a file or a database. If you want to create large volumes of quiz questions, you may want to consider putting the XML data in a database.

### Example 4: Specifying Learner Information

You can store information about specific learner preferences in XML and use that information to tailor the course to better meet the learner's needs. For example, this XML file contains information about the audience and the language. We can extract that information and adjust the course accordingly.

```
<profile>
   <user firstname="Janet" />
   <user lastname="Lee" />
   <user audience="admin" />
   <preference language="spanish" />
</profile>
```

# Basic Steps to Creating an XML-based Course Architecture

The possible applications of Flash and XML are virtually limitless, so let's narrow down our wish list for the purposes of this chapter. Let's suppose we want the architecture to:

- Dynamically load external Flash movies to provide the content for each page.
- Load the page title into a dynamic field.
- Load the page instructions into a dynamic field.
- Display a progress counter that displays the current page number and the total number of pages (i.e. 4 of 9).
- Dynamically create a Table of Contents.

Once we create an architecture that works, we can create all of the content outside of the course structure.

To create this kind of architecture we are going to follow these high-level steps:

**1** Manually create the basic user interface, including background elements, Next and Back buttons, and a Table of Contents button.

It is even possible to create these elements dynamically, but there are a couple of reasons we are not going to incorporate them at this time. First, you want to get the most bang for your buck. In other words, you only have to create these elements once, so why not do them manually? The content pages are what you would normally have to spend time creating and modifying. Second, we want to make this chapter more approachable. The simpler we keep it, the more understandable the concepts will be.

**2**   Load the XML data into Flash so we can work with it.

**3**   Create the sequential Next/Back navigation system using the XML data.

**4**   Create the Table of Contents using the XML data.

Seems simple enough, doesn't it? Well, in concept it is. However, getting it to actually work can be a bit tricky, so be sure to work through the hands-on exercises so you get a good grounding before trying something on your own.

## Manually Creating the User Interface

We aren't going to spend much time explaining how to create the user interface in this chapter since most of the UI is up to you. However, in order for it to work with the concepts we discuss in this chapter you should have, at a minimum, the following elements on the Stage:

- Next button
- Back button
- Table of Contents button
- An empty movie clip into which instructional content will be loaded. Give this movie clip an instance name of *Presentation*. (This can of course be called anything you want as long as you reference it properly in the code.)
- An empty movie clip into which the Table of Contents will be loaded. Assign this an instance name of *courseMapClip*.
- A dynamic field in which the content page title will be placed with a variable name of *contentTitleText*. You assign variable to a Dynamic Text field using the Properties Inspector.
- Two dynamic fields linked to the variables *currentPage* and *totalPages*
- A dynamic field linked to the variable *contentInstructionText*

## Getting XML Data into Flash

Once you have an XML document, you can load it into Flash and store the data in a Flash object. Generally you do this in the first keyframe of the movie. There are three steps you need to take to get XML data into Flash:

**1**   Create an XML object that will store the loaded data.

**2**   Define a function that will process the data once it has been loaded.

**3**   Load the data and call the function.

Note: In this chapter we decided to focus on using ActionScript to communicate with XML. You can use the ActionScript method in MX, and MX 2004. Flash MX Professional comes with an XMLConnector component, which reduces the amount of coding that you need to do. In some cases you may find the component easier to use than coding it yourself, or you may find that coding is just as easy. Either way, to learn more about the component, go to: http://www.macromedia.com/devnet/mx/flash/articles/xmlconnector.html

## Creating and Loading the XML Object

Before you can manipulate the XML data within Flash, you need to create a container in which the XML data can reside. You do this by creating a special object called, not surprisingly, an XML object.

To create an XML object, add this line of script on the main timeline:

myXML = new XML();

This code creates an empty container into which you then load the XML data. To load the data into the object, call the XML object's **load** method (command):

myXML.load("[path to filename].xml");

## Processing the Information

Once you have loaded the XML object, you are ready to do something with all of the information you imported. The **onLoad()** event handler lets us know when it is safe to start processing the data loaded using the **load()** method. To start processing the data, respond to the **onLoad** event handler by assigning a function like this:

MyXML.onLoad() = myFunctionName;

Of course you need to create the function that will process the data. You'll learn more during the hands-on exercises later in this chapter about how to work with the data.

Here is the beginning of some sample code that could be used to create a Table of Contents based on an XML file.

```
// create an XML object to store the Table of Contents elements
tocElements = new XML();

// set ignore white space to true, which tells flash to ignore the
// carriage returns white space in the XML file
tocElements.ignoreWhiteSpace = true;

//run the processTOC function once the elements are loaded
tocElements.onLoad = processTOC;

// load the XML document toc.xml into the XML object
tocElements.load("toc.xml");

// list the elements in the trace window
trace("tocElements contains" tocElements);
```

Notice that the onLoad event handler calls the *processTOC* function. This function loads the content of the XML document into an array. An array is a powerful kind of variable that allows you to store multiple pieces of data in an organized fashion. (You may want to refer to a book on ActionScript for more information on working with arrays.)

In this code example, the function first determines whether the data loading has been "successful." If successful it loads the array, if not it displays an error message.

```
function processTOC(success) {
  if (success) {
    //load array
    pageElements = this.firstChild.childNodes;
    totalPageElements = pageElements.length;
    }
  else {
      trace("Error 01: Error loading XML data");
    }
}
```

**Note:** You may have noticed that the **processTOC( )** function has a parameter called *success*. This parameter is automatically passed by the onLoad event handler and has a value of either true if the XML object loaded data successfully or false if it did not.

# Creating the Sequential Next/Back Navigation System

In this chapter we are going to assume that we are building an architecture that is similar to the one we built in Chapter 17: *Creating a Custom Flash-based Architecture*, but with some differences. In that chapter we created a shell into which we loaded external SWF movies for the content. This architecture does the same, except that instead of using code on every frame to tell Flash which movies to load, the XML file contains the paths to the external movies.

To create the Next/Back navigation, we need to create a function that knows what the current content movie is so that when the Next or Back button is clicked, it can go look at the XML data and find the previous or next movie to load into the presentation area.

You will learn more about this as you work through the hands-on exercises later in this chapter.

# Creating the Dynamic Table of Contents

Your Table of Contents can look and work however you like. Just remember these basic steps:

**1**   Create a separate Flash FLA file so you can use this object with any course you create.

**2**   In the FLA file, create a movie clip that will serve as the template for each Table of Contents entry. This movie clip will be duplicated each time a entry needs to be created. When the user clicks this movie clip, the correct external content movie will be loaded into the Presentation movie clip on the Stage and the Table of Contents will close.

**3**   Create an ActionScript function that reads the XML data. Every time a new entry needs to be created it duplicates the movie clip template you created in step one, loads the correct text label into it, and repositions it below the previous entry.

**4**   Publish this as an SWF file.

**5**   In the main course architecture FLA file, add code to the **Course Map** button to load the Table of Contents SWF movie into the CourseMapClip movie clip.

You will learn more about each of these steps as you work through the hands-on exercises later in this chapter.

# Creating Your First XML-based Course Architecture

In this section you will create a custom XML-based course architecture.

## Viewing the Finished Exercise

Before you begin, take a moment to view the completed exercise on the CD-ROM.

**On CD**: Explore an XML-based architecture by opening **samples/Chapter18/xml_arch_pageloader.fla** on the CD-ROM. Also look at **architecture2.xml** on the CD-ROM. You may also want to open the **xml_arch_pageloader.swf** experiment with it.

**Tip**: While you can read an XML file by looking at the tags, you may also want to take a look at the XML file with an XML editor that is more visual, such as Microsoft XML Notepad. You can download this free application at **http://www.webattack.com/get/xmlnotepad.shtml**.

When viewing the source file, here are some things to look for:

- What objects have instance names?
- Are the fields in the layout static or Dynamic Text fields?
- Where is the ActionScript stored?
- In the XML file, what is the hierarchy of elements?
- In the XML file, what attribute points to the content movie?

## Creating the Architecture

In this exercise you'll create an XML-based architecture that loads external SWF content movies into a presentation area. The movies will be loaded when the learner clicks the Next or Back buttons, creating a sequential navigation experience.

**To create a custom XML-based architecture, follow these steps:**

**1** Open *samples/Chapter18/xml_arch_pageloader_start.fla*.

We've created the user interface elements for you, but you still need to set up those interface elements to be "code ready". This means giving instance names to some objects and linking Dynamic Text fields to variables that we can reference when we add the ActionScript code.

**2** Select the **Next** button and give it an instance name of *next_btn*.

Because ActionScript is case sensitive, make sure to type instance names exactly as they appear in this book—in this example it's lower case.

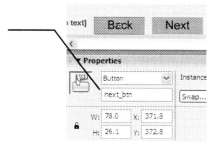

**3** Select the **Back** button and give it an instance name of *back_btn*.

Now that we have our buttons set up, we need to set up the text fields. To be able to populate the text fields with information from the XML file, we need to first make the fields Dynamic Text fields (as opposed to Static Text fields) and then associate a variable with the text field that we can reference using ActionScript.

**4** Select the title field near the top of the user interface and select the **Dynamic Text** option from the Field Type dropdown list.

To link a text field to a variable, first make it a Dynamic Text field.

Type the variable name here.

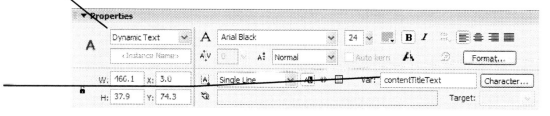

**5** Now link the field to a variable by entering *contentTitleText* in the Var textbox.

Note: We don't need to give fields that are linked to a variable an instance name because Flash automatically creates a reference to the text of the field when we enter a variable name. We could have coded this sample exercise to use the text property of the dynamic text field instead of the variables. This example shows you another approach.

**6**  Select the instruction text field near the bottom of the user interface. Make it a Dynamic Text field, and associate it with a variable named *contentInstructionText*.

**7**  Select the leftmost text field in the 0 of 0 group. Make it a Dynamic Text field, and associate it with a variable named *currentPage*.

Associate this field with the variable *currentPage*.

Associate this field with the variable *totalPages*.

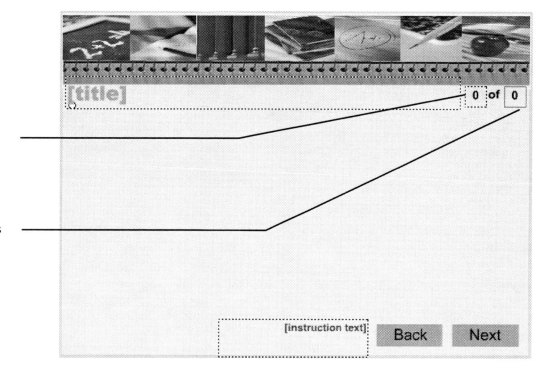

**8**  Select the rightmost text field in the 0 of 0 group. Make it a Dynamic Text field, and associate it with a variable named *totalPages*.

The last element we need to finish setting up is the empty movie clip into which we are going to load the external content SWF files. We have to name the instance of the movie clip in order to reference it using ActionScript.

**9** Select the empty movie clip just under the title text field and give it an instance name of *presentation*.

Select this movie clip and give it an instance name of *presentation*.

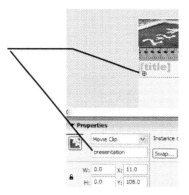

With the user interface elements ready to go, we're all set to add the code that communicates with the XML file.

**10** Select the first frame of the Scripts layer and open the Actions panel.

We first need to create the XML object and load the XML data into that object.

**11** Add this code to the *scripts* layer:

```
myXML = new XML();
myXML.load("architecture2.xml")
myXML.onLoad = startCourse;
myXML.ignoreWhite = true;
```

**Note:** Instead of typing this code, you may want to copy the existing code from the **samples/chapter18/xml_arch_pageloader.fla** file and paste it into the file you are working with. This would help eliminate typing errors.

Let's take a look at each line of code that you just inserted:

| Code | Explanation |
|------|-------------|
| **myXML = new XML();** | Creates a new XML object in Flash. As we explained earlier, this is a special object set up to hold XML data. In this example, the object is called **myXML**. Once the data is in this object you can |

| Code | Explanation |
|------|-------------|
|  | load all or parts of it into variables that you can then use to populate fields or load content. |
| **myXML.load("architecture2.xml")** | Use the **load( )** method of the XML object to point to the external XML file. Remember that if the XML file is not in the same directory as the Flash file, you need to create a relative link to the file (for example, **xml_content/architecture2.xml**). |
| **myXML.onLoad = startCourse;** | This line is an event handler that tells Flash what ActionScript function to execute once the XML file loads. Because this is not a normal function call, you do not need to add parentheses after the function name. This event handler automatically passes a *true* or *false* to the function, indicating whether the XML file loaded successfully. |
| **myXML.ignoreWhite = true;** | The **ignoreWhite** property of the XML object tells Flash to ignore any white space between XML tags. It is almost always a good idea to set this to *true*. |

At this point it is probably a good idea to test the code to make sure the XML file is loading correctly.

**12** Test your Flash movie (Control → Test Movie).

**13** In test mode, display the variable values (Debug → List Variables).

Flash displays the Output window:

If the XML file loaded correctly, you will see a reproduction of your XML file listed here as the value of the variable **_level0.myXML**.

```
▼ Output
Level #0:
Variable _level0.$version = "WIN 7,0,14,0"
Variable _level0.currentPage = "0"
Variable _level0.totalPages = "0"
Variable _level0.contentTitleText = "[title]"
Variable _level0.contentInstructionText = "[instruction text]"
Variable _level0.myXML = [object #1] {

    <architecture>
        <pages>
            <page tocEntry="true" tocDefinition="Find out what you&apos;re going to learn in this mini-lesson"
filename="content/objectives.swf" title="Learning Objectives" instructions="" />
            <page tocEntry="true" tocDefinition="Learn how the user interface is separated from the content."
filename="content/step1.swf" title="Step 1: Create the User Interface" instructions="" />
            <page tocEntry="true" tocDefinition="Learn how to load the external XML file into the Flash XML
object." filename="content/step2.swf" title="Step 2: Loading the XML File" instructions="" />
            <page tocEntry="false" tocDefinition="" filename="content/step2a.swf" title="Step 2: Loading the XML
File" instructions="" />
            <page tocEntry="false" tocDefinition="" filename="content/step2b.swf" title="Step 2: Loading the XML
File" instructions="" />
            <page tocEntry="true" tocDefinition="Learn how to create a sequential navigation system based on the
sequence of pages in the XML file" filename="content/step3.swf" title="Step 3: Next/Back Navigation"
instructions="" />
            <page tocEntry="true" tocDefinition="Learn how to create the Table of Contents based on the sequence
of pages in the XML file" filename="content/step4.swf" title="Step 4: Creating the TOC" instructions="" />
            <page tocEntry="true" tocDefinition="Quiz yourself on what you&apos;ve learned" filename=
"content/quiz_question.swf" title="Quiz" instructions="Choose the correct answer and click Check Answer." />
        </pages>
    </architecture>
}
Button: Target="_level0.btn_next"
Variable _level0.btn_next.tabIndex = [getter/setter] undefined
Button: Target="_level0.btn_back"
Variable _level0.btn_back.tabIndex = [getter/setter] undefined
Edit Text: Target="_level0.instance1"
    variable = "currentPage",
    text = "0",
    htmlText = "0",
    html = false, textWidth = 14, textHeight = 18, maxChars = null,
    borderColor = 0x000000, backgroundColor = 0xFFFFFF, textColor = 0x000000, border = false,
```

Now that we've loaded the XML data into the XML object, we are ready to work with that data. In other words, we need to create the **startCourse( )** function that we referenced in the **myXML.onLoad = startCourse** line.

**14** Add the following code to the Scripts layer:

```
function startCourse(loadOK) {
    if (loadOK == true) {
        rootNode = myXML.firstChild;
        pagesNode = rootNode.firstChild;
        totalPages = pagesNode.childNodes.length;
        currentPage = 1;
        firstPageNode = pagesNode.firstChild;
        currentPageNode = firstPageNode;
        loadCurrentPage(firstPageNode);
    }
}
```

By populating variables that we have already associated with Dynamic Text fields Flash autmatically displays this text in those fields. In this example **totalPages** and **currentPage** make up the page counter.

This function checks to see if the XML file was loaded successfully. If it was, it assigns different parts of the XML data to corresponding variables. Each XML data hierarchy can be divided into sub-elements (called *children*). You can refer to the first sub-element or tag within any given element by using the **firstChild** property.

The whole <architecture> tag is placed in the variable **rootNode**

The <pages> tag is placed in the variable **pagesNode**

The first <page> tag is placed in the variable **firstPageNode**

```
<architecture>
  <pages>
    <page tocEntry="true" tocDefinition="Find out what you're going to learn in th
    <page tocEntry="true" tocDefinition="Learn how the user interface is separated
    <page tocEntry="true" tocDefinition="Learn how to load the external XML file :
    <page tocEntry="false" tocDefinition="" filename="content/step2a.swf" title=":
    <page tocEntry="false" tocDefinition="" filename="content/step2b.swf" title=":
    <page tocEntry="true" tocDefinition="Learn how to create a sequential navigati
    <page tocEntry="true" tocDefinition="Learn how to create the Table of Content:
    <page tocEntry="true" tocDefinition="Quiz yourself on what you've learned" fil
  </pages>
</architecture>
```

Now that we've loaded ActionScript variables with the XML data, we're ready to start using those variables to display the course content. The last line of code calls the **loadCurrentPage()** function, passing it the contents of the first page element, or *node*. The **loadCurrentPage()** function is the code that displays the course content based on the **<page>** tag in the **firstPageNode** variable.

**15** Add this code to the Scripts layer:

```
function loadCurrentPage(newPageNode) {
    contentMoviePath = newPageNode.attributes.filename;
    contentTitleText = newPageNode.attributes.title;
    contentInstructionText = newPageNode.attributes.instructions;
    if (contentInstructionText == "") {
        contentInstructionText = "Click Next to continue."
    }
    loadMovie(contentMoviePath,presentation);
}
```

If there aren't any page-specific instructions, use default instructions.

The **firstPageNode** variable becomes the **newPageNode** parameter passed to this function. While we have the whole node, what we really need to access is individual attributes within the node.

Each node in the XML file contains the following attributes:

- **tocEntry** – Set to *true* if this entry should be included in the Table of Contents. (See the hands-on exercise following this one for more information)
- **tocDefinition** – contains text associated with the Table of Contents entry, if applicable
- **filename** – contains the path to the external SWF file that is the content for this page
- **title** – contains the title for this page
- **instructions** – contains any page-specific instructions

The first thing we want to do is access the **filename** attribute. To access an attribute, use dot syntax to reference the **attributes** property of the element. So we references the filename attribute like this:

```
contentMoviePath = newPageNode.attributes.filename;
```

We then use the **contentMoviePath** variable in the last line of the function to load the external Flash movie into the empty movie clip *presentation*:

```
loadMovie(contentMoviePath,presentation);
```

**16** Test the movie (Control → Test Movie) and make sure that the movie content is loading for the first movie.

Beyond the text fields getting populated, you should be able to see the first content movie, *objectives.swf*, loaded into the presentation movie clip.

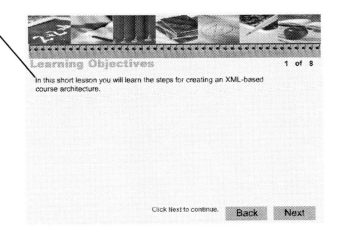

Now that we've got the pieces of the first XML page element loaded, we need to add the final functionality, getting the Next and Back buttons to load the appropriate movies and content.

**17**  Add this code to the Scripts layer:

```
next_btn.onRelease = function() {
    nextPageNode = currentPageNode.nextSibling;
    if (nextPageNode == null) {
        break;
    } else {
        currentPage++;
        loadCurrentPage(nextPageNode);
        currentPageNode = nextPageNode;
    }
};

back_btn.onRelease = function() {
    nextPageNode = currentPageNode.previousSibling;
    if (nextPageNode == null) {
        break;
    } else {
        currentPage--;
        loadCurrentPage(nextPageNode);
        currentPageNode = nextPageNode;
    }
};
```

Remember when we gave the **Next** and **Back** buttons instance names? Here is where naming instances comes in handy. We could have added **on (release)** functions to each button, but instead we've added them here in the Scripts layer by using the following syntax:

```
[instance name].[event name] = function() {
    [function code]
}
```

Placing the code in the same area as the rest of the code prevents the need to go digging around through different objects to find the relevant code. It's not necessarily a better way of doing it, but it does offer the advantage of the code being stored in a single location.

In the code you added, we introduce another XML object property: **nextSibling**. The **nextSibling** property refers to the next XML node on the same hierarchical level. In this case we use the **nextSibling** property to load the content of the next or previous **<page>** node into the variable **nextPageNode**.

Once we have that variable loaded we check to see if it is empty. If it is we don't do anything (i.e. break). That will only happen at either the beginning or end of the page nodes. If there is some data there, we increment the page counter and send the data to be loaded into the presentation area.

**18** Test your Flash movie (Control → Test Movie).

The movie is now complete and you should see different content loaded in every time you click **Next** and **Back**. This content should correspond with the different **<page>** elements in the XML file.

## Adding Content to this Architecture

Before moving onto the next section, you may want to create your own external SWF file(s) to see if you can get them working with this current architecture. If you've set up everything correctly, you should be able to add an other **<page>** node to the XML file that points to your new SWF file(s). Re-open the published SWF file of the architecture and the SWF should display at the appropriate place in the navigational sequence.

# Enhancements to the Basic XML–based Architecture

So far in this chapter you've learned to create a linear navigation system based on an external XML file. However, how do you give the learner an opportunity to jump from one topic in the course to another topic without having to click Next or Back over and over? In this section you'll learn how to add:

▪ A Course Map that will allow learners to move non-sequentially through the content.

## Creating a Course Map Based on an XML File

There are many different ways you can create menu systems for e-learning courses. At the very least you should allow the learner to jump from the current topic to another topic in the course or lesson. You can accomplish this with a simple course map.

Course maps can range from one-level to multi-level menu systems. In this section you will learn how to create a one-level course map that is based on the same XML file you used in earlier exercises in this chapter. By keeping it simple we hope that you will become familiar with the techniques and concepts used to create the course map and be able to apply those skills to creating your own system, whether it be simple or complex.

**On CD**: Before getting into the details, open and explore the **samples/chapter18/xml_arch_pageloader_wCourseMap.fla** file. Publish it and see how it works.

First lets review the high-level steps needed to create a Course Map based on an XML file:

**1**    Create a separate Flash FLA file so you can use this object with any course you create.

**2**    In the FLA file, create a movie clip that will serve as the template for each Table of Contents entry. This movie clip will be duplicated each time an entry needs to be created. When the user clicks this movie clip, the correct external content movie will be loaded into the Presentation movie clip on the Stage and the Table of Contents will close.

**3**    Create an ActionScript function that reads the XML data and every time a new entry needs to be created it duplicates the movie clip template you created in step one, loads the correct text label into it, and repositions it below the previous entry.

**4**    Publish this as a SWF file (File → Publish).

**5**    In the main course architecture FLA file, add code to the **Course Map** button to load the Table of Contents SWF movie into the *CourseMapClip* movie clip Stage.

## Step 1: Create a Separate FLA File

Course maps can be designed to incorporate any number of different elements. For the purposes of this book we've created a course map that displays page titles. When the learner places the mouse over the page title a description of the page title appears to the right. When the learner clicks the page title the appropriate external content, based on the XML file, is loaded into the course presentation area.

**On CD**: Open and explore the file titled **samples/chapter18/toc.fla**.

In this file we have three layers: MainEntry, Scripts, and Background.

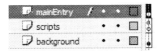

### The MainEntry Layer

The MainEntry layer contains all user interface elements of the course map except the background elements. It contains the movie clip that you use as a template to create each course map entry. We've given the movie clip an instance name of *mainEntryMC*.

This movie clip gets duplicated for each page entry in the XML file that indicates it should be in the course map.

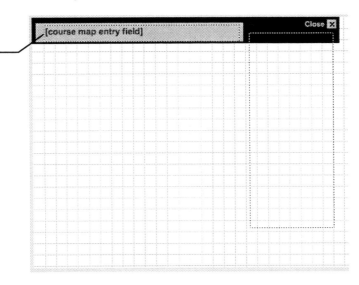

If you edit the movie clip you'll find that it contains a Dynamic Text field associated with the variable *mainTOCtext*. This is the variable that changes based on the title in the XML file:

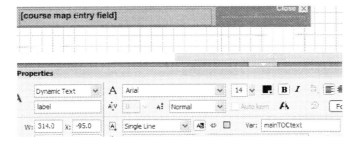

The main movie also contains two other movie clips. The course map entry description is displayed in the *tocDefArea* movie clip when a learner places the mouse over the course map entry. Inside this movie clip there is a Dynamic Text field that is associated with the *tocDefText* variable.

Finally, when the learner clicks the movie clip that acts as a **Close** button, the course map hides.

The *tocDefArea* movie clip

This movie clips acts as a **Close** button, hiding the course map when clicked.

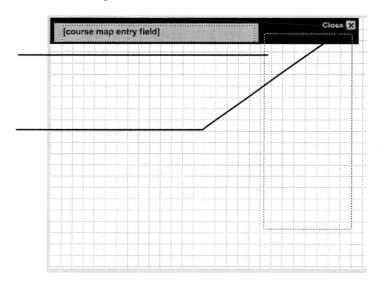

### The Scripts Layer
The Scripts layer contains code with three main sections:

- XML object initialization
- XML variable loading
- Course Map entry duplication

We'll explain some overarching concepts in step 3, but see the inline comments in the code itself for a more detailed explanation of how it works.

### The Background Layer
The Background layer contains a movie clip with a black rectangle. This movie clip gets resized to the combined height of the course map entries. This provides a good background for all the course map entries.

## Step 2: Create a Movie Clip Template to be Duplicated as Course Map Entries

This step is easier than it sounds. Simply create a movie clip symbol, place a Dynamic Text field inside the movie clip that is linked to a variable. That's about it.

You may also want to add visual elements to it, such as a color background (in this case green).

Finally, add any code to this movie clip that will make it behave how you want it to behave:

```
on (rollOver) { //causes movieclip rollover color to change and positi
    this._y = this._y-1;
    this._x = this._x+1;
    this.label.textColor = "0x000000";
    _parent.tocDefArea.tocDefText = this.tocDefinition;
}

on (rollOut) {
    this._y = this._y+1;
    this._x=this._x-1;
    this.label.textColor = "0x000099";
}

on (release) { //"choice" property set in root level function
    currentPageNode = _root.pagesNode.childNodes[this.choice-1]; //bec
    _root.currentPageNode = _root.pagesNode.childNodes[this.choice-1];
    _root.currentPage = this.choice;//change currentPage so the progre
    //trace(this.choice-1 + "/" + currentPageNode)
    _root.loadCurrentPage(currentPageNode); //calls function from root
    _parent._visible = false; //once it is clicked we want TOC to hide
}
```

In this case we have three event handlers. The first makes the movie clip change position and displays a description when the cursor hovers over it. The second moves the movie clip change back to its original location when the mouse moves off of it. The third event handler calls the function of the root movie (remember this course map movie is getting loaded into a higher-level movie) to load in the appropriate content. It also changed root level variables and hides the course map.

## Step 3: Create ActionScript Code that Reads the XML and Creates the Course Map

The ActionScript that creates the TOC is located in the Scripts layer. We give a brief overview here, but see the inline comments in the code itself for more details.

This first section loads the XML object:

```
//Copyright Rapid Intake Inc., 2004
//This code may be reused without permission
//Please leave a reference to Rapid Intake Inc. (www.rap

//load XML file
topicNum = 1;
//This variable keeps track of which topic number in the
//Some entries in the XML file may not be in the TOC, so

myXML = new XML(); //creates a new XML object into which
myXML.load("architecture2.xml"); //loads the external XM
myXML.onLoad = createTOC; //what to do once the external
myXML.ignoreWhite = true; //tells Flash to ignore any wh

function createTOC(loadOK) { //called after xml file loa
    if (loadOK == true) { //testing to see if xml file l
        loadTOCvariables(); //loads XML "node" variables
    } else {
        trace("the xml file did not load correctly"); //
    }
}
```

Notice that we are using the same XML file that we used to load the content in the hands-on exercise earlier in the chapter. You could use a separate XML file, but using the same file when possible makes maintaining the course a lot easier. The one time you might want to split up the files is if the main source file contains so much data that loading the course map takes too long.

Also note that the only thing we are doing in the initial function called after the XML object is loaded is checking to see if it loaded correctly. We could have placed this IF statement inside the **loadTOCvariables( )** function to have one less function. It's really a programming design question and would work either way.

The next section loads the XML variables and starts the loop that ends up creating the course map:

```
function loadTOCvariables() {
    rootNode = myXML.firstChild; //refers to the entire contents of th
    pagesNode = rootNode.firstChild; //loads all content in "pages" no
    currentPageNode = pagesNode.firstChild; //loads the first "page" n
    total = pagesNode.childNodes.length; //counts total "page" nodes..
    entryNum = 1;
    for (i=1; i<=total; ++i) { //loop through all "page" nodes
        isTocEntry = currentPageNode.attributes.tocEntry; //get attrib
        //trace(i + "    " + isTocEntry)
        if (isTocEntry == "true") { //some entries might not be in TOC
            //trace(topicNum);
            this["text"+topicNum] = currentPageNode.attributes.title;
            //trace(this["text" + i]);
            createTOCentry(topicNum,entryNum); //this function actuall
            entryNum++;
        }
        topicNum++; //increases topicNum for the next go around
        currentPageNode = currentPageNode.nextSibling; //nextSibling r
    }
    mainEntryMC._visible = false; //to hide the first one that we copi
}
```

The **For** loop calls the **createTOCentry( )** function each time the loop cycles through. Notice that we use the square brackets to create variables that have the loop number added to them (i.e. variables named *text1*, *text2*, *text3*, and so forth). Also, the last line of the function hides the **mainEntryMC** movie clip template since it is no longer needed.

The last section of the code establishes the movie clips.

```
function createTOCentry(topicNum,entryNum) {
        newName = "mainEntryMC"+entryNum;
        mainEntryMC.duplicateMovieClip(newName, entryNum);
        this["mainEntryMC"+entryNum]._y =
this["mainEntryMC"+(entryNum-1)]._y+this["mainEntryMC"+(entryNum-
1)]._height+2;
        this["mainEntryMC"+entryNum].choice = topicNum;
        this["mainEntryMC"+entryNum].tocDefinition =
currentPageNode.attributes.tocDefinition;
        this["mainEntryMC"+entryNum].mainTOCtext =
this["text"+topicNum];
        blackBack._height = mainEntryMC._height*(entryNum+1);
}
```

This section of the code duplicates the course map entry movie clip template, gives it a new name, positions it below the previous entry, and loads the **tocDefinition** dynamic text variable. It also puts the contents of the *n* variable created in the

**loadTOCvariables()** function into the **mainTOCtext** dynamic field variable. Finally, it resizes the black background, named *blackBack*, to be larger than the number of course map entries.

## Step 4: Publish the Course Map as a SWF File

This is the easiest step. Just publish the course map FLA file as you would any other Flash file. Just make sure you place it either at the root level or lower level of the main movie that will be calling it.

## Step 5: Add Code to the Course Map Button in the Main Movie to Load the Course Map Movie

Open the main movie file (**samples/chapter18/xml_arch_pageloader_wCourseMap.fla**), select the Course Map button and add an event handler like this:

Be sure to point to SWF file here, not the FLA. Also, make sure to point to whatever you named your file—*toc.swf* is just an example.

```
on (press) {
    loadMovie("toc.swf","courseMapClip");
}
```

Once you've complete these five steps correctly, you have a simple one-level course map, based on the external XML file:

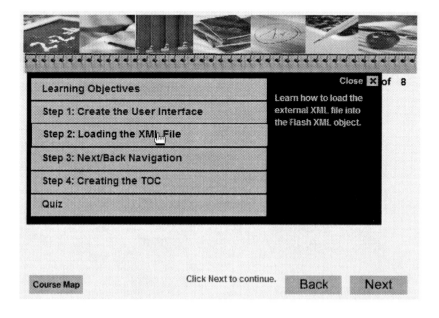

**Tip:** Now that you understand the basics, you can either create your own or leverage someone else's design by working with one of several commercially available menu systems that are XML-driven. Some are even available as free downloads on the Macromedia Flash Exchange.

# Summary

You can greatly increase the power and flexibility of your e-learning courses by storing data externally to Flash. Using this technique enables you to build course elements dynamically rather than having to account for all possibilities at design time.

While there are several ways to store external data, this chapter focused on how to use an XML file as the external storage mechanism.

# Section IV:
# Tracking Student Data

**If you need to track quiz results in an LMS, this section will show you how easy it is with the Flash Learning Interactions**

Chapter 19: Data Tracking with e-Learning
            Standards

# Data Tracking with e-Learning Standards 19

Up to this point in the book you have learned a number of different ways to include Flash in e-learning. If you decide to use Flash as the main e-learning development tool, you may be wondering how you can integrate a course with a Learning Management System (LMS) for the purpose of tracking data. Developing your course around e-learning standards will allow you to do just that.

The two main e-learning standards for course development and data tracking are the Sharable Content Object Reference Model (SCORM) and the Aviation Industry CBT Committee (AICC). In this chapter we do not attempt to completely explain these two standards. What we hope to accomplish is to make you aware of what is required and give you some basic instructions for making courses that are SCORM or AICC compliant.

In this chapter you will learn:

- How to prepare Flash learning interactions for data tracking using SCORM or AICC.
- An overview of SCORM and what it defines.
- About requirements for making a SCORM conformant course.
- How to publish a course using the SCORM template.
- How to create a SCORM content package.
- How to test a SCORM SCO or content package for conformance.
- An overview of AICC.
- How to publish a course that will track data using AICC standards.

# Preparing Interactions in the Course

Before you prepare to publish a course for SCORM or AICC, you need to make sure that any Flash interactions you have included in the course are set up to communicate with an LMS. By default the interactions will not send data to an LMS. You must activate **Knowledge Track** option for each interaction.

## Setting Up the Knowledge Track Option for Individual Interactions

As you have learned in previous chapters, you can establish learning interaction parameters that affect the way those interactions function. You do this in the Component Inspector.

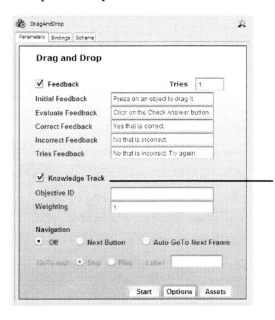

When you check the Knowledge Track option, it causes the interaction to pass data to the LMS. Some data is sent automatically, while other data (such as the Objective ID and Weighting) you can set up so it will be sent to the LMS.

When you check the Knowledge Track option, each interaction will calculate automatically and send the following data to the LMS:

- Question Type
- Correct Response
- User Response
- Result

- Date/Time
- Latency (the amount of time to complete the question)

## Setting Optional Data Tracking Parameters

The Objective ID and Weighting can be used as way to specify how the information is tracked. These parameters are important in AICC and SCORM compliant Learning Management Systems.

| Parameter | Description |
|---|---|
| Objective ID | Enter an identifier for the course objective that this interaction is developed for. |
| Weighting | Specify a value that determines the importance of a particular question. If the question posed by the interaction is twice as important as other questions, you can assign a weight of 2 while all other interactions use a weight of 1. In most cases you will probably assign the same weight for each interaction. |

The Interaction ID is another parameter that contains data that is sent to the LMS. Each interaction should have a unique Interaction ID so that you can use the reports from the LMS to determine which interactions the learner did not complete. As you learned in previous chapters, you can set this parameter on the Start tab of the Component Inspector.

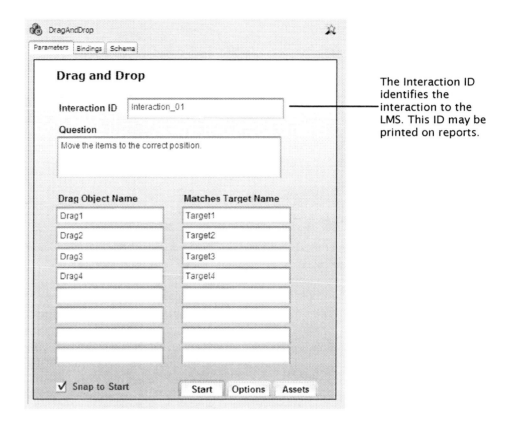

The Interaction ID identifies the interaction to the LMS. This ID may be printed on reports.

# Quiz Templates

Developing a quiz using the Quiz templates provides a little more information to track than using individual interactions without a Quiz template. Not only is the question data for stand-alone interactions sent to an LMS, but so is the total score and total time spent in the quiz.

If you developed a course with a Quiz template, there are a few additional parameters you may want to establish. These parameters include those that control the way the quiz functions, but some of these parameters may also be sent to the LMS. For example, you can enter the Activity ID and Activity Name to identify the course in the LMS.

Login File URL,
Activity ID, and
Activity Name are
parameters that the
LMS may use.

**Note:** If you are publishing to an AICC standard, you may want to enter a Login File URL. When an AICC-compliant LMS starts a quiz, it includes parameters that the HTML code looks for. These parameters have to do with login information. If no parameters are specified, the user is redirected to the URL specified in the Login File URL field. If this field is blank, the redirect does not occur.

In this section you have learned about some of the settings you may want to change when publishing for a standard. Now let's take a look at those standards. First, we will discuss SCORM.

# Introducing SCORM

SCORM is a set of specifications for developing and packaging courses. SCORM has borrowed from previous work on standards and compiled those standards into a reference model. This reference model aids developers in the labeling, storing, and presentation of learning content. The most recent release of SCORM (SCORM 2004 or version 1.3) builds upon and adds to work already completed and adopted by numerous vendors in version 1.2.

According to the *SCORM 2004 Overview* document, published by Advanced Distributed Learning (ADL www.adlnet.org), the main purpose of SCORM is to make-learning content:

- **Accessible**. This refers to the ability to access learning components from one remote location and distribute them to many other locations.

- **Adaptable**. This refers to the ability to tailor instruction to individual or organizational needs.

- **Affordable**. This addresses the need to decrease the time and cost involved in delivering instruction.

- **Durable**. This refers to making e-learning able to endure technology evolution without costly redesign.

- **Interoperable**. This refers to the ability to move content developed for one platform or one set of tools to another platform or another set of tools without changing the content.

- **Reusable**. This refers to the ability to take content already developed and incorporate it into additional courses.

At this point you may be saying to yourself, "I just wanted to track learner data. How did I get mixed up into all of this?" SCORM can track learner data for you, but there is a lot more to it than that. SCORM was not developed simply as a data tracking standard. That is only a part of the SCORM reference model. In the sections that follow we will clarify additional advantages the SCORM model provides and how to implement them.

# What Does SCORM Define?

SCORM 1.2 dealt with the following main areas of course development: The creation of learning content into learning objects, the packaging and distribution of that content and the run time environment that is required to track information about a learning object or collection of learning objects. With the release of SCORM 2004, SCORM now addresses how the developer can specify the sequencing and navigation between learning objects.

Although not everything that is defined by SCORM is necessary to implement in order for a course to run on a SCORM compliant LMS, you will want to know how to implement all aspects of SCORM. We will cover some of the terms and some of the main areas addressed by SCORM.

## Learning Objects and Content Packages

There are multiple definitions used to describe e-learning objects. For our purposes we will call it a unit of content that can be delivered to a learner.

In SCORM a learning object that can be delivered by and communicate with a SCORM compliant LMS is called a Shareable Content Object (SCO). A single course or learning experience may consist of one or more SCOs. A SCORM course may also consists of assets, which are electronic learning resources that can't communicate to the LMS. Therefore, in order for a SCO to be a SCO it must communicate with the LMS. The specifications that identify how this communication occurs is collectively called the SCORM Run Time Environment.

Here is a graphical representation of a possible SCORM course that includes two SCOs and some assets.

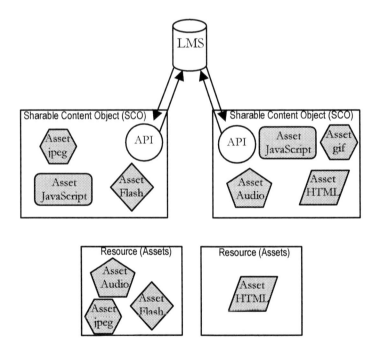

## Run Time Environment

The Run Time Environment (RTE) is what you normally think of when you think of data tracking. (How will my course communicate with the LMS?) The RTE specifications define how a SCO is to establish communication with an LMS, pass or retrieve data from the LMS, and end the communication once the SCO is no longer active.

To be SCORM conformant a SCO only needs to communicate twice to the LMS: when it starts (initialize) and when it finishes (finish). Some of the extensions available to make a Flash course SCORM conformant only provide these two calls and nothing else. Although this is all that is required, you will want to do more. You will want to track scores and other data. Luckily the SCORM template provided with Flash does more than just initialize and finish.

Once a SCO is communicating with the LMS, it must be packaged in a way that it can be delivered to the LMS. The Content Aggregation and Distribution standards address content packaging.

## Content Aggregation and Distribution

Content aggregation and distribution identifies how to package content for delivery to a SCORM compliant LMS. It address these three main areas:

- Meta-data
- Content Structure
- Content Packaging

Meta-data is used to describe a course and its components. By thoroughly labeling a course and its contents, you make it possible to reuse these components. Although extensive meta-data is not required, the more you incorporate meta-data into a course the more reusable it becomes. This meta-data makes it possible to search for and extract learning elements from a repository.

Content structure describes how a SCORM course should be organized using SCOs and assets. In a content structure SCOs and assets are considered resources. The organization of each resource and the resources that are a part of the course are identified in a manifest file.

In order for any LMS to be able to load a SCORM course it must be packaged a certain way. A course that is ready to be delivered and used by any SCORM compliant system is called a content package. A content package consists of these items:

- **Manifest File**: A manifest file is an XML document named *imsmanifest.xml*. This file is the main controlling file for the content package. It identifies all the e-learning resources (assets and SCOs) that are included in the package. It specifies the course organization (how the resources should be organized for the e-learning experience). It also includes information on the meta-data for describing the course and all the resources. In SCORM 2004 the manifest file can also specify how sequencing is to occur between SCOs.

- **Learning Resources**: The e-learning resources are all the electronic files (e.g. gif, jpeg, swf, html and so forth) that are a part of and required by the package. The e-learning resources are organized as assets or SCOs.

- **Schema Files:** The schema files are XML controlling files that are required to interpret the manifest file. These files are discussed later.

Later in this chapter we will look how to put together a content package.

### Sequencing and Navigation

The Sequencing and Navigation piece is new to SCORM 2004. It contains many standards for LMS vendors so that instructional designers and developers can identify how sequencing is to happen. Prior to SCORM 2004, LMS vendors could implement navigation between different SCOs according to the method they thought was best. As LMSs become compliant with SCORM 2004, developers will be able to identify within the manifest file how this sequencing should occur.

## Which SCORM Version Should You Develop Use?

As of the publication of this book, most LMSs and support tools only support SCORM 1.2. Version 1.3 is still fairly new. So if the course you are developing will be deployed in the near future you will want to develop to version 1.2.

However, if you plan to deploy a course in the distant future, you will want to take advantage of version 1.3. The only problem with developing to 1.3 is the current Flash SCORM extension available for Flash only supports 1.2. Therefore, keep a vigilant watch for version 1.3 tools.

## How Does a Learner Take a SCORM Course?

Once you have created a SCORM content package and placed that course on the appropriate server, the learner will need to access the LMS in order to take the course. As mentioned earlier, a single SCORM conformant course may consist of one or more SCOs assembled into a content package. (For purposes of developing in Flash, remember that each SCO must be a separate Flash movie published with the SCORM template).

These steps summarize how a SCORM course may be taken:

**1**    The learner logs into the LMS.

**2**    The learner selects that course to be taken.

**3**    The LMS opens a SCORM compliant frameset and displays the course inside that frameset. The frameset contains the necessary functions for communicating with the LMS. Because SCORM has standardized these function calls, any course published using the SCORM template available in Flash will be able to communicate using the RTE. The first command sent will initialize the SCO that was launched.

**4**    The learner moves through the SCO answering questions as necessary. Whenever data needs to be tracked, the SCO sends that data to the LMS using the functions mentioned.

**5**    When the learner is finished with the course, a command is sent to sever the communication link between the SCO and the LMS.

**6**    If another SCO is chosen from the course, the process begins again. The learner proceeds through each SCO that is available in the course.

# Making Your Flash Course a SCORM Course

Now that you have a basic introduction to SCORM, let's address a more hands-on topic: How do you make your Flash course a SCORM course?

**Note:** In this section we will address making a course version 1.2 conformant. The same procedures will apply once version 1.3 tools become available.

If you have already developed a course and you just want to make it run on a SCORM compliant LMS, you can convert the entire course to a single SCO by completing the steps discussed in this section. However, if you are still in the planning stages, design your course to take advantage of SCORM. The ADL web site (www.adlnet.org) provides suggestions for designing SCOs. Instead of making the entire course a single SCO, think about which pieces can be reusable and design your course using a series of multiple SCOs. To make each SCO conformant you will need to repeat these steps for each movie (SCO).

**Caution:** We have simplified the process of creating a SCORM conformant course so that it is easier to learn. Keep in mind that there is more to SCORM than is presented in this chapter. Once you become more comfortable with this standard, you can expand the possibilities.

Once you have developed the course, you need to take some additional steps to make your course run on a SCORM compliant LMS. Here is a quick overview of the tasks you should consider finishing:

**1**  Make sure the interactions are set up for the **Knowledge Track** option.

**2**  Publish your course using the SCORM template.

**3**  Create the course manifest file.

**4**  Package your course for delivery to the LMS.

**5**  Test your course using the testing suite provided from the ADL web site.

Each task is covered in more detail in the sections that follow.

**Caution:** When you name a Flash movie that you will publish using the SCORM template, make sure you avoid any arithmetic symbols as a part of the name (e.g. +, -, * and so forth). When the course is published, JavaScript functions are created in which these symbols could cause JavaScript errors. These errors are very difficult to debug.

## Planning Your Course

In Section III: *Creating Course Architecture with Flash* we discussed several methods for setting up course architecture and navigation. Which one of these methods is best suited for creating a SCO?

Actually, the creation of course architecture is not entirely necessary when creating a SCO. When a SCO or a series of SCOs are delivered on an LMS, the LMS takes care of navigation between SCOs and other elements of the architecture like course maps. However, as a developer, you are responsible for inner SCO navigation. For example, if you have created a SCO that contains several frames of content, you need to provide a way for the learner to move between those frames. You can borrow any of the techniques presented in the architecture section for setting up a SCO, but the simplest technique and the technique that requires minimal ActionScript is to place all content within a single Flash movie.

**Note:** The one architecture technique that will not work for creating SCOs is using a separate HTML pages for each course topic. This will not work if you want to include multiple topics in a single SCO. Only if each topic (HTML page and associated movie) is a single SCO, can you use this method.

## Preparing the Interactions in Your Course

If you have used the Flash Learning Interactions as a part of your course, you need to make sure that the appropriate settings are established so that data from these interactions is tracked. This includes selecting the Knowledge Track option and filling in the Objective ID and the Weighting.

**More Information:** The tasks required to establish these settings were discussed earlier in the Prepare Interactions in the Course section.

## Publishing with the SCORM Template

Flash MX 2004 comes with a SCORM template. When you publish a course using this template, it generates an HTML file that contains the necessary Application Program Interface (API) calls for the SCORM Run Time Environment (RTE). HTML and JavaScript are considered a standard way to communicate with the SCORM API.

When you publish a course using the Flash with SCORM Tracking template, several files (SWF and HTML) are created. The main HTML that performs the API calls is named **coursname_content.htm**. This HTML file consists of numerous JavaScript functions. These JavaScript functions are called from the Flash movie using the Flash **fs_command**. This command was developed to allow Flash movies to communicate with external resources. Once a JavaScript function is called, it sends the correct API call so that data is sent or received from the LMS.

If you have developed the course using the Flash interactions, these JavaScript function calls are made automatically for you once you enable the Knowledge Track option. There is no need to do any additional scripting. However, as you become familiar with the **_content.htm** file, you could initiate your own calls using ActionScript.

The **_content.htm** file also initializes and terminates the SCO communication for you. These functions are required by SCORM.

**Note:** An important concept to remember is that each Flash movie you publish with the SCORM template is considered a separate SCO. Therefore, if you design your course with multiple SCOs, you will need to develop each SCO as a separate Flash movie.

## Publishing a SCO

Once you have developed a movie that will become a SCO, you are ready to publish it using the Flash with SCORM Tracking template. In this section you will publish a simple quiz that we have included on the CD-ROM.

**On CD**: To complete this exercise, open samples\chapter19\sample19.fla from the CD-ROM.

**Use these steps to publish a Flash movie using the SCORM template:**

**1**   Open the movie you would like to publish. For this exercise, open *sample19.fla* from the CD-ROM.

**2**   Access the Publish Settings (File → Publish Settings).

Flash displays the Publish Settings dialog:

Select the Flash with
SCORM Tracking ——————
template.

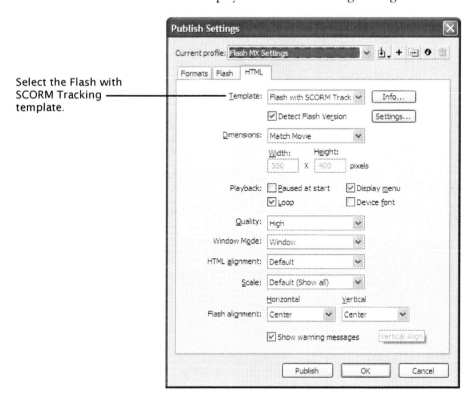

**3**   In the Templates drop down, select the Flash with SCORM Tracking template. Choose any other settings you would like to use.

**4**   Click **Publish**.

**5**   Click **OK** to close the Publish Settings dialog window.

Once the publishing is finished, you will find several new files have been added in the same directory with the FLA file. Here is a list of the new files created:

- alternate.gif
- flash_detection.swf
- sample19.html
- sample19.swf
- sample19_alternate.html
- sample19_content.html

The file that contains the necessary JavaScript to make the appropriate SCORM API calls is the **sample19_content.html** file. We will look at this file in a little more detail in a later section.

The **_content.html** file contains several variables that you may want to change. These variables control how the SCO will function. You will need to edit the code of this file to make changes. All of the variables are towards the top of the document as shown here:

In JavaScript any line of code that declares a variable begins with var. You can see several variables in this screen shot.

```
26  //        Fragments Copyright 2002 Pathlore Software Corporation All rights Reserved
27  //        Fragments Copyright 2002 Macromedia Inc. All rights reserved.
28  //        Fragments Copyright 2003 Click2learn, Inc. All rights reserved.
29  //        Developed by Tom King, Macromedia.
30  //                    Leonard Greenberg, Pathlore,
31  //                    and Claude Ostyn, Click2learn, Inc.
32  //        Includes code by Jeff Burton and Andrew Chemey, Macromedia (01/06/02)
33  // --------------------------------------------------------------------
34  // Change these preset values to suit your taste and requirements.
35  var g_bShowApiErrors = false;    // change to true to show error messages
36  var g_bInitializeOnLoad = true;  // change to false to not initialize LMS when HTML page is
37  // Translate these strings if g_bShowApiErrors is true
38  // and you need to localize the application.
39  var g_strAPINotFound = "Management system interface not found.';
40  var g_strAPITooDeep = "Cannot find API - too deeply nested.';
41  var g_strAPIInitFailed = "Found API but LMSInitialize failed.';
42  var g_strAPISetError = "Trying to set value but API not available.';
43  var g_strFSAPIError = 'LMS API adapter returned error code: "%1'\n When FScommand called AP
44  var g_strDisableErrorMsgs = "Select cancel to disable future warnings.';
45  // Change g_bSetCompletedAutomatically to true if you want the status to
46  // be set to completed automatically when calling LMSFinish. Normally,
47  // this flag remains false if the Flash movie itself sets status
48  // to completed by sending a FScommand to set status to "completed",
49  // "passed" or "failed" (both of which imply "completed")
50  var g_bSetCompletedAutomatically = false;
51  // This value is normally given by the LMS, but in case it is not
52  // this is the default value to use to determine passed/failed.
53  // Set this null if the Flash actionscript uses its own method
54  // to determine passed/fail, otherwise set to a value from 0 to 1
55  // inclusive (may be a floating point value, e.g "0.75").
56  var g_SCO_MasteryScore = null;  // allowable values: 0.0..1.0, or null
57  // ====================================================================
58  // WARNING!!!
59  // Do not modify anything below this line unless you know exactly what
```

The comments in the code explain the variables and how you may want to make changes. We have also provided a summary of each variable and how you may want to change it in the following table.

| Variable | Description |
|----------|-------------|
| g_bShowApiErrors | This variable determines whether or not error messages are displayed. If you would like to see the error messages, change this value to true. If you don't want to see any error messages, change it to false. |
| g_bInitializeOnLoad | This variable determines whether or not the SCO should initialize with the LMS. If you plan to run the SCO outside the LMS, you may want to change this value to false. |
| g_bSetCompletedAuto matically | This variable determines whether or not to set the status of the SCO to "completed" when the SCO is exited. You can use ActionScript to set the status of a SCO. If you have not done this you may consider changing the value of this variable to true. |
| g_SCO_MasteryScore | One of the settings SCORM allows you to set is the mastery score. Normally this is set by the LMS based upon the contents of the manifest file, but if this is not being done you can enter a default value that will determine pass/fail status. You must enter a value from 0 to 1. |

## Packaging the SCO

All the files that are created during publishing are necessary for the movie to function as a SCO. Those files in conjunction with your Flash movie become a SCO that can communicate with a SCORM compliant LMS. The SCO may be used or reused in any SCORM conformant course.

To create a SCORM conformant course that any SCORM compliant LMS can launch, you must package the SCO and any other SCOs or assets you want to include in the course into a SCORM-conformant content package. The next section describes this process.

# Creating a SCORM-conformant Content Package

SCORM specifies how to package e-learning objects so that they can be shared, stored, uploaded and delivered to a learner by any SCORM-compliant LMS. The SCORM content package consists of these elements:

- An XML manifest file that describes the organization, content resources, and metadata for the course.
- All files (e.g. Flash, HTML, images and so forth) associated with each resource (SCO). It is a good idea to place these files in a sub-directory.
- The XML manifest control files that are provided by ADL. These are also referred to as schema files and come with a *.xsd* extension.

All these files are zipped together into a single zip file that can be easily passed to an LMS.

## Creating the Manifest File and Metadata

The Manifest file is an XML document that identifies all the pieces of a content package. The contents of the manifest file consist of metadata, course organization, and resources. The manifest file may also identify and link to sub-manifests.

Providing all the information necessary to create a conformant manifest file is beyond the scope of this book. We suggest that you investigate the information provided by at ADL web site as well as find party tools that will help create a manifest file.

**More Information:** More information on creating a manifest file is available from the ADL web site: http://www.adlnet.org.

Some third party developers have created tools that can help create a manifest file, metadata, and even create an entire SCORM package. Some of these tools are free, some are commercial. Here is a short list to help you in finding the necessary tools to complete the job:

- Macromedia provides an extension to Dreamweaver that creates a manifest file based upon the contents of a Dreamweaver site. The name of the extension is Manifest Maker. The one downside of this tool is that it identifies each individual web page as a SCO. So if you have a SCO that is made up of more than one HTML file (like would happen when publishing a Flash movie to the SCORM template), you will need to make modifications to the manifest file. For more information visit: http://www.macromedia.com/resources/elearning/extensions/dw_ud/manifest.html.

- RELOAD (Reusable e-learning Object Authoring & Delivery) offers a couple of tools for SCORM developers. The RELOAD editor will assist you in creating a content package that includes a manifest file, resources and meta-data. This is an open source product and is free for download. The tool was initially built to support the IMS content packaging specifications, which the SCORM content packaging specifications were derived from. It has been updated to create SCORM packages. The tool comes with documentation and is not difficult to learn. For more information visit: http://www.reload.ac.uk/.

- The AltEd SCORM Editor is a commercial tool with a 14-day free trial. This product is feature rich. It was originally developed in Korean, but they have since created an English version. You can download a free trial at: http://www.alted.com/product/download/download.htm.

- JCA Solutions provides a couple of commercial tools plus training on SCORM. Meta Data Generator and Manifest Generator are the two tools that can help create a manifest file and meta data. For more information visit: http://www.jcasolutions.com/.

Even though each of these tools helps you create a manifest file and in some cases the entire content package, you still need to have a basic understanding of how a manifest file is created and the type of information that needs to go into a manifest file. We suggest that you spend some time with the documents found on the ADL web site.

**On CD**: To give you an idea of what a manifest file looks like, you can view a sample manifest file in the samples\chapter19\sample19-1test folder. This manifest file is simple. It doesn't include any meta-data. Many times it is better to start with a simple example and learn the basics first. Remember, the name of the manifest file is imsmanifest.xml.

**More Information**: If you would like to view additional samples of manifest files, you can find several examples on the ADL web site: http://www.adlnet.org.

# Packaging the Course

Once you have the manifest file created you are ready to package the course. To package the course correctly you need to organize the files. You also need to add the schema files to the course. Remember, some of the tools presented in the previous section will also help you package the course. Follow these guidelines when packaging a course:

- Organize all the SCOs with all the assets into a single location. If you have been working on a single SCO or have been keeping multiple SCOs organized together, this step may already be completed. Place the course files in a subdirectory

- Place the imsmanifest.xml file at the root of the course organization. This file must always be at the root.

- Retrieve and place the control files (.xsd files), also known as schemas, into the course. The latest files are available as a download from the ADL web site.

- Zip all the files together.

Once the files are zipped together, the content package is ready to deliver to the LMS. Before uploading to an LMS, you may want to take some time and test the content package as described in the next section.

 **Tip:** Several of the tools mentioned in the previous section will create a manifest file, meta-data, and package the course as well. It can simplify the process a great deal.

# Using the ADL Testing Suite

ADL provides a testing suite that will allow you to test a content package and make sure it is SCORM conformant. If the content package passes the ADL test, it should function on any SCORM conformant LMS. All the steps provided in this section are for the SCORM 1.2 test suite. However, the ADL web site provides good instructions for any of their tools. This includes instructions for installing and using a test suite.

The test suite allows you to run four different tests:

- LMS Run-Time Environment Conformance Test
- Sharable Content Object (SCO) Run-Time Environment Conformance Test
- Meta-data Conformance Test
- Content Package Conformance Test

You will not need to worry about the first test, it is for an LMS. When creating SCORM content you will want to use at least one of the last three tests. If you are testing a SCO that you have not packaged yet, then use the SCO test. If you have included a lot of meta-data then you will want to use that conformance test. If you have a content package that you want to make sure works, use the content package test.

## Installing the ADL Testing Suite

Before you can use the ADL testing suite, you must download it from the ADL web site and then install it.

**More Information:** To download the testing suite, go the resource center on the ADL web site: http://www.adlnet.org/index.cfm?fuseaction=rcbrowse. The testing suite comes with a ReadMe document that provides more information if you need it.

**Note:** The ADL only recommends running the testing suite on a Windows 2000 or Windows XP platform. No other platforms have been tested.

**Use these steps to install the SCORM 1.2 test suite:**

**1** Download the SCORM 1.2 Conformance Test suite from the resource center of the ADL web site (http://www.adlnet.org/index.cfm?fuseaction=rcbrowse). You will need to unzip the file.

**2** Download and install Sun Java 2 Standard Edition Runtime Environment Version 1.3.1_02 from http://java.sun.com/products/archive/j2se/1.3.1_02/jre/.

**Caution:** Make sure you install the correct version of the Sun Java 2 Standard Edition Runtime Environment. The correct version is 1.3.1_02. This is not the latest version, but it is the version required for the test suite to function properly.

**3** Double click the test suite setup file and run the installation.

**Note:** In order to run the Meta-data Conformance test or the Content Package Conformance test, the control files (.xsd files) must be copied to the desktop. This is necessary because of a limitation in the testing suite.

**4** Copy the control files (.xsd extension) to the desktop of your local machine. You can obtain those files from the ADL web site. (The installation file may copy these to the desktop for you.)

## Running the Content Package Conformance Test

The Content Package Conformance Test will test the content package, any referenced or in-line meta-data and any SCOs that are a part of the content package. If you are preparing a package to run on an LMS, this is generally the test you will want to use.

**Use these steps to run the Content Package Conformance Test**

**1**   Select the test suite program from the Start menu.

The test suite displays an HTML menu:

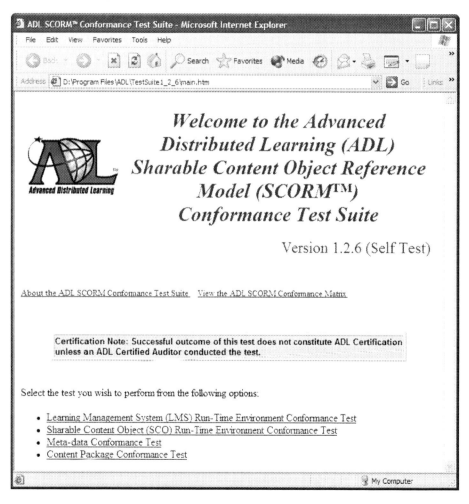

**2**   Click Content Package Conformance Test.

A Java security warning will display.

```
Java Plug-in Security Warning                                    [X]

        Do you want to install and run signed applet distributed by
        "Concurrent Technologies Corporation"?

        Publisher authenticity verified by :
        "VeriSign, Inc.".

        ⓘ   The security certificate was issued by a company that is trusted.

        ⓘ   The security certificate has not expired and is still valid.

        Caution: "Concurrent Technologies Corporation" asserts that this content is
        safe. You should only install/view this content if you trust
        "Concurrent Technologies Corporation" to make that assertion.

    [Grant this session]   [Deny]   [Grant always]   [View Certificate]
```

Because the test suite is reading and writing files from your local system, this warning displays.

**3**   Click **Grant this session** to continue.

The Instructions screen displays.

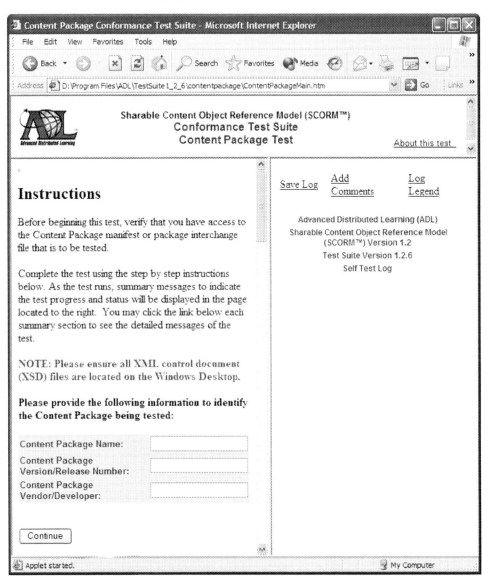

**4** Enter the content package name. For this example enter *sample19test*.

**5** Enter the content package version number. For this example enter *1*.

**6** Enter the content package developer. For this example enter *Rapid Intake*.

**7** Click **Continue**.

The next step in the testing process is to choose the correct package format for the test. Three options are available. If you have zipped the package using the correct format shown, you can choose the Package (PIF) option. If you have not zipped the package or you are not sure of the format, use one of the non-PIF options. For this example you will choose the second option.

**8**   Choose the correct package format and click **Continue**. For this example choose **Package (non PIF)**.

In the next step you will need to choose the package type. If you have assembled a course, you will want to choose the Content Aggregation Package instead of the Resource Package. A resource package simply provides resources that can be used by other SCOs.

**9**   Choose the package type and click **Continue**. For this example select the **Content Aggregation Package**.

**10**  Browse for and select the content package. For this example select the manifest file within the **sample19–1test** folder provided on the CD. You will need to copy these files to your hard drive.

**11**  Click **Begin Test**.

The testing suite informs you that the parsing and testing may take a while.

**12**  Click **OK** to start the test.

The testing suite first tests meta-data and the manifest file. As issues are found they are recorded in the log and the progress is displayed in the right-hand pane.

Note: The sample course used in this exercise has minimal information in the manifest file. No meta–data is provided.

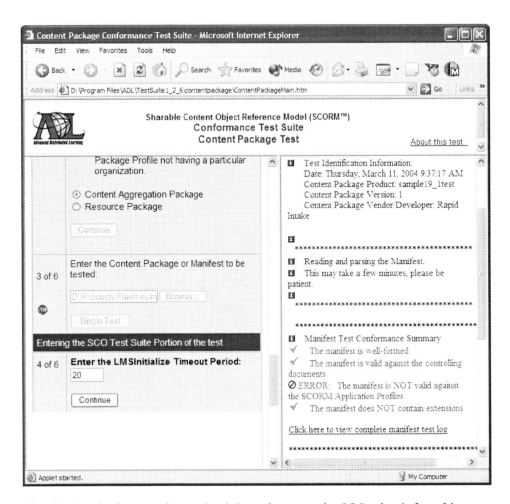

The display also lets you know that it is ready to test the SCOs that it found in the content package. If there are issues with the manifest file, the testing suite may not be able to locate the SCOs. You may need to fix the manifest file before you can test the SCOs.

**13**  To test the SCOs that are included in the content package, click **Continue**.

You are prompted to enter Login data for a user. This data is normally provided by the LMS, but you must provide it to continue testing.

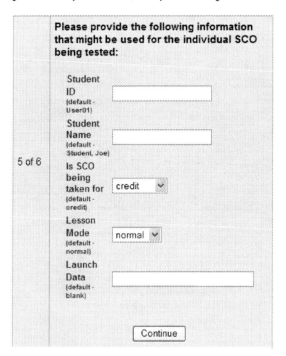

You can just use the defaults if you would like.

**14**  Click **Continue** to use the defaults for the test.

**15**  Click **Launch SCO** to begin the test.

The course will launch in a separate browser window. You can work through the course if you wish. As you try different interactions, you can see the results of the LMS communications show up in the testing suite. The results let you know whether or not the communication was successful.

**16**  When you are finished with the test, click **Complete Test**.

If the test was successful, the testing suite informs you that the package is conformant. However, this does not mean that the package is compliant. For that to occur, it must be tested by ADL.

If errors occurred, you can access a log of those errors by clicking the associated link. The errors do a pretty good job at pointing out problems. However, if you are having difficulty resolving those problems, you may want to deliver the log to a SCORM consultant.

## Trying Your Course in a Run Time Environment

As a part of the testing process you may also want to try your course in a simulated run time environment. It is a good idea to try out your course before you start working with the LMS.

There are a couple of tools that allow you to do this. The testing suite discussed earlier lets you run your course while testing. Here is one more tool that will act as a single-user, local LMS to run your SCORM course:

- RELOAD (Reusable e-learning Object Authoring & Delivery), mentioned earlier as a manifest and packaging tool, also offers a SCORM player. The player will act as an LMS and display and navigate between multiple SCOs. The tool is open source and free to download. For more information visit: http://www.reload.ac.uk/.

If you are new to SCORM, testing is a necessity. You want to find out if things are working like they should, and you don't want to place things in the LMS just to do that. Hopefully the resources provided in this section will help you accomplish that goal.

# Introducing AICC

The AICC (Aviation Industry CBT Committee) has developed guidelines for the aviation industry that guides the development, delivery and evaluation of CBT. Even though the AICC has developed standards specifically for the aviation industry, these standards have been adopted by other industries.

## What Does the AICC Standard Define?

The AICC hopes to accomplish three main goals:

- Assist airplane operators in development of guidelines, which promote the economic and effective implementation of Computer-Based Training (CBT).
- Develop guidelines to enable interoperability.
- Provide an open forum for the discussion of CBT (and other) training technologies.

The AICC has developed technical recommendations named AGR (AICC Guidelines & Recommendations). Each AGR addresses a specific area where a standard is suggested. There are a total of 10 AGRs. Here is a brief list as provided from the AICC web site (www.aicc.org):

- **AGR 001 - AICC Publications**: This document summarizes all of the publications issued by the AICC.

- **AGR 002 - Courseware Delivery Stations**: This document contains recommendations for the acquisition of a computer-based training student CPU.

- **AGR 003 - Digital Audio**: This document recommends guidelines that promote the interoperability of digital audio.

- **AGR 004 - Operating/Windowing System:** This document provides a formal recommendation for an operating and windowing system used for delivery of CBT.

- **AGR 005 - CBT Peripheral Devices**: This document recommends guidelines that promote the interoperability of the following peripheral devices: video overlay card, videodisk player, and XY input device (such as a touch screen, mouse, or trackball), and part task trainers.

- **AGR 006 - Computer-Managed Instruction (CMI)**: This document recommends guidelines that promote the interoperability of CMI systems. Interoperability means the ability of a given CMI system to manage CBT lessons from different origins. It also includes the ability for a given CBT lesson to exchange data with different CMI systems. Many of these standards have been adopted by SCORM. When you create a course that can run on an AICC compliant LMS, you need to follow these guidelines.

- **AGR 007 - Courseware Interchange**: This document recommends guidelines for the interchange of the elements that occur in CBT courseware.

- **AGR 008 - Digital Video**: This document recommends guidelines for the creation, distribution, and use of digital video in CBT courseware.

- **AGR 009 - Icon Standards: User Interface**: This document recommends guidelines for the functions of the student interface.

- **AGR 010 - Web-Based Computer-Managed Instruction**: This document recommends guidelines that promote the interoperability of web-based CMI systems. The purpose of this AGR is to promote the same kind of interoperability as described AGR006 for Web-based CBT courseware and CMI systems. As with AGR 006 many of these standards have been adopted by SCORM. When you create a course that can run on an AICC compliant LMS, you need to follow these guidelines.

The templates discussed later in this chapter assist you in creating a Flash movie that meets the guidelines established in the AGR 010 and AGR 006. Those guidelines, if followed, allow the course to communicate with the LMS.

## How Does a Learner Take an AICC Course?

It can help during development to understand how and AICC course is taken once it is delivered to the LMS. When a student takes an AICC-compliant course, these events occur:

**1** The learner logs in to the LMS.

**2** The student finds an Assignable Unit (AU) to take. The Assignable Unit is the Flash course that was published using the template.

**3** The content is located on a web server. To track properly, the Flash file needs to be embedded in the Flash AICC tracking frameset. Which we will cover later in this chapter.

**4** The LMS creates two parameters that are appended to the end of the URL: AICC_URL and AICC_SID. The final URL when the content is launched may look something like this:
```
http://myserver/flashcontent.htm?AICC_URL=http://mylmsserver/trackingu
rl.asp&AICC_SID=12345
```

**5** The learner moves through the course answering questions.

**6** The Flash learning interaction sends the tracking data to the LMS through the HTML/JavaScript tracking files. The tracking data is sent when the learner answers a question or progresses to the next page.

# Making Your Flash Course an AICC Compliant Course

To send tracking data to an AICC-compliant LMS, there are three main things that you need to do:

- Prepare the Flash learning interactions by enabling the Knowledge Track option for each interaction.
- Publish the Flash course using the Flash with AICC Tracking template.
- Modify the frameset file and place all files on the LMS server.

The sections that follow discuss each of these tasks in more detail.

## Preparing the Interactions in Your Course

If you have used the Flash Learning Interactions as a part of your course, you need to make sure that the appropriate settings are established so that data from these interactions is tracked. This includes selecting the Knowledge Track option and filling in the Objective ID and Weighting.

**More Information:** The tasks required to establish these settings were discussed earlier in the Prepare Interactions in the Course section.

## Publishing with the AICC Template

Flash MX 2004 comes with an AICC template. When you publish a course using this template, it generates HTML files that contain the necessary functions to communicate with an AICC compliant LMS.

When you publish a course using the AICC Tracking template, several files (SWF and HTML) are created. The main HTML file that contains a lot of the function calls is named coursname_content.htm.

If you have developed the course using the Flash interactions, these JavaScript function calls are made automatically for you. There is no need to do any additional scripting. However, if you become familiar with the _content.htm file, you could also initiate your own calls using ActionScript.

**On CD**: To complete this exercise, make sure you have access to *sample19.fla* that is available on the CD-ROM. Copy this file to your hard drive.

**Use these steps to publish a Flash movie using the AICC template:**

**1**   Open the movie you would like to publish. For this exercise, open
samples/chapter19/sample19.fla.

This is the same file that you used to publish in the SCORM exercise. The nice thing about developing a course using Flash Learning Interactions is that you can publish to both AICC and SCORM.

**2**   Access the Publish Settings (File → Publish Settings).

Flash displays the Publish Settings dialog:

Select the Flash with AICC
Tracking template

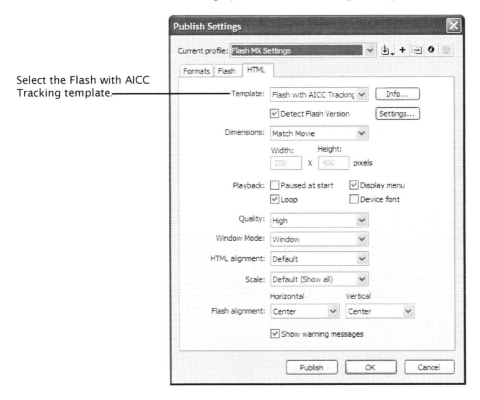

**3**  In the Templates drop down of the HTML tab, select the Flash with AICC Tracking template. Choose any other settings you would like to use.

**4**  Click **Publish**.

**5**  Click **OK** to close the Publish Settings dialog window.

Once the publishing is complete, you will find several new files have been added to the directory that contained the FLA file. Here is a list of the new files created:

- alternate.gif
- flash_detection.swf
- sample19.html
- sample19.swf
- sample19_alternate.html
- sample19_content.html

These are the same files that are created if you publish to SCORM. However, the contents of the HTML files are different.

# Preparing a Frameset and Delivering to the LMS

Before delivering the AICC compliant course to an LMS you must complete one more task. It is necessary to set up a frameset that will be used with the HTML and SWF files.

The purpose of the frameset file is to track data across multiple pages and then display the results to the learner. A sample frameset file comes with the learning extensions. You can change this sample file and then deliver all of the files to the LMS.

**Use these steps to prepare the frameset file:**

**1** Find and retrieve the frameset file (frameset.htm), the results file (results.htm), and the scripts subfolder located in the Flash MX 2004 program folder. Place these files and folder with the other files created when you published the Flash movie.

As mentioned these files are located in the Flash MX 2004 program folder. Here is a sample path:

```
D:\Program Files\Macromedia\Flash MX 2004\en\First
Run\HTML\Learning Extensions Srvr Files
```

This folder also contains a ReadMe file with a few instructions.

**2** Open the **frameset.htm** file in Dreamweaver or another HTML editor. (The change you need to make is small enough that you can use Notepad if you would like.)

**3** In the frameset file, you will find these two lines of code:

```
<frame src="Untitled-1.htm" name="content" frameborder="0">
<frame src="results.htm" name="cmiresults" scrolling="0"
frameborder="0">
```

**4** In the first line is a reference to **Untitled-1.htm**. Change this to the name of the HTML file you published. The name will correspond with the Flash file name. For the previous example you need to enter **Sample19.html**. This HTML file will call the **_content.html** and **_alternate.html** as necessary.

You have now prepared the frameset. At this point you can test the course for AICC compliancy or place the files on the LMS to be delivered to the learner.

**Use these steps to deliver the files to the LMS:**

**1** Make sure all the files produced when you published the Flash movie along with the frameset file the results file and the scripts folder are all contained in the same directory.

**2** Place these files on the web server.

**3** In the LMS or the AICC Course Descriptor files make sure to reference the frameset.htm file.

## Testing Your AICC Course

As with SCORM courses, the AICC provides a testing suite you can use to test your courses for compliancy. This type of testing can help you verify that the e-learning application will work correctly once you place it on the LMS.

Unlike the SCORM testing suite, the AICC testing suite is not as easy to acquire or install. You will need to plan ahead in order to have the testing suite available when you need it.

Before you can use the testing suite you need to obtain a user id and password. To obtain this information you must complete and sign an agreement form. You must then send that form to the AICC. They will respond with the user id and password. Then you can download and use the testing suite.

**Note:** In addition to installing the testing suite, you will need to install the Apache server and Apache server version 1.3. You may also need to install the Macromedia Shockwave plugin. Both of these are available as a free download.

**More Information:** For more information on the testing suite, the license agreement, and download locations, visit http://www.aicc.org/pages/aicc_ts.htm.

# Summary

In this chapter we covered two methods for tracking learner data. These two methods require the use of SCORM or AICC standards.

You should now understand a little more about the SCORM and AICC standards. You also learned how to package your Flash movies for delivery using these two standards.

In many ways SCORM is the currently preferred standard, so we spent more time discussing SCORM. You learned about several tools that can aid in SCORM development work. We also went through a SCORM testing scenario.

Any LMS that is SCORM or AICC compliant can run courses created with the methods described in this chapter.

# Section V: Unlocking the Power of Components for e-Learning

Components open new avenues for e-learning development. In this section learn to work with and create e-learning components.

---

# Using Flash Components in e-Learning **20**

One of the most useful features of Flash is components. Components let you add complex functionality of UI elements to your movie by simply dragging an object to the Stage and establishing some settings.

Even though most components are created for uses other than e-learning, those components may still be useful to e-learning developers. In order to reduce the amount of time it takes to create e-learning, developers of e-learning need to use existing components and create new components that target e-learning.

The information provided in this chapter focuses on components delivered with Flash MX 2004. The functionality of components has changed with subsequent releases of Flash.

In this chapter you will learn:

- What a component is and how it can save time.
- About advantages of using components.
- How to use some of the standard components provided with Flash.
- About component resources.

# What is a Component?

In Flash 5, Macromedia introduced SmartClips as a way to package animation and content for reuse. With the release of Flash MX, Macromedia enhanced the SmartClip idea and called them components. Now with Flash MX 2004, Macromedia has implemented version 2 components, which expand on the functionality of version 1.

**Note:** Components are only available in Flash MX and Flash MX 2004. You can still create and use SmartClips in Flash 5, but you will be missing some of the functionality that is provided in components.

**Caution:** Mixing version 1 and version 2 components in a single project is not recommended and may cause problems.

A component is a complex movie clip that you can use over and over again to speed up development. Components are reusable, extensible, and distributable. These three features make components invaluable for e-learning developers for the reasons described here:

- **Reusable**: In the development of e-learning there are several things that you do over and over again. For example, every course uses navigation buttons; most courses also include quiz questions and Table of Contents. If these elements are converted to components, you can use them over and over again and greatly decrease your development time.

- **Extensible**: Components generally come with parameters that let you make modifications to how it will work in your application. This means that you can adapt components to fit each e-learning course without writing additional code.

- **Distributable**: Because components are separate movie clips it is quite easy to distribute them among other e-learning developers. This ensures that certain elements of the e-learning course are consistent. You can distribute components as installable extensions or simply pass the appropriate files from one developer to the next.

You have already worked with components as a part of this book. The Flash Learning interactions are components that you can use to create a quiz. These components come with changeable parameters. If you think about how much time it would require to create those quiz questions yourself, you get a sense of the power of components.

**Note**. The Flash Learning interactions in many cases combine UI components with other objects to create a new component: the learning interaction. For example, the Multiple Choice interaction includes several Checkbox components, a PushButton component, plus a couple of fields, and other graphic images. The instructions that appear with a learning interaction is the actual component for the learning interaction. It controls how all these elements act together to make the learning interaction work.

Most components are not created with e-learning in mind, but that doesn't mean they are not usable for e-learning. Also, you can create your own components for your e-learning development.

In this chapter we will look at some of the components that come with Flash and how to use them in an e-learning course. In later chapters we will address the topics of creating your own components and changing existing components.

# Using Flash Components in e-Learning

Flash MX 2004 comes with numerous UI (user interface) components. Flash MX 2004 Professional comes with even more components. These components are categorized as follows:

- **UI components** allow you to build interfaces quickly.
- **Data components** allow you to connect to a data source, pull down data, store it locally in Flash, and update it remotely. (Only available with Flash MX 2004 Professional.)
- **Media components** make it easy to add audio and video to Flash projects. (Only available with Flash MX 2004 Professional.)

You might find some of these components useful during e-learning development. You can also install additional components created by other developers using the Extension Manager.

 **More Information**. For more information about where you can get components and how to install them, see the Resources for Additional Component section later in this chapter.

Some of the components that come with Flash MX that you might find useful in e-learning are described here:

| Component | Description |
|---|---|
| Button | The Button component functions like a standard button and is used as a submit button in the learning interactions.<br><br>Button |
| Checkbox | A Checkbox indicates that there may be one or more options to choose from. This component lets you add check boxes to your e-learning application. You have already seen this component used as a part of the Multiple Choice learning interactions.<br><br>✓ CheckBox |
| ComboBox | A ComboBox lets the learner select from a list or provide an entry.<br><br>one ▼<br>one<br>two<br>three<br>four |
| ListBox | A Listbox lets a learner select one or more choices from a list. A Listbox displays a scrollable list and allows single or multiple selections of the items listed. This is similar to a ComboBox except that it does not drop down.<br><br>one<br>two<br>three<br>four |

| Component | Description |
|---|---|
| Menu | A Menu lets the learner choose different topics or lessons from a pop-up list. It functions like menus you are used to in other applications. This component requires scripting to set up and is only available with the Flash MX 2004 Professional version. |
| MenuBar | A MenuBar lets the learner choose different topics or lessons from a list that appears vertically on the Stage. This component is only available with the Flash MX 2004 Professional version. |
| RadioButton | A Radio Button indicates a mutually exclusive choice. You have already seen radio buttons used in the True/False learning interaction. |
| TextArea | The TextArea provides an easy way to add a text field with or without a horizontal scroll bar. |
| Alert | The Alert provides an easy way to create dialogue boxes (alerts) to present to the learner. |

**Note:** These are just some of the components that are available. You may find applications in e-learning for the other components. The Media components available with the Flash MX 2004 Professional version are especially helpful if you need to add video to your e-learning course.

**More Information:** The learn more about how to use each of the components provided with Flash, open the Using Components help (Help → Using Components).

To access any of these components, you must open the Components panel (Window → Components).

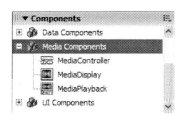

The Components are available using a tree view.

**Note:** As you install additional components, they will show up in new categories in the Components panel.

To use any of the components displayed in the Components panel, you drag the component to the Stage and establish the parameters. In the next couple of sections we will look at how you can use some of these components in e-learning applications.

# Publishing Version 2 Components

All of the components that come with Flash MX 2004 are version 2 components. These components are written in ActionScript 2.0. Macromedia recommends that you do not mix version 1 and version 2 components in a single project.

In order for version 2 components to work effectively and without problems, you should choose Flash Player 7 and ActionScript 2.0 as publish settings (File → Publish Settings).

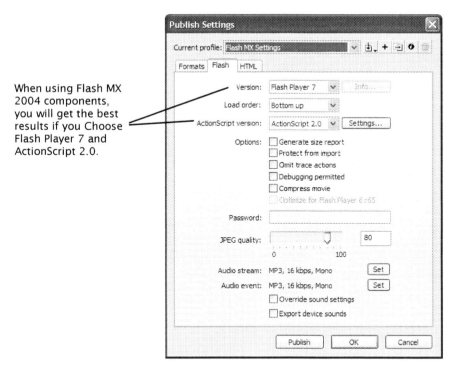

When using Flash MX 2004 components, you will get the best results if you Choose Flash Player 7 and ActionScript 2.0.

**Note:** All UI components will function properly if published using Flash Player 6 and ActionScript 2.0. Only the Media and DataSet components require Flash Player 7.

# Component Example: Using the Button

In the first example we will look at how you can use a Button component. There are numerous places where buttons are helpful in e-learning. It is not difficult to create the buttons on your own so why would you want to use the Button component? The simple answer is that it is already created for you and can save you some time.

In this example you will learn some of the ins and outs of working with components by creating a simple interaction using the Button component. In this interaction, the learner will click the button to see a movie demonstrating a task.

### Viewing the Finished Button Interaction

Before you begin creating this simple interaction, take a moment to view how it will look.

**On CD.** To view the finished interaction, open **samples/chapter20/sample20-1.swf** and try out the interaction.

This simple interaction consists of a one-frame movie that loads another Flash movie when the button is clicked. This single frame could easily be a part of an entire e-learning course.

## Creating the Button Interaction

Most of this interaction has already been created for you in the **samples/chapter20/sample20-1_start.swf** file. Use this file as a starting point for this exercise. Let's first take a look at what has already been done.

- All the background graphics have been created for you. These graphics are contained on three layers that have been grouped under the NavBar folder.

- Four additional layers have been created and grouped in the Content folder. These layers are Action, Buttons, Movie, and Text.

- The initial text for the training page has already been added.

To finish this interaction you will need to create a blank movie clip to display the demonstration. You will then add and configure the PushButton component.

**Use these steps to create a blank movie clip and add it to the Stage:**

**1**   Open **samples/chapter20/sample20-1_start.fla**.

   The background graphics and the text have already been created. You will add the blank movie clip to the Movie layer.

**2**   Create a new symbol (Insert → New Symbol).

**3**   Name the new symbol *Demo* and make sure that the **Movie Clip** behavior is chosen.

Enter the name and select the *Movie Clip* behavior.

**4**   Click **OK**.

Flash displays the first frame for the Demo movie clip. That is all we need to do to create the blank movie clip so you can now return to the original timeline.

**5** Return to Scene 1 so you can add this movie clip to the Stage.

**6** Open the library (Window → Library).

**7** Select the first frame in the Movie layer. Find the Demo movie clip and drag it onto the Stage. Position the movie clip so it is just to the right of step 3.

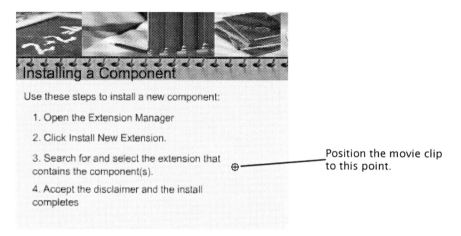

Position the movie clip to this point.

**8** In the Properties Inspector, enter *demo1* as the instance name.

**Note:** Be careful when entering instance names. ActionScript is case sensitive.

You will use the instance name later on to refer to this movie clip.

Now you are ready to add the component and set the parameters so that it will start the demonstration playing.

**Use these steps to add and configure the Button component:**

**1** Open the component panel if it is not already open.

**2**    Select frame 1 in the Buttons layer and drag the Button component onto the Stage. Position it below the text.

**3**    Give the component and instance name of *showDemo*.

Each component comes with a set of parameters that you can define. For some components, you may need to display the Component Inspector (Window → Development Panels → Component Inspector) to access those parameters.

You may need to display the Component Inspector for some components.

You can also change parameters by accessing the Parameters tab in the Properties Inspector. Here is what the Parameters tab contains for the Button component:

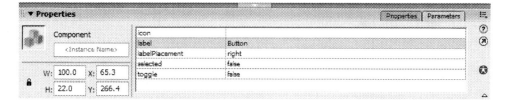

As you can see, there are five parameters for the Button component. You won't need to use all of them in this exercise.

**4**   To change the caption of the button, enter *Show Demo* as the Label parameter.

Leave the other settings as they are. You can add an icon to the button, determine the label placement in relation to the icon, indicate whether the button is selected, and change the button to a toggle.

There are two ways to enable a component with Action Script. The easiest way is to add script directly to the component using the **on( )** event construct. This method is pretty straightforward and easy to understand.

The second way to enable a component is by adding a listener. This is done on the first frame of the movie. A listener is some code that will tell the component to listen for a particular event to occur. Whenever that event happens, the appropriate code is executed.

**Note:** In Flash MX components, you use a Click Handler to enable the component. A click handler is just a reference to an ActionScript function.

**5**   Use one of these methods to add code to the button:

■   To add script directly to the component using the **on( )** event construct, select the component and display the Actions panel. Enter the code as shown here:

```
on(click){
        loadMovie("installcomp.swf","_root.demo1");
}
```

This is a simple **on (click)** handler added directly to the component. The **loadMovie** action loads a demo movie that has already been created into the blank movie clip demo1. Although not necessary in this case, we have used the full path to the movie clip: _root.demo1.

**More Information:** For more information on the loadMovie function, see Chapter 16: Creating a Custom Flash-based Architecture.

In order for this action to work, the **installcomp.swf** file must be located in the same directory as this movie. If not, you would need to enter a path that accounts for the different directory.

■   To add a listener, select the first frame of Action layer and insert this code:

```
newlistener = new Object();
newlistener.click = function(evt){
        loadMovie("installcomp.swf","_root.demo1");
}
showDemo.addEventListener("click", newlistener);
```

The first three lines of code create the listener function. The last line of code assigns the listener to the component using the instance name we assigned earlier. The **loadMovie** action is used in both the **on( )** event construct and the listener. Many ActionScript developers prefer using listeners because the code is centralized in one frame instead of spread across multiple objects.

**6**   Save the movie and test it to see if the Show Demo button is working.

**Note:** The *installcomp.swf* file was created using Camtasia Studio. Camtasia is one of many products that will record screen activity and export the resulting movie as a Flash file. For more information on other products see the appendices on the CD-ROM.

That is all that is required to use the Button component for this type of example. However, there are many ways you can enhance this simple interaction.

# Enhancing the Functionality of the Button Component

The simple interaction you created in the previous section works well. However, there are a few things you may want to do to enhance how it works. For example, when the learner first clicks the Show Demo button, you may want to change the button text to "Stop Demo". If they click it again, the demonstration should stop. You can do this by making changes to the listener function or the **on(click)** handler. These changes will take advantage of some of the Button component's built in properties.

Each Flash component comes with properties and methods that you can use to manipulate the component.

**More Information.** To find out the properties and methods that are available for each component, search for the component name in the Using Components help.

In this section we will look at using the **Button.label** property.

The label property specifies the text label for the button. You can use this property to dynamically change the label and the function of the button. For example, you can change the listener function or the **on(click)** handler to be more dynamic:

```
if (showDemo.label == "Show Demo") {
    loadMovie("installcomp.swf","_root.demo1");
    showDemo.label="Hide Demo";
} else {
    unloadMovie("_root.demo1");
    showDemo.label="Show Demo";
}
```

As you can see we have made a few changes. First, we have included an *if statement*. The if statement uses the label property to get the current label of the button. If the label is "Show Demo" then the movie is loaded and the property is changed to *Hide Demo*.

If the label is set to *Hide Demo*, then the movie is removed using unloadMovie and the label property is used to set the label to "Show Demo". This creates a button that lets the learner hide and show the demonstration at will.

**On CD**. You can view a sample of the interaction using this new function by opening **samples/chapter20/sample20-2.swf.** You can view the code by opening **samples/chapter20/sample20-2.fla.**

This provides one example of how you can use the properties that come with the Flash components to enhance their functionality. An entire book could be written on using the components that come with Flash. In this section we hope you have seen how to work with Flash components in an e-learning application. You can use the Component help to learn more. As you learn more about the available methods and properties, you will discover many ways to use components.

**More Information**. You can make changes to how the component looks as well. For more information see Chapter 21: Customizing Flash Components.

# Resources for Additional Components

Components are a fairly new idea, but the idea has really caught on. Other development environments come with objects that you can use to quickly develop applications. That is the purpose of components in Flash.

Additional components are being created by developers other than Macromedia, and you can find many of these components on the web for free. In this section we will take a look at where you can find additional components that may help reduce e-learning development time.

**Caution:** Remember that there are version 1 components and version 2 components. Don't mix the two types of components in a single project. Version 1 components work best if published using ActionScript 1.0. Version 2 components work best if published using ActionScript 2.0.

The first place you will want to look for e-learning components is the Flash Exchange on the Macromedia web site. You can access the Flash Exchange by choosing Help → Flash Exchange or by visiting **http://www.macromedia.com/** and clicking the Flash exchange link.

The Flash exchange contains Flash 5 SmartClips (the predecessor of the component), version 1 components, and version 2 components. Only a few of the components are created by Macromedia. Other developers submit components to be included on the site.

The components found on the exchange are classified into categories. One of those categories happens to be e-learning. Although there are not a lot of components in that category, it does aid in finding those that may be helpful with e-learning development. Even though other components are not specifically created for e-learning, they may also be helpful.

To make use of these components, you simply download them and install them using the Extension Manager.

## Installing Components

Once you have downloaded a component, you can install it using the Extension Manager. After installation many of the components will show up in the Components panel. There are some components that will not. For more information you need to check the documentation for the component.

**Use these steps to install a component:**

**1**　Download the component to your computer.

**2**　Open the Extension Manager.

　　You can open the extension manager from the Start menu or you can choose Help → Manage Extensions.

**3**　Select Flash from the drop-down menu.

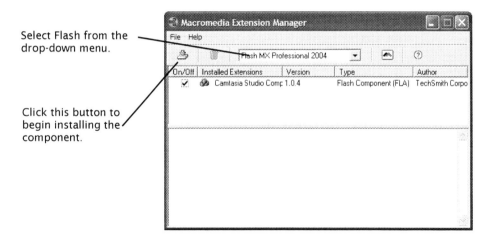

Select Flash from the
drop-down menu.

Click this button to
begin installing the
component.

**4**   Click the Install New Extension button or choose File → Install Extension.
Search for and select the MXP file (extension) that you downloaded.

**5**   When prompted to accept the disclaimer, click **Accept**.

Once the installation is complete, you may need to shutdown and restart Flash.

## Learning Components

On the Flash exchange you can access learning components by selecting the
learning category. This will display all components that Macromedia determines
belongs to the learning category. Components are added to this category all the
time, so you will want to visit the Flash exchange occasionally and determine
whether any learning components might help with your development efforts.

## Other Components

When developing e-learning using Flash, you should not limit yourself to just
looking at the components available in the learning category. There are many other
components, and you may find some of them useful.

In the first part of this chapter we discussed the use of some of Macromedia's UI
components that are delivered with Flash MX 2004. Macromedia has continued to
develop UI components and makes the available on the exchange. These
components are all found in the User Interface category.

A component that we like to use for e-learning that is not found in the learning category is the Camtasia Studio Components. You can find this component in the User Interface category. We use Camtasia Studio™ to create Flash-based demonstrations of software programs. This set of components lets you easily enhance the look of these Flash demonstrations by adding a pre-loader, a controller bar, or a duration counter.

The Flash Exchange is not the only place to find components. There are other locations on the Internet. Some are commercial and some are free. As components spread there will undoubtedly be additional sites that popup. Here are a few sites you can take a look at.

- www.flashcomponents.com
- www.flashcomponent.com
- www.flashkit.com
- www.flashcomponents.net

To find additional sites, perform an Internet search on Flash components.

# Summary

The use of components in e-learning is advantageous in order to reduce the amount of time development can take. In this chapter you learned what a component is, how to find them and how to install them. You also learned how to use the Flash UI components in an e-learning course.

In the next couple of chapters we will look at how you can create and customize components.

# Customizing Flash Components **21**

As you learned in Chapter 20, there are numerous components available that you can use in your e-learning projects. However, some components may not do everything you would like them to do or look the way you want them to look. In most of these situations, it is much easier to make a few changes to a component than trying to recreate your own.

In this chapter we will look at how you can customize components. We will look at customizing the UI components as well as the learning interactions.

In this chapter you will learn:

- About different ways you can customize components.
- How to work with the UI component styles.
- How to use themes with components.
- About the structure of learning interactions.
- How to customize the Multiple Choice interaction.
- How to rename a customized learning interaction.

# Customizing Components

Many of the components provided by Macromedia or other developers can save you a lot of time. The UI components come with another nice feature: you can easily change the appearance of the component. You may want to change the appearance of a single component you have used in an e-learning application, or you may want to change the appearance of multiple components. For example, the Flash learning interactions use many of the UI components. You can change the appearance of these components.

We will discuss three different ways you can change components:

- Component styles
- Component themes
- Component skins

The styles associated with components have ActionScript methods and properties that allow you to change the color and text formatting of a component.

A theme is a collection of styles and skins that make up a component's appearance. Themes let you apply changes to a series of components. You can only change styles that are supported by the theme the component is using.

Skins are graphic symbols used to display components. Skinning is the process of changing the appearance of a component by modifying or replacing its source graphics (the skin symbol). A skin can be a small part of the component, like a border's edge or corner, or a composite piece like the entire image of a button in its up state. A skin can also be a symbol without a graphic, which contains code that draws a piece of the component.

**Note:** Using component styles and applying a theme is only possible with version 2 components. Version 2 components come with Flash MX 2004. Flash MX delivers version 1 components. For more information about customizing version 1 components see the appendix on the CD-ROM.

After learning to change the appearance of Flash UI components, we will also look at how you can customize the functionality of Flash learning interactions.

# Using Component Styles

One of the really nice things about version 2 components is that they are built so the appearance can be quickly changed using ActionScript. You can make these changes at the start of a Flash movie or any time during the movie.

When you find that you need to change the appearance of UI components, you may want to change a single component or multiple components. We address methods for doing both.

Every component instance has style properties and **setStyle()** and **getStyle()** methods. You use these methods to modify and access style properties. In this section we will look a customizing the styles of a component in 3 ways:

- Change styles for a single component instance. This is effective in some situations, but it is not the best method if you need to change the style on all the components throughout a movie.
- Change the style for all components in a movie using the **_global** style declaration.
- Change the style for multiple components by creating a custom style declaration.

**More Information:** For more information about customizing UI components, see the Using Components help in Flash MX 2004.

# Styles and Themes

Themes determine which styles a component comes with. In order for a component to use a style, it must be associated with the theme assigned to that component. The default theme for Flash MX 2004 components is the halo theme.

In the next section we list multiple styles that are associated with components. Some of the styles listed are not supported by the halo theme. Therefore, in order to use those styles you will need to create a new theme.

**More Information:** See the Using Themes section for more information about creating and using themes.

# Style Properties

Before we look at how to make changes to components using styles, you need to become familiar with the styles that are changeable. This table lists some of the available styles as identified in the Component Help of Flash MX 2004. Remember, in order for a component to use a style, it must be associated with the theme assigned to that component.

| Style | Description |
| --- | --- |
| backgroundColor | The background color of a component. The default value is transparent. This style is used by List and Accordion components that use the default halo theme. |
| borderColor | The black section of a three-dimensional border or the color section of a two-dimensional border. The default value is 0x000000 (black). The Accordion, Loader, TextInput, MenuBar, and List components that use the default halo theme use this style. |
| borderStyle | The component border. Possible values are *none*, *inset*, *outset*, or *solid*. The default value is *solid*. The Accordion and List components that use the default halo theme use this style. |
| buttonColor | The face of a button and a section of the three-dimensional border. The default value is 0xEFEEEF (light gray). This style is not supported by the halo theme. |
| color | The text of a component label. The default value is 0x000000 (black). The Alert, Accordion, Button, CheckBox, DateChooser, DateField, NumericStepper, ProgressBar, TextInput, TextArea, RadioButton, MenuBar, Menu, Label, and ComboBox components that use the default halo theme use this style. |

| Style | Description |
|-------|-------------|
| disabledColor | The disabled color for text. The default color is 0x848384 (dark gray). The Alert, Accordion, Button, CheckBox, DateChooser, DateField, NumericStepper, ProgressBar, RadioButton, MenuBar, Menu, and ComboBox components that use the default halo theme use this style. |
| fontFamily | The font name for text. The default value is _sans. The Accordion, Alert, Button, CheckBox, ComboBox, DateChooser, DateField, Label, Menu, MenuBar, NumericStepper, ProgressBar, RadioButton, TextArea, and TextInput components that use the default halo theme use this style. |
| fontSize | The point size for the font. The default value is 10. The Accordion, Alert, Button, CheckBox, ComboBox, DateChooser, DateField, Label, Menu, MenuBar, NumericStepper, ProgressBar, RadioButton, TextArea, and TextInput components that use the default halo theme use this style. |
| fontStyle | The font style. Possible values are *normal* or *italic*. The default value is *normal*. The Accordion, Alert, Button, CheckBox, ComboBox, DateChooser, DateField, Label, Menu, MenuBar, NumericStepper, ProgressBar, RadioButton, TextArea, and TextInput components that use the default halo theme use this style. |
| fontWeight | The font weight possible values are: *normal* or *bold*. The default value is *normal*. The Accordion, Alert, Button, CheckBox, ComboBox, DateChooser, DateField, Label, Menu, MenuBar, NumericStepper, ProgressBar, RadioButton, TextArea, and TextInput components that use the default halo theme use this style. |
| highlightColor | A section of the three-dimensional border. The default value is 0xFFFFFF (white). A Loader component that uses the default halo theme uses this style. |

| Style | Description |
|---|---|
| marginLeft | A number indicating the left margin for text. The default value is 0. This style is not supported by the halo theme. |
| marginRight | A number indicating the right margin for text. The default value is 0. This style is not supported by the halo theme. |
| scrollTrackColor | The scroll track for a scroll bar. The default value is 0xEFEEEF (light gray). This style is not supported by the halo theme. |
| shadowColor | A section of the three-dimensional border. The default value is 0x848384 (dark gray). This style is not supported by the halo theme. |
| symbolBackgroundColor | The background color of check boxes and radio buttons. The default value is 0xFFFFFF (white). This style is not supported by the halo theme. |
| symbolBackground DisabledColor | The background color of check boxes and radio buttons when disabled. The default value is 0xEFEEEF (light gray). This style is not supported by the halo theme. |
| symbolBackground PressedColor | The background color of check boxes and radio buttons when pressed. The default value is 0xFFFFFF (white). This style is not supported by the halo theme. |
| symbolColor | The check mark of a check box or the dot of a radio button. The default value is 0x000000 (black). This style is not supported by the halo theme. |
| symbolDisabledColor | The disabled check mark or radio button dot color. The default value is 0x848384 (dark gray). This style is not supported by the halo theme. |

| Style | Description |
|---|---|
| textAlign | The text alignment. Possible values are: *left*, *right*, or *center*. The default value is *left*. The Label, NumericStepper, TexArea, and TextInput components that use the default halo theme use this style. |
| textDecoration | The text decoration. Possible values are: *none* or *underline*. The default value is *none*. The Accordion, Alert, CheckBox, ComboBox, DateChooser, DateField, Label, Menu, MenuBar, NumericStepper, ProgressBar, TextArea, and TextInput components that use the default halo theme use this style. |
| textIndent | A number indicating the text indent. The default value is 0. This style is not supported by the halo theme. |
| themeColor | The background of a component. Possible values are: *haloGreen*, *haloBlue* and *haloOrange*. The Accordion, Alert, Button, CheckBox, ComboBox, DateChooser, DateField, Menu, MenuBar, NumericStepper, ProgressBar and RadioButton components that use the default halo theme use this style. |

These are not all of the available styles and properties. Individual components may have styles not shared by other components. For a complete list of styles for each component, see the Using Components help information for a specific component.

You will learn how to use these properties in the sections that follow.

# Change the Style of a Single Component Instance

In this section we will look at how to change the style for a component instance. You will use this technique if there is a single instance of a component that you want to change. In this example you will change the control button in a learning interaction.

## Viewing the Changed Control Button

If you would like to see how the changed control button will look, take a moment to open the sample Flash movie on the CD-ROM.

**On CD**: To see the changed control button open *samples/chapter21/sample_21-1a.swf*. To view the code that was added to the Flash movie open *samples/chapter21/sample_21-1a.fla*.

While viewing the sample file notice that when you roll over the control button, the highlight color is now blue.

## Making the Change to the Control Button

In this section you will add an interaction to a Flash movie and then add ActionScript to change a couple of styles for the control button (button component instance). You will change the **themeColor** and the **color** of the text.

**Use these steps to change styles to a single component instance:**

**1**  Open a new Flash file, add a multiple choice interaction to the Stage and break it apart so it is ready to modify.

   Before you can enter ActionScript to change the style of the control button, you must get the instance name of the button.

**2**  Select the control button at the bottom of the interaction and retrieve the instance name from the Properties Inspector.

   In the case of the control button the instance is always Template_ControlButton. Remember that ActionScript 2.0 is case sensitive.

**3**  Select the frame that contains the learning interaction and open the Actions panel (Window → Development Panels → Actions).

   When creating a full course you will want to create a separate layer for the ActionScript code.

   To change the **themeColor** and the **color** of the text (two styles) requires two lines of ActionScript.

**4** Enter these two lines of ActionScript.

```
Template_ControlButton.setStyle("themeColor","haloBlue");
Template_ControlButton.setStyle("color","blue");
```

The **setStyle** method is used to change a style. You must use two parameters. The first parameter is the name of the style. The second parameter is the value. In the second line we set the color to blue. We are able to use the term *blue* because it has been established as a standard color. For most colors you will need to use a number that represents the RGB value of that color: (0xRRGGBB). For example, you could replace the second line with this to give it a lighter shade of blue:

```
Template_ControlButton.setStyle("color",0x0066ff);
```

When indicating RGB colors no quotes are placed around the color.

Colors that are already defined are: black, white, red, green, blue, magenta, yellow, and cyan.

**5** Test the movie so you can see the change in the control button. You will need to select one of the responses before the control button will become active.

# Using Global Styles to Change All Components

There may be some situations where you want to change a style that is used by multiple components. For example, you may want to have all the components that support themeColor to using the same themeColor.

## Viewing the Changed Components

You may want to view a sample learning interaction that has had the **themeColor** changed for all components.

**On CD**: To see a sample interaction with the **themeColor** changed for all components open **samples/chapter21/sample_21-1b.swf**. To view the code that was used open **samples/chapter21/sample_21-1b.fla**.

## Using the Global Style

In this example you will add a Multiple Choice learning interaction and change the **themeColor** style for the control button and the checkboxes using a single line of ActionScript. This is done using the **_global** style.

**Use these steps to change a global style:**

**1**     Open a new Flash file, add a multiple choice interaction to that Stage and break it apart so it is ready to work on.

**2**     Select the first frame and open the Actions panel (Window → Development Panels → Actions).

**3**     Enter this line of ActionScript code.

```
_global.style.setStyle("themeColor", "haloBlue")
```

We still use the **setStyle** method to change the style. The main difference is that we are assigning this change to **_global.style**. This change will affect the control button and the check boxes that exist in the interaction.

**4**     Test the movie so you can see the changes. Place the cursor over the check boxes. You will need to select one of the responses before the control button will become active.

# Creating a Custom Style to Change Multiple Components

If you want to change multiple components in a Flash movie without changing all components, you need to create a custom style. A custom style is a new instance of the CSSStyleDeclaration object. A new instance lets you establish a set of custom styles that will be used by any component instance you assign it to.

You can then make changes to custom styles in the same way you made changes to the **_global style** in the previous section.

**Use these steps to create a custom style:**

**1** To begin creating a custom style, you must create a new instance of the CSSStyleDeclaration object using syntax like this:

**var styleObj = new mx.styles.CSSStyleDeclaration;**

This creates a new instance of the CSSStyleDeclaration object. The new instance is stored in the styleObj variable. (You can choose a different variable name if you wish.)

**2** If you want the ability to assign this custom style to individual instances of components, you will also want to apply a name to the custom style using this syntax:

**styleObj.styleName = "customStyle";**

**3** You also need to add the custom style to the global style list so that you can make changes on a global level:

```
_global.styles.customStyle = styleObj;
```

**4** Now that everything is established, you can define the custom style using syntax similar to it:

```
styleObj.fontSize = 14;
styleObj.fontWeight = "bold";
styleObj.textDecoration = "underline";
styleObj.setStyle("themeColor", "haloBlue");
```

The custom style is created and defined. You can use more style definitions if you want. Remember, the styles you use must be a part of the theme assigned to the component or they will not show up.

**5** To apply the custom style to a single component instance use syntax similar to this:

**Template_ControlButton.setStyle("styleName", "customStyle");**

In this example, *Template_ControlButton* is the instance name of the component that the **customStyle** is being applied to.

**6** To apply the custom style to all components of a particular component type, use syntax similar to this:

_global.styles.CheckBox = styleObj;

This statement applies the styleObj custom style to all CheckBox components. You can replace CheckBox with any component name (for example, Button, RadioButton, TextArea, and so forth).

If you would like to change a style property associated with a custom style that has been applied to a component type, you can use syntax similar to this:

_global.styles.CheckBox.setStyle("fontSize", 20);

Although creating a custom style requires more ActionScript and may be a little more complex, it does provide more flexibility when assigning styles.

 **On CD**: To see an example of custom styles applied to a learning interaction open *samples/chapter21/sample_21-1c.fla*.

# Using Themes

Themes are a collection of styles and skins. In order to apply a style to a version 2 component, the component must first be associated with a theme that contains that style.

By default all version 2 components that come with Flash MX 2004 are associated with the halo theme, but you can change this. Some of the styles listed in the table in the previous section are not part of the Halo theme collection. Therefore, you may want to create a new theme to take advantage of those styles. For example, the color style, which represents the background color of check boxes and radio buttons, is not available in the halo theme.

Flash MX 2004 comes with 2 themes: halo and sample. The sample theme provides support for all the styles that have been created for the components. Halo is the default theme.

The 2 themes that come with Flash MX 2004 are stored as FLA files in the **First Run\ComponentFLA** folder. To locate this folder, do a search on your hard drive. The FLA file that stores the halo theme is named **HaloTheme.fla**. The FLA file that stores the sample theme is named **SampleTheme.fla**. To create a new theme, you will copy one of these themes and use it as a starting point.

In this section you will first learn how to create a new theme. Then you will learn how to apply that theme.

# Creating a New Theme

When you create a new theme you always start with an existing theme and then start making changes. To make changes to the theme, you must edit the skins that make up a theme. Graphic skins are the images that are put together to make up the look of a particular component. For example, the check box consists of several skins. The check mark that shows up when the checkbox is clicked is one of those skins. The box itself is made of several skins to show the different states.

In this section you will create a new theme that will support more styles. You will also edit the check box skins. You will create a check box that displays an X when clicked instead of a check mark. The new style we will use will make the X display in red.

**Use these steps to create a new theme:**

You will create a new theme by copying the Sample theme that is provided with Flash MX 2004.

**1**   Find the **SampleTheme.fla** file in the **First Run\ComponentFLA** folder. Make a copy of the Flash file and name it *newTheme.fla*.

The location of the **First Run\ComponentFLA** folder may be different depending upon your operating system and installation choices. Therefore, to locate the folder it is best to do a search. Generally you will find it inside the installation folder. On certain operating systems you may locate more than one ComponentFLA folder. Use the folder that is located inside the First Run folder.

**2**   Open the *newTheme.fla* file.

**3**   Open the library if it isn't already opened (Window → Library).

The Flash UI Components 2 folder contains all the library items. The skins that you may want to change are located inside **Themes\MMDefault**. Inside the MMDefault folder is a folder for each component. You will find the skins you want to change inside one of those folders. In this example you will change the check mark for the CheckBox component. There are two elements that will need to be changed: the normal check mark and disabled check mark.

**4**   Open the cb_check_ symbol that is inside the **Checkbox Assets\Elements** folder.

**5**   You may want to zoom in on the check mark to make it easier to work with.

**6** Select the check mark and delete it.

**7** Select the line tool and change the stroke height in the Properties Inspector to **2**.

**8** Draw a black angled line. Select the line and position it at **X=0,Y=0**. Set the width of the line to be **7.0** and the height **6.9**.

These dimensions should make the X fit inside the box.

**9** With the line selected duplicate it (Edit → Duplicate). Rotate the line 90° clockwise (Modify → Transform → Rotate 90° CW). Make sure the position of the line is **X=0,Y=0**.

**10** Repeat steps 5-9 for the *cb_ckeck_disabled* symbol.

This symbol skin is for the check mark that displays when the button is disabled.

That is all that is required to change the check mark. To make the mark red you need to use one of the styles that comes with the sample theme. Here is a line of ActionScript that will set the mark to red.

```
_global.style.setStyle("symbolColor", "red");
```

# Applying a Theme

If you have an e-learning course you have created, you can apply your own theme to the Flash movies that make up that course. Each Flash movie you create will need to have the theme applied. Once the theme is applied, the skins you have modified with show up. Also the new styles will be accessible from ActionScript.

In this section you will modify the **sample_21-1b.fla** movie so that the interaction will display an X instead of a check mark.

**On CD**: To see a sample interaction with the new theme applied, open **samples/chapter21/sample_21-1d.swf**. To view the code that was used open **samples/chapter21/sample_21-1d.fla**.

**Use these steps to apply a theme to a Flash movie.**

**1**    Open **samples/chapter21/sample_21-1b.fla**.

You will add the sample theme to this movie.

**2**    Open the Flash file that contains the new theme (newTheme.fla) as an external library (File → Import → Open External Library).

**3**    In the theme's Library panel, open **Flash UI Components 2\Themes\MMDefault** and drag the CheckBox Assets folder from the *newTheme* library to the current movies library. If the library of the movie is not open, make sure to open it (Window → Library).

When you are applying a new theme, you need to copy over any asset folder that has changed. In this case we just copy the CheckBox assets.

**Tip**: It may be difficult to drag the folder from one library to the other unless you have detached one of the library panels. This causes it to float over the Stage and makes it easier to work with both libraries.

The new folder should now show up in the library panel.

**4**    Inside the Checkbox Assets folder find the **CheckBoxAssets** symbol and right-click (CONTROL-click on the Macintosh). Select Properties from the pop-up menu.

**5**    Make sure that the **Export in first Frame** option is checked.

Check the Export in first frame option.

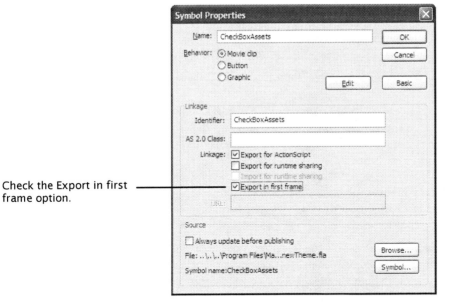

If the Symbol Properties window only shows the top portion of the window, click the Advanced button.

**6**    Click **OK** to Close the Symbol Properties window.

Now you can make the X red.

**7** Select frame 1 of the **Sample_22-1b** file and open the Action panel (Window → Development Panels → Actions).

**8** Enter this ActionScript code:

```
_global.style.setStyle("symbolColor", "red");
```

This line of ActionScript code causes the check mark on the CheckBox component to change colors. Since we have replaced the check mark with an X, the X changes to red.

**9** Test the movie (Control → Test Movie) to see the new look of the check boxes.

# Skinning a Component

Each skin element is a symbol. By changing the symbol, you change the look of the component.

In the previous section you learned how to change skins when creating a new theme.

The skins to a component are found in the library. The skins used in Macromedia components are organized so that they are easy to work with. Any conscientious component developer will follow this same type of organization.

**More Information:** See Chapter 11 and the previous section for more information about changing assets of a learning interaction.

# Customizing Learning Interactions

The changes that we have discussed so far in this chapter have dealt specifically with the UI components that come with Flash MX 2004. Making changes to these components will also change the way the Flash learning interactions look because they are made up of UI components.

However, changing the UI components is not the only way you can change the Flash learning interactions. Once you become more familiar with the ActionScript that controls those learning interactions, you can change the way individual interactions function.

In this section we will show you an example of the types of changes you can make by changing a Multiple Choice interaction. Before making the actual changes, we will take a look at how the interaction is structured.

# Learning Interaction Structure

Before we take a look at a specific example of changing the multiple choice interaction, we will discuss the structure of learning interactions so that you can better transfer the information from this example to other interactions you may want to make changes to.

The first thing you need to be aware of when working with learning interactions is that a learning interaction consists of a component plus a collection of several other components and objects. This is the reason you must break apart the component before you can set the parameters. As we have mentioned several times in earlier chapters, the actual component is represented by the set of instructions.

The instructions represent the component for learning interactions.

By default, a Multiple Choice component consists of these elements:

- 5 CheckBox components
- 2 Dynamic Text fields
- 1 Button component
- 1 graphic symbol for the background
- The Multiple Choice interaction component (the instructions)

**Note:** The learning interactions that come with Flash MX 2004 are made up of version 2 components while the learning interactions that come with Flash MX are made up of version 1 components.

To change the look of any UI components, you can use the techniques discussed in the previous sections.

If you need to change the scripts associated with a learning interaction, there are two main places that the scripts are stored. First, each interaction has scripts associated with the component. You can access these scripts by right-clicking (CONTROL-clicking on a Macintosh) the learning interaction component and selecting Edit from the pop-up menu. In the symbol edit mode you will see three layers. The first frame of the middle layer contains the ActionScript code as shown here:

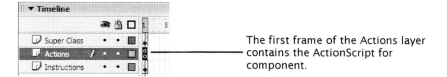

The first frame of the Actions layer contains the ActionScript for component.

The second place is actually the class definition for the component. This code is contained in another symbol that is placed in the Super Class layer. You must edit that symbol to access the code for the component class. We will not make any changes to the class definition code.

# Customizing a Multiple Choice Interaction

Now that you understand some of the structure inherent in a learning interaction, we will use a specific example to apply some of this information. In this section you will modify a multiple choice interaction so it will provide immediate feedback. In all the Flash learning interactions, the learner has to click a Check Answer button before feedback is provided. With Multiple Correct questions (more than one right answer) clicking a button to submit the answer makes sense. But sometimes it is nice to have the feedback provided immediately once a response is clicked. In this exercise you will change a multiple choice question so it will provide immediate feedback.

### Viewing the Finished Interaction

To see an interaction that responds with feedback as soon as the learner clicks a response, you can view the sample on the CD.

**On CD**: Open **samples/chapter21/sample_21-2.swf** to view an example of the finished interaction.

To successfully complete this customization, there are two main tasks that you must perform:

- **Part 1: Change the CheckBox Components to RadioButton Components**. Checkboxes denote that there might be multiple correct responses, so the learner may not expect immediate feedback when a checkbox is used. Therefore, we will look at how you can change the checkbox components to RadioButton components.

- **Part 2: Changing the Script of the Learning Interaction**. To force the learning interaction to provide feedback as soon as the learner clicks a radio button, you need to make some changes to the script associated with the component. You will also need to change the script so that the Next Question button becomes active as soon as feedback is displayed.

Each task is addressed in a separate section.

## Changing the CheckBox Components

In the previous section we mentioned that checkboxes generally send the message that the learner may click one or more responses. Therefore, the first step to make an interaction respond immediately is to change the checkbox components to radio buttons. This is a simple process of deleting the checkbox buttons, adding the radio buttons and naming them correctly.

 **On CD**: For this exercise use *samples/chapter21/sample_21-2_start.fla* as a starting point.

**Use these steps to change the CheckBox components to RadioButton components:**

**1** Open *samples/chapter21/sample_21-2_start.fla*.

**2** Access the Multiple Choice interaction in frame 1 of the Interactions layer.

**3** Select each CheckBox component and note the instance name. (The names should be Checkbox1 through Checkbox4). Delete all four CheckBox components.

**4** Drag four RadioButton components to the Stage. Space and align them as necessary.

**5** Name the RadioButton components using the same instance name used by the CheckBox components (Checkbox1, Checkbox2, Checkbox3, and Checkbox4).

It is important that the instance names are the same so that the code will still function properly. You can choose to change the names in the Component Inspector as well. Remember ActionScript 2.0 is case sensitive.

The interaction should now look like this:

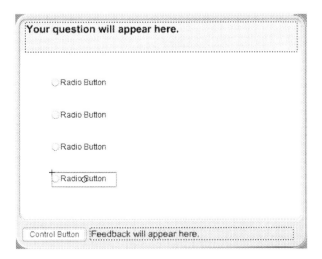

That is all that is required. You are now ready to begin changing the scripts. The reason we are able to change checkbox components with radio button components is that all the properties and methods used by the learning interaction are common between these two components.

## Changing the Scripts

In this section you will make slight modifications to the scripts that control the Multiple Choice learning interaction.

**Use these steps to customize the scripts in the Multiple Choice interaction:**

To make changes to the scripts of the learning interaction, you will need to edit the component script.

**More Information:** For more information about the component script see Chapter 11: Customizing Learning Interactions.

**1**   Right-click (CONTROL-click on a Macintosh) the learning interaction component (the instructions) and select **Edit** from the pop-up menu.

**2**   Select the frame in the Actions layer and display the Actions panel (Window →
Development Panels → Actions).

The first part of the code explains all the code that follows:

A description of the code
that follows.

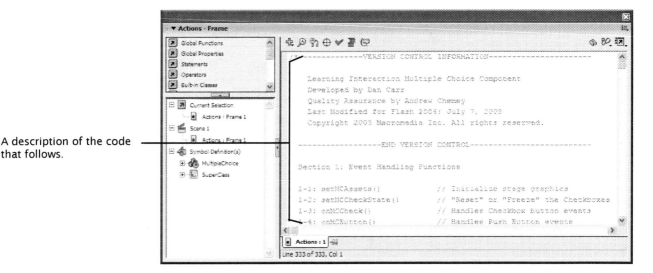

At about line 36 you should find the **setMCAssets( )** function. This is the first
place you will make a change.

**3**   In the last line of the **setMCAssets** function, change the **onMCCheck** reference
to **onMCButton**. The line of code should now look like this:

```
router.setComponentListener(router.Checkboxes[i], onMCButton);
```

The purpose of this line of code is to establish a listener function for each
checkbox. Since we replaced the checkboxes with radio buttons and gave them
the same instance name, the listener is established for the radio buttons. The
listener function is executed whenever one of the radio buttons is clicked. By
default the listener function is **onMCCheck**. This function does two things: it
enables the control button and changes the feedback to tell the user to click the
**Check Answer** button for feedback.

The **onMCButton** function is a function that gets called whenever the learner
clicks the **Check Answer** button. When the Check Answer button is clicked,
this function provides feedback. Therefore, by replacing the **onMCCheck** with
**onMCButton**, we have skipped a step so the feedback is provided immediately.

**4**   Save the file (File → Save) and test it (Control → Test Movie).

When you test the movie you will notice that feedback is provided immediately. However the Next Question button is not active so the learner cannot continue to the next page. The reason it did not become active is because we skipped that step when we changed the listener function. Therefore we need to modify the **onMCButton** function so it will also activate the **Next Page** button.

The first step will be to copy the line of code that is used to activate the button.

**5** Find the **onMCCheck** function (about line 72) and copy this line of code (you will paste it in the next step):

```
router.setComponentState(router.Assets.ControlButton, true);
```

This line of code is used to activate the **Next Page** button. Since we skipped the **onMCCheck** function, we will add this line of code to the **onMCButton** function.

**6** Find the **onMCButton** function (about line 85). Paste the line of code directly beneath the line that begins **var router =**.

The start of the function should now look like this:

```
85  function onMCButton(){
86
87      var router = _parent.SessionArray[_parent.session];
88      router.setComponentState(router.Assets.ControlButton, true);
89      if(router.buttonFlag == false){
90
```

If you now test the interaction you will see that the button now becomes active at the same time the feedback is displayed. However, there is still one more issue. When you first come to the interaction the button says Check Answer. Since we will never click the button to have it check the answer we should change this so it always says Next Question. This can be done with the component parameters.

**7** Click **Scene1** to return to the main timeline.

**8** Select the learning interaction component (the instructions) and open the Component Inspector (Window → Development Panels → Component Inspector or click the button in the Properties Inspector).

**9** Click the Assets tab to change the Control Button Labels.

**10** Change the **Check Answer** label to *Next Question*.

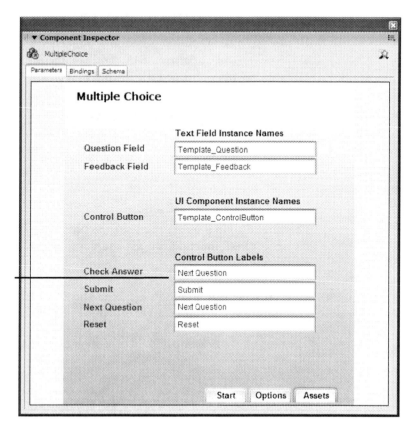

Change the **Check Answer** label to *Next Question*.

**11**  Save the movie (File → Save) and test it (Control → Test Movie).

That works pretty well. However, a problem arises when you add another Multiple Choice interaction to the movie. When you try to add another interaction you will receive this prompt:

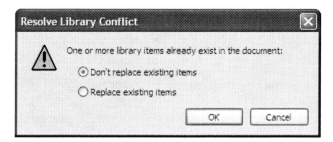

If you choose not to replace existing items, the new interaction will function like the interaction just changed. If you choose to replace existing items, the interaction just changed will no longer provide immediate feedback.

In the next section we look at how you can fix this problem.

# Renaming a Customized Component

As illustrated in the previous section, there are some problems with leaving the Multiple Choice component in its current state. Additional Multiple Choice learning interactions added to the movie will function as the modified interaction. To prevent this from happening you must complete three tasks:

- Rename the modified Multiple Choice symbol.

- Rename the modified Multiple Choice component

- As you should do anytime you use multiple interactions of the same type, rename the assets.

**On CD**: To see the sample exercise with these changes already made, open **samples/chapter21/sample_21-3.fla**.

**Use these steps to rename the symbol and component:**

In this section continue with the same exercise that you completed in the previous section. A lot of the work that needs to be done to rename a component is done from the library.

**1**  Open the library (Window → Library).

**2**  In the library, find the Multiple Choice symbol. Right-click (CONTROL-click on a Macintosh) the symbol and choose Properties from the pop-up menu. (The Multiple Choice symbol should be at the root level of the library.)

The symbol Properties window displays:

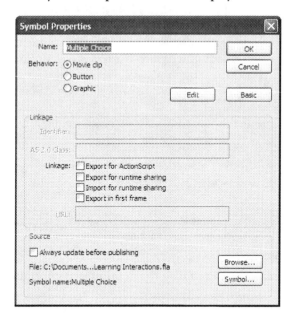

**3** Change the name to *Multiple Choice Immediate Feedback*.

**4** Click **OK**.

**5** Find the Multiple Choice component and right-click on it (CONTROL-click on a Macintosh) and choose Properties from the pop-up menu. The component is inside the **Assets\Controls\Components** folder.

**6** Change the name to *MultipleChoiceIF*.

The IF stands for immediate feedback.

**7** Click **OK**.

**Use these steps to rename the assets:**

**1** Access the learning interaction on frame 1 of the Interactions layer.

**2** In turn select each radio button and give it a new instance name (for example, *IF1*, *IF2*, *IF3*, and *IF4*).

**3** Select the component (the instructions) and access the Components Inspector (Window → Development Panels → Component Inspector or click the button in the Properties Inspector).

**4**   In the Start tab of the Component Inspector enter the instance name for each response.

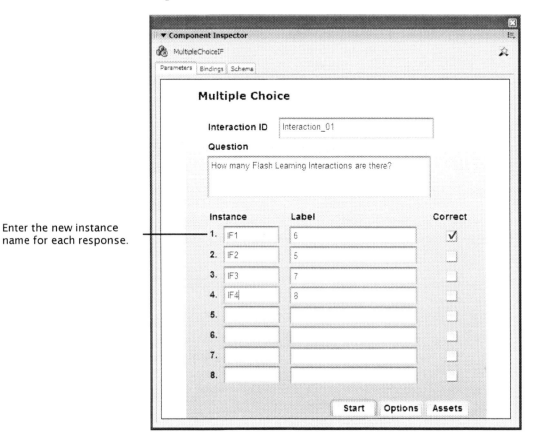

Enter the new instance name for each response.

**5**   Close the Component Inspector.

You can now add additional Multiple Choice interactions to this movie without them taking on the behavior of the customized interaction. You can also use this customized interaction in other places in the movie by dragging the symbol from the library.

You can follow this same process for other components you customize.

# Customizing a Learning Interaction on Your Own

You have now successfully changed the way a learning interaction functions. At this point you may be asking yourself "How would I figure this out on my own?" There are a few skills that are necessary to be able to complete these types of changes:

- **Knowledge of ActionScript:** You need to have a good understanding of ActionScript. To determine where and how a script can be changed, you need to become familiar with the component's code. To do so you must understand ActionScript. Macromedia has done a good job of commenting the code. The comments can help you determine what a particular piece of code is doing.

- **An Understanding of how Components Work:** Hopefully, the chapters in this book will provide you with the information you need. You can apply this information to other situations.

- **Persistence:** Sometimes it is not a simple process to figure out how a component should be changed. If you keep digging, you can eventually find the answer.

It may take some time to figure out how to customize a component, but once you have it figured it out you can continue to reuse that information.

# Summary

The UI components provided with Flash MX 2004 can save a good deal of time during development. They are also versatile enough that you can change they way the look. In this chapter you learned how to change UI components by changing styles, creating new themes and customizing component skins.

You can also change the learning interaction components. If the component doesn't provide the functionality you would like, you can customize that component. Many times it is much easier to customize an existing interaction than trying to create one on your own. You learned how to customize a Multiple Choice interaction so that it would provide immediate feedback.

Once you have customized a learning interaction you can rename it so that you can add additional learning interactions to the same file.

 **On CD**: For more information about customizing version 1 components (components delivered with Flash MX) see the appendix on the CD-ROM.

# Developing e-Learning Components 22

Components are the answer to rapid e-learning development. However, the number of components created specifically for e-learning is rather small. As more e-learning developers see the value of components, that should change.

In this chapter we provide some basic information about developing components. Creating quality components requires a good knowledge of Flash and ActionScript 2.0 as well as Object Oriented Programming (OOP). Those topics are beyond the scope of this book, but we provide an example to walk through to get you started creating components.

In this chapter you will learn:

- Why components are the future of e-learning.
- About the knowledge required to develop components.
- An overview of the tasks required to develop components.
- How to create a simple e-learning component.
- About resources to learn more details about developing components.

# Components and e-Learning Development

If Flash is the future of e-learning development, as we believe, then components are going to help make this possible. In the previous chapters we hope you have seen the value of components for e-learning development. The Flash learning interactions are necessary for e-learning development. The UI and other components help make development easier.

Even though most of the components available for Flash are not specific to e-learning, most can be used in an e-learning application to save development time. Also, component developers can adapt current components and make them more specific to e-learning which will speed up development time even more.

For example, a component developer may adapt the button component to create several navigation buttons specific to e-learning. The addition of navigation buttons to an e-learning course is then simply a matter of dragging a component to the Stage. Having multiple components like this will cut down on the time required to develop e-learning applications.

# Introduction to Creating Components

Creating components requires some background knowledge.

## Knowledge Needed for Component Development

To create quality version 2 components requires a good grounding in these areas:

- **ActionScript 2.0:** Creating quality components requires the writing of ActionScript code. The more familiar you are with ActionScript the better off you will be.
- **Component Structure:** Macromedia recommends a structure for how components are built. These recommendations should be followed.
- **Object Oriented Programming:** An understanding of Object Oriented Programming (OOP) concepts and how they apply to ActionScript 2.0 is important.

- **ActionScript Classes:** A familiarity with ActionScript classes, including those created for components, can also be very helpful.

 **More Information:** For information on creating version 1 components (Flash MX) see the appendix on the CD–ROM.

## Basic Steps to Creating Components

Version 2 components (Flash MX 2004) have simplified some tasks associated with creating components. However, it has also made it necessary that you have a better understanding of ActionScript and creating classes. Here is an overview of the tasks that you must complete to create a version 2 component. Some of these tasks may be completed in a different sequence than presented here.

**1** Create the component symbol.

**2** Create the component assets and add them to the component symbol.

**3** Create a class or subclass for the component. Include in the class definition the properties and functionality (methods) required by the component.

**4** Define class properties and component.

**5** Create the component definition.

**6** Compile the component to create a live preview and package it as an extension for distribution.

# Creating a Simple e-Learning Component

In this section we will go through some of the basics steps for creating a component. Although this example is quite basic and could be enhanced in a number of ways, it should give you a good understanding of the process required to create a version 2 component.

A progress meter is an element found in many e-learning courses. In the sections that follow you will create a basic progress meter. Once the component is finished, you will be able to drag this component to the Stage, set the colors you would like for the progress meter, and it will begin working.

## Viewing the Finished Component

On the CD-ROM we have included a packaged component. If you place this component into the Components folder, the component will appear in the component panel and you can try it out.

**On CD**: Create a folder named My Components in the **Macromedia\Flash MX 2004\en\First Run\Components** and copy **samples/Chapter22/progMeter.swc** to that folder to view this sample component.

# Creating the Component

In this section you will create a progress meter component. The steps in this section are divided into five areas:

- Create the component symbol.
- Create the component assets.
- Attach the component class file.
- Describe the component class file.
- Compile and package the component.

## Creating the Component Symbol

The first step is to create a component symbol. We begin from scratch so that you can see all the steps involved.

**Use these steps to create a component symbol:**

**1** Create a new Flash file and save it as *New Components.fla*.

**2** Create a new symbol (Insert → New Symbol).

The Create New Symbol dialog displays.

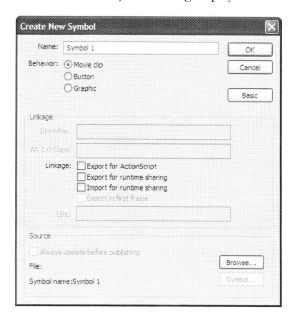

**3** If the Linkage and Source areas of the dialog are not visible, click **Advanced**.

**4** Fill out the Create New Symbol dialog using the settings in this table.

| Setting | Value |
|---|---|
| Name | progMeter |
| Behavior | Select Movie Clip |
| Linkage | Check the *Export for ActionScript* option. |
| Linkage | Uncheck the *Export in First Frame* option. |
| Identifier | progMeter |
| AS 2.0 Class | progMeter |

When you have created symbols in the past, you have not entered information into the Linkage area. Several of these options become important when creating components. Exporting for ActionScript and assigning an identifier makes it possible to address this symbol using ActionScript. It is not necessary to export this component in the first frame and so we deselect this option so as not to over burden the Flash movie on the first frame. Finally, we associate this symbol with an ActionScript class file. The purpose of the class file is to define a new ActionScript class. The class file is a separate document with a .as extension. You will see this file later.

**5**    Click **OK** to close the Create New Symbol dialog.

**6**    Open the library (Window → Library), right-click (CONTROL-click on a Macintosh) the progMeter symbol and select Component Definition from the pop-up menu.

The Component Definition window displays:

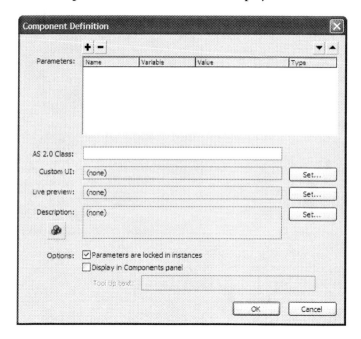

The component definition window lets us define this symbol as a component.

**7**    Enter *progMeter* in the **AS 2.0 Class** field.

**8**    Check the **Display in Component panel** option.

**9**    Enter *Progress Meter* as the tool tip and click **OK**.

In the library you should see the icon change to indicate that the symbol is now a component. You still need to define the look and functionality of the component, but you have just created a blank component.

## Creating the Component Assets

Now that you have a component symbol created, you need to create the assets (graphic elements that make up a component) and place them on the component symbol timeline. You will first create 2 movie clip symbols that you will use to create the assets.

**Use these steps to create the component assets:**

**1**    Create a new movie clip symbol and name it *progressFill* (Insert → New Symbol and choose movie clip as the behavior).

**2**    Check the **Export for ActionScript** option, uncheck the **Export in First Frame** option, and enter *progFill* as the identifier.

**3**    Click **OK**.

**4**    On the Stage draw a white rectangle without a border. Size it to 100 X 100 and position it at 0,0.

**5**    Repeat steps 1-3. Name the new  symbol *progressOutline* and enter *progOutline* as the identifier.

**6**    In the new symbol draw a white rectangle without a fill, just the border. Size it to **100 X100** and position it at **0,0**.

The reason we had you create these symbols using white and a size of 100 X 100 is that we can then use them to create the assets. A rectangle with the size of 100 x 100 is a much better base for scaling than a smaller sized rectangle. Also, since we want to change the color of these assets, we make them white (a neutral color) to begin with.

**7**    Right-click (CONTROL-click on the Macintosh) the component symbol in the library and choose Edit.

**8**    Enter *fill* as the name for the layer.

**9**	Drag on instance of the progressFill symbol to the Stage. Use the Properties Inspector to change the Tint to **#FF9900**.

Change the tint on the movie clip.

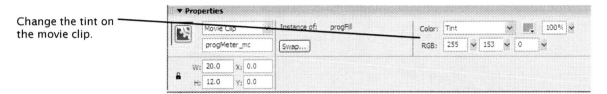

**10**	Enter *progMeter_mc* as the instance name. Resize the movie clip to **20 x 12** and position it at **0,0**.

**11**	Create a new layer named *outline* directly above the fill layer.

**12**	Drag a copy of progressOutline to the Stage. Enter an instance name of *progOutline_mc*. Change the tint to **black (#000000)**. Size the movie clip to **200 x 14** and position it at **0, -1**.

Now the only assets left to add are the text fields that read *Start* and *Finish*.

**13**	Create a static text field at the start of the progress meter and enter *Start*.

**14**	Create another static field at the end of the progress meter and enter *Finish*.

The component should now look like this:

The assets have now been added and you are ready to set up the ActionScript class.

## Attaching the Component Class File

When creating a component, you need to enter the code that will create the component class file in a separate ActionScript file. You can create this file using Flash Professional or another text editor. If you do not have Flash Professional there isn't an option to create an ActionScript file. You can, however, use a regular text editor to enter the code. The only trick is to assign the file a .as extension and a file name that matches the class file you entered in the linkage field.

Because of the complexity of programming a class file, we have already created it for you. You will need to copy this file into the same directory as your component in order for things to work correctly.

**Use these steps to attach the ActionScript class file:**

**1**  Copy **sampes/Chapter22/progMeter.as** from the CD-ROM to the current directory of your component.

When you created the component symbol you entered *progMeter* as the AS 2.0 Class. So as long as this file resides in the same folder, Flash will find it. The component should now be functional.

**2**  Click **Scene 1** to return to the main timeline.

**3**  Right-click (CONTROL-click on the Macintosh) the component in the library and select Component Definition. When the Component Definition dialog displays, click **OK**.

Opening and closing the Component Definition causes the component parameters to show up in the Properties Inspector.

**4**  Drag the component to the Stage to test it. Add several frames to the movie and test it (Control → Test Movie). If the progress bar grows as the movie plays, you know it is working correctly. You may also want to change the colors in the Properties Inspector.

Now that the component is working we will package it, but first let's take a closer look at the code.

## Describing the Progress Meter Class Code

This class file is quite basic when compared to some components. As we describe the different parts of the class file, you may want to open it and follow along with the code. In order to make the code easier to describe we have divided it into section using comments.

The first line of the file creates a new class named *progMeter*. This class becomes a sub-class of the Movie Clip class because we include *extend MovieClip* with the code. Everything between the curly braces belongs to the progMeter class.

The first three variables are required by the component architecture to establish the connection between the component and the symbol. This code lets developers create instances of this class using ActionScript.

The next section contains four variables that are used by the component. The two movie clip variables are used to identify the **progressFill** and **progressOutline** movie clips that are included as assets. The two color variables are used to change the color of the progress meter. These variables are identified as private. This means that only code inside the class definition can change these variables.

The next section defines what are called *getter* and *setter* properties. This is the preferred method for providing a way for the user to change component properties. The defineable attribute that appears on the line before each set function causes these attributes to show up in the Properties Inspector when the component is selected. Using this structure it is pretty easy to set up component parameters.

The constructor function comes next. This function is called anytime a new instance of the class is created. Notice that the constructor function name is the same as the class name. In most components this function is used to initialize the component by drawing assets. For simplicity sake we have manually drawn the assets for the component, but there are several good reasons to draw those assets dynamically using the constructor function.

In the constructor function for the progress meter component, we simply set the color of the progress meter based on the settings chosen by the user.

The final function makes the progress meter work. Since this class is an extension of the MovieClip class, it will receive **enterFrame** events. We have written a function based on the **enterFrame** event. Each time this event is sent, the progress meter evaluates the **startframe** and **endframe** of the parent movie and resizes the progress bar accordingly.

**Note:** As we have mentioned this is a basic ActionScript class. Its purpose is to get you started. As you learn more about the structure of components you may want to improve upon this.

## Compiling and Packaging the Component

Compiling and packaging a component provides three benefits:

- A compiled version of the component protects the code and cuts down on compile time in the final course.

- A live preview is created that dynamically updates on the Stage. A live preview shows what the final component will look like when it is played. For example, when you change a component attribute, that change is reflected in the version that is shown on the Stage. You don't have to wait until you test the movie. For the progress meter component, this functionality will not be available. We created all the assets manually instead of having the constructor function do it.

Therefore, the live preview will not update until the component is redrawn, which will happen when the Flash movie plays. Even though the live preview may not be perfect, the component will still work fine when the Flash movie is played. The Flash learning interactions also lack a live preview.

- An SWC file is created that you can distribute and place in the component folder so that your components will show up in the Component panel.

**Use these steps to compile and package the component:**

**1** Right-click (CONTROL-click on a Macintosh) the component in the library and select Export SWC File.

**2** Save the file as *progMeter.swc*.

This places the progMeter.swc file in the same directory as the current Flash file. The SWC file is the file you place in the component directory so that you can access the component from the Components panel.

**3** Create a new folder named *My Components* in the Flash MX 2004 Components directory and copy the progMeter.swc file to that directory.

**Note:** The Components directory may exist in one of several places. Perform a search to locate the component directory on your hard drive. It is generally located inside the Flash MX 2004 program directory.

**4** Close and re-open Flash MX 2004 and the new component will display in the Components panel.

You have created a simple component and packaged it for distribution.

# Resources for Learning to Create Components

Resources for learning how to create components fall into two categories: learning ActionScript 2.0 and its OOP features, and learning to create components. The Macromedia web site, under the Flash development center, has a number of good articles on ActionScript 2.0 (www.macromedia.com). The *ActionScript Reference Guide* that comes with Flash help contains a section on creating classes and a section on Object Oriented Programming. The *ActionScript Dictionary* and the *Using Components* sections of the help files provide information about current classes. There are also many good articles available on the Internet. The Flash developer center on the

Macromedia web site also provides some good articles. Many books on Flash also provide information on creating components.

Remember the process for creating version 1 and version 2 components is different.

 **More Information:** For information on creating version 1 components (Flash MX) see the appendix on the CD–ROM.

# Summary

In this chapter you learned what is possible with components and e-learning. Components will help make Flash the e-learning development tool of choice. You learned basic information about what is required to create components. You created a basic e-learning component to familiarize yourself with the process. If you are serious about creating e-learning components, you will want to access the resources mentioned in the last section of this chapter.

# Index

# F

# Looking for e-Learning Development Assistance?

Rapid Intake designs and develops computer-based training (CBT) and web-based training (WBT), and for all types of organizations. We can assist you from the first concept to the finished training product or program.

# Hosts of e-LearnDevCon (the e-Learning Developers Conference)

Rapid Intake organizes and hosts the e-Learning Developers Conference each year. This one-of-a-kind event focuses on techniques specific to e-learning developers. It is the only event in the United States that focuses exclusively on e-learning developers. Check it out at **www.elearndevcon.com**!

# WBT Tips

WBT Tips is a free periodic email loaded with valuable tips about web-based training design and development. Our tips emphasize techniques in Dreamweaver, Coursebuilder, Learning Site, Flash and other web development tools and technologies. Sign up at *www.rapidintake.com/wbttipsSignup.htm*

# www.rapidintake.com

See our web site for a list of clients and other organizations for whom we've created e-learning solutions. Among others you'll find such companies as HP, Lockheed-Martin and Intel who have used Rapid Intake's services to achieve their e-learning goals.

# Call Us Toll Free (866) 231-5254